PREVENTING VIOLENCE AT WORK

A STEP-BY-STEP PROGRAM TO PROTECT YOUR EMPLOYEES, COMPANY AND ASSETS

JOSEPH A. KINNEY

PRENTICE HALL
Englewood Cliffs, New Jersey 07632

Prentice-Hall International (UK) Limited, *London*
Prentice-Hall of Australia Pty. Limited, *Sydney*
Prentice-Hall Canada, Inc., *Toronto*
Prentice-Hall Hispanoamericana, S.A., *Mexico*
Prentice-Hall of India Private Limited, *New Delhi*
Prentice-Hall of Japan, Inc., *Tokyo*
Simon & Schuster Asia Pte. Ltd., *Singapore*
Editora Prentice-Hall do Brasil, Ltda., *Rio de Janeiro*

10 9 8 7 6 5 4 3 2 1

ISBN 0-13-317901-X

PRENTICE HALL
Career & Personal Development
Englewood Cliffs, New Jersey 07632
A Simon & Schuster Company

Printed in the United States of America

PREFACE

In recent years, violence has been spreading through our workplaces, becoming more pervasive with each passing day. All-too-familiar horror stories of stalkings and shootings, mayhem and murder fill our daily newspapers and nightly television news broadcasts, serving as constant reminders that we are no longer safe on the job. The growing problem of workplace violence imposes substantial costs and risks on employers, workers, and American society.

The culture of violence that has been spawned in the United States is unique in the industrialized world. External factors, such as the glamorization of violence by the media and the availability of guns, contribute to this problem, but fundamental changes in the workplace itself have created an entirely new atmosphere where violence can breed and flourish. Levels of stress are explosive in countless work environments. Survivors in downsized corporations are asked to fill multiple jobs. The comity that may once have existed between managers and the managed is gone.

Management, workers, researchers, government and the general public must work together to chart a course to return the work environment to a stable and secure place, where people come to work, and believe in the enterprise and its role in their lives. The failure to move in this direction will impose social and economic costs that our society cannot afford to shoulder.

It is crucial to note that violence is an issue that must be addressed by both workers and management in strategies that are genuinely inclusive. Workers who have experienced violence are terrified and firmly dedicated to seeing violence end. From a legal perspective, both employers and unions are targets for lawsuits, emphasizing the need for cooperation. Managers who seek to impose top-down solutions without employee input are likely to see their efforts questioned and, possibly, rejected as illegitimate. This is especially true in organizations where labor-management relations suffer.

Our society must come to grips with this issue as an unbearable crisis. This book is intended to begin the process of understanding what violence is doing to and costing America in its work environments. I have two simple but challenging objectives: (1) to measure and explain the phenomenon of workplace violence and (2) to identify and describe the measures that have the promise of reducing such incidents. In meeting these goals, we will examine a number of critical issues in this book:

- First, we will explore the scope and magnitude of the problem of workplace violence.

- Next we will provide some theories about perpetrators before moving on to discuss the special problems of women.

- Further on, we will look at downsizing and how some firms are mitigating the human problems that come with restructuring.

- In the final chapters, we will consider a menu of options that employers have for addressing violence, with a special focus on threat management.

As you will see, there are ways to manage the risks that violence poses. There is a process that each employer can follow in developing the most appropriate program. By following the steps outlined in this book, employers can begin to take the bite out of violence that is so badly damaging our workplaces.

ACKNOWLEDGMENTS

This book could not have been written without the encouragement, love, and support of Stefani, first my partner and now my wife. Stefani is a very intelligent, perceptive woman who sees the conflicts and dilemmas that are unseen by others. Stefani has done her best to meet our little family's shifting needs while ensuring that I meet the challenge of writing this book.

Together, Stefani and I have seen firsthand just how precious life is. During the early stages of planning this book, our son, Ralph, was born prematurely while we were on vacation. For 47 days, our lives were like a roller coaster, as Ralph struggled for life. His valiant battle will always inspire me. Ralph's short life and the interaction of those around him are very much at the heart of this book.

There are many people whom I would like to thank. Our two children, Joshua and Paul-Claude (alphabetical order) who teach us a little each day of their lives. Then there are our parents. Jennifer and Gary have helped shaped Stef into the special person that she is. My Dad and Mom have shown me the value and lessons of unconditional love, standing by my side through thick and thin. Jennifer (Mom Jenny), Gary, Dad, and

Mom, along with Josh, Paul-Claude and Ralph's memory, have made life worth living.

There are some beyond this close circle. My brother Chris has always been there for me, as was Paul, my baby brother, before he lost his life in 1986 in an incident that involved a collapsed scaffold. My friends Carl and Cathy Bates, Tom Geoghegan, Steve Petry, Carolyn Potts, Helen Bensimon, Mary Helen Yarborough, Gerry Scannell, Bill Moseley, Matt Piers, Chuck Hurley, Jim Bradtke, and dozens of others too numerous to mention in this book have been very helpful. Certainly, I value the contributions and especially the criticisms of all of those who helped shaped the National Safe Workplace Institute since its inception in 1987.

There are some individuals I have learned from who should be mentioned. These include Jim Royer of FMC Corp. and Judy Alberio at the St. Paul Company, superb security directors who are very much at the heart of their profession; Joanne Colucci of American Express, who is intelligent, informed and balanced in her approach to this problem; Jean Lambkin and Gary Royce of the Norfolk Naval Air, who typify professionals and a "can-do" spirit that should be a model for both the public and private sectors; and Dr. Sue Cassidy, IBM Medical Director, who has taught me that balance is the only way to approach violence prevention at work.

There are some very special people in government who are trying to be leaders and partners with business in eradicating violence at work. Alan Friedrich of the New Jersey Department of Labor, Cal OSHA chief John Howard, and Harry Payne and Sharon Tarlton in the State of North Carolina have been partners in my work on these issues.

Jim Powell, Jim Lee, and Steve Seeburger are with the Pinkerton Services Group in Charlotte, a company that is on the cutting edge of workplace violence prevention. PSG will be a leader for many years to come on workplace issues.

Deserving of special mention is Garry Mathiason of the law firm Littler, Mendolson of San Francisco. Garry is a lawyer with vision, intelligence and thoughtfulness. His writing about the legal implications of workplace violence is very compelling and thoughtful. Chris Hatcher, Ph.D., National Assessment Services is a superb clinician who has fostered my understanding of these issues. In that same vein, Dennis L. Johnson, Ph.D., President of Behavior Analysts & Consultants. Dennis contributed to the landmark study by the National Safe Workplace Institute, *Breaking Point—The Workplace Violence Epidemic & What to Do About It*. Dennis taught me a lot about behavior observation systems and other early interventions.

Moreover, I have had two very special editors: Karen Hansen, whose vision and professionalism are second to none, and Barry Richardson, who constantly but politely kept me moving toward completing this project. Karen and Barry make writing a book much easier than it would be without their help and encouragement.

There are other people that should be acknowledged. I hope that they know who they are and that they will accept my personal thanks.

Joseph A. Kinney

CONTENTS

INTRODUCTION

Growing Hopelessness
and the Disintegration
of the American Dream

The deadly violence that was once remote to U.S. workplaces is now an increasingly grim and painful reality to all of us. Until recently, violence was thought by most Americans to be limited in our society to urban ghettos. Violence was considered barbaric and foreign to a civilized people in a post-industrial nation. Our language took note of this divided reality. In the United States, we did not have guns, we had "Saturday Night Specials" that were reserved for those who made their living from crime and intimidation. Even occupational injury and disease have been largely limited to blue collar workers, a small part of our increasingly service- and information-focused nation. Granted, in recent years, our culture has begun to take note of white collar workers suffering from occupational stress, the acute pain of repetitive motion injuries, and even from the poison of polluted air in modern office buildings. However, until the past decade, workplaces—both blue and white collar—have been free from the threat of violence, except for robbery. The feeling of sanctuary has now passed. The workplace no longer provides a safe haven in a violent world.

The first landmark case of non-robbery, workplace violence occurred on August 20, 1986 in Edmond, Oklahoma, with the fatal shootings of thirteen postal workers. Sure, there had been workplace homicides before, but few in number and scattered over long periods of time. Before the tragic explosion in Edmond, workers vented their anger and frustration in non-fatal acts—fist fights, pushing and shoving, typically taking place across the street following a hectic workday. Workplaces were generally free from the threats of disgruntled employees, dismissed workers full of outrage, or violent intruders seeking spouses or others with whom there had been real or imagined romantic entanglements.

Now, and perhaps for many years to come, workplace violence has become established, an all-too-commonplace event. The sanctity of the work environment is now fragile. Once trusting workers are now looking over their shoulders, paranoid and fearful about co-workers who fit profiles of likely perpetrators or individuals who they just feel may explode. Frightened employees phone psychiatrists on radio call-in shows to discuss their workplace fears.

The inevitable result of violence is that many Americans can no longer feel safe when they go to work. The threat of violence, even death, has become omnipresent. Guns, the preferred tool of violence, are available in abundance. While guns have always been available in modern America, the use of such weapons was limited outside the ghetto to hunting, skeet or target shooting. Now, in the minds of the emotionally unstable or the acutely angry, the use of guns or other weapons is seen as an acceptable way to resolve conflict. Weapons are considered to be an equalizer between those who have power and those without power—a way to level the playing field. In today's world, angry individuals see guns as tools to be used to resolve a conflict or to seek justice from those who have offended them.

There are two compelling reasons why guns have become the tool of choice for violence. First, many people have experience with guns. Millions of Americans, including a majority of adult males, have knowledge and experience firing many types of guns ranging from pistols to machine guns. The new aspect of the violence phenomenon is the willingness of certain individuals to use weapons to resolve conflicts or disputes in a work environment. For many people, the use of such weapons against those who they feel are truly their enemies involves only a small step in logic.

Second, the mass media—especially television and motion pictures—have portrayed the use of guns as glamorous and acceptable. There are now 3,000 studies which demonstrate a positive relationship between the depiction of violence in the media and increased incidents of violence in society.[1] The availability of guns, the experience that people have in using such weapons, and the perception that such use is legitimate have created circumstances encouraging weapons abuse.

There are other factors that make workplace violence a national phenomenon that must be addressed. For example, many workers can no longer expect to make economic progress in their lives. Much of the work force has not experienced real income growth for almost two decades. In fact, substantial numbers of workers have had steep declines in their income during the past decade. As we end the 20th century, we are experiencing the first generation in more than a half-century where primary breadwinners of the current generation are not likely to exceed the wealth of their parents.

To make this situation worse, workers in the 1990's face a much smaller and less rewarding job market than a decade ago. A worker who loses a job and is in financial jeopardy is often also at risk of losing house, car, and more. For many members of the Baby Boom Generation, the painful reality that they will not surpass their parents in wealth or social status creates an acute feeling of frustration and failure. This is especially true for men who have carried rifles in battle.

GROWING HOPELESSNESS

In the 1990's, there is a strong and growing feeling of hopelessness among many middle class citizens. The American dream of economic advancement has evaporated for many. The momentary euphoria of Desert Storm exists no more as America journeyed from wartime triumph into economic recession before the victory parades had ended.

Workplace violence is now part of our lives. To be sure, non-robbery violence stems from many sources. It is not unusual for fired employees to return many years later to bring violence and destruction. Recently, a person who was fired from a job eight years earlier wandered into the suburban Philadelphia offices of a $6 billion corporation to fatally gun down the Vice Chairman before committing suicide.

The prospect of violence has grown as dreams of advancement in economic and social status have been shattered. With these shattered dreams have come changed horizons. Now Americans go to work with a far different objective: to earn the money to meet their immediate financial obligations rather than to achieve distant aspirations. The meaning of work as a vehicle for economic and social progress has been lost for too many.

EMPLOYER OBJECTIVES

As we will see in this book, violence can be prevented. Most angry people give us warnings that can be heeded by those who care. Employers have both a business interest and a legal obligation in trying to prevent workplace violence. The prospect of injury has serious implications not only for those directly affected, but for the morale and productivity of the entire work force. An incident of violence can disrupt the workplace enormously, tarnish an employer's reputation, and contribute to long-lasting productivity problems. The costs beyond injury and even death are often hidden, but real and damaging.

Employers are being forced to come to grips with the prospect of violence in the workplace. Law firms are now warning their corporate clients of the legal implications of failing to respond to clearly recognizable threats. Others in the corporation—security, human resource, safety, etc.—are beginning to understand and respond to violence from their unique vantage points. We can no longer lull ourselves into thinking that violence is a random, uncontrollable and unmanageable event in our lives. We cannot afford to blind ourselves to the possibility of this infection.

It is easy to focus on homicide. In reality, homicide is just part of the violence problem. Numerous studies show that non-lethal physical violence and threats can be enormously damaging to the welfare of individuals and the organization. While there is no question that non-robbery homicide is a new and growing concern, other forms of violence must not be ignored.

GOVERNMENT'S LIMITATIONS

Government is finally beginning to address the problem of workplace homicide. In 1992, Centers for Disease Control (CDC) epidemiologists declared the increasing spiral of workplace homicide as a serious national public health problem[2] and as an issue worthy of public and private interventions and study. Government is now considering the types of interventions by employers that would reduce this tragic toll. As this is being written, there are three different legislative proposals in California alone.[3] The Federal Department of Labor is considering both legislative and regulatory proposals. In fact, a small number of employers have been issued citations for failing to protect employees in situations where there were recognized threats.

Trial lawyers have also noticed that workplace violence can be the source for litigation. Hundreds of lawsuits have been filed embracing numerous legal doctrines, resulting already in a number of sizable awards and settlements to victims of non-robbery violence and aggression.

Even a dedicated government, however, will have limitations. Government agencies simply do not have the resources to adequately pursue a meaningful anti-violence strategy in our workplaces. Its role in the short-term will most likely remain modest, with investigations and enforcement actions pursued in only the most egregious cases.

1

VIOLENCE AT WORK

Examining the Scope of the Crisis

Our workplaces should be free from harm. This is only natural in a post-industrial society. None of us, from the entry-level, blue collar worker to the millionaire executive, expects to go to work to become ill or injured. Neither do we expect violence or intimidation to be a part of our work life, but now we must be realistic. Violence pervades our workplaces, threatening us all. Horror stories of bloodshed at office towers, on factory floors, in post offices, and other workplaces are all too vivid. Memories of these episodes enter our thoughts, especially when a co-worker explodes with anger. After all, it seems only reasonable to think that anger can evolve into physical attacks or even murder.

As we will see in this chapter, violence involves a range of acts and behaviors. Homicide is just one form—perhaps the tip of the violence iceberg. Fear and intimidation are other examples. Low-level violence threatens our spirit and diminishes our productive nature in the process. When we feel threatened, we cannot focus on work. None of us is immune from the threat of violence. We must come to grips with this reality and begin to reshape our workplaces into environments where productive relationships can be pursued and renewed, where trust is restored and where we can reach our collective potential.

In this chapter we define what we mean by violence. Clear definitions are essential to appreciate the nature of this problem, its impact on our lives and its scope. This is important if we are to be rational in developing a response. Many senior managers, skeptical about the size of the problem, fail to discuss it and thereby allow denial and neglect to flourish.

Parallels exist between the denial that surrounded the early dialogue on sexual harassment and the incipient exchange on workplace violence. There are always those who are skeptical each time a new problem emerges. They believe that a problem cannot be a problem unless and until they have experienced it and declare it so. Many senior executives thought that discussion of the harm related to sexual harassment was overblown and not worth their time. They think the same about violence at work. They think that policies meant to bar fighting are sufficient to address violence and aggressive behaviors.

Still others want to believe that the violence that exists in society somehow should also naturally exist in the work environment. There are plenty of examples of causes of violence well beyond the control of employers, such as domestic violence, demented customers, and gang rituals.

Nevertheless, an unwillingness to address issues and problems that lie within the control of employers is unforgivable. It ignores the fact that people go to work to earn a living that will help them meet their financial obligations and, hopefully, help in retirement. People do not go to work to die, become injured or sick. They want and deserve workplaces that are free from physical attacks, menacing behaviors, and threats.

Physical attacks and other types violence at work are on the rise. While it is unusual for most workers to ever witness an occupational fatality, many individuals are increasingly experiencing assaults, threats, verbal abuse, and other forms of violence at work. People intuitively feel that these are associated with or can lead to physical attacks. Fear and anxiety are rising at work since the late 1980's, imposing substantial burdens on us as individuals, on our employees, and on communities in which we live. The physical, psychological, and productivity costs are large, even if hidden. The prospect of violence at work has given our lives a new source of fragility, with anxiety and uncertainty never experienced before.

In our effort to understand the problem, we will begin by defining the types of violence that exist at work.

DEFINING THE PROBLEM

There are three types of violence: attacks, threats, and harassments. These are consistent with the basic dictionary definition of violence as unwanted aggression or anger. Evidence from the medical sciences demonstrates that even threats and harassment leave us emotionally injured. And in the eyes of medicine, emotional or psychological injury is physical injury. The expression that "sticks and stones may break my bones but words will never hurt me" is no longer literally true (if it ever was). Employers have paid enormous judgments in learning this painful lesson. The admonition that "an ounce of prevention is worth a pound of cure" is crucial here. Let us define each type of violence.

ATTACK

To attack is "to use force against in order to harm." Physical forms of attack involve assault and the most brutal assaults result in homicide.

THREAT

Threats involve an expression of one's intention to inflict injury. The difficulty with threats is that they may be very subtle. Indeed, sometimes threats are meant to frighten without the use of words that make one's intention clear to the victim. Adequate threat documentation, which is covered in detail later in this book, is very important to determining how to manage individuals who are the source of threats.

HARASSMENT

Harassment involves behaviors that are designed to trouble or worry the victim. Such behaviors may not mean the same to perpetrators as they do to victims. However, their abusive nature is well established and, as a result, must not be tolerated.

In this book, we will be concerned with all types of violence. As we will see, the possibility of being murdered on the job is remote. Nevertheless, other non-lethal forms of violence are very damaging and need to be prevented. Likewise, there is reason to believe that perpetrators who become lethal often engage in threats and harassing behaviors before killing. By stopping violence early in its evolution, we may be preventing a murder—of ourselves, a co-worker, or another individual. We also are defining new values and boundaries at work, making our work environments free from violence and the fear of violence.

MEASURING THE PROBLEM OF WORKPLACE VIOLENCE

In this chapter, we will examine what is known about the scope of violence in our work lives. This knowledge is essential to understanding the steps that must be taken at all levels—corporate, government, and individual—if we are to halt this epidemic.

Americans have endured, however reluctantly, blue-collar death as part of industrial progress and the perceived risk of work life, especially in high risk industries. Many people believe that workers, especially those in hazardous jobs like mining, steel-making or construction, are paid to accept high levels of risk and that this risk of injury and death will be limited to a small part of the population. Such a belief unwittingly contributes to hundreds of worker deaths each year and to hundreds of thousands of agonizing injuries that could be prevented. Our public policies have lulled us into believing that unsafe work will be regulated, and, should injuries occur, that the injured will be adequately and fairly compensated.

Much the same logic has been applied to "hidden" epidemics in the workplace, including occupational diseases like cancers and respiratory ailments and, more recently, occupational stress. Our culture leads us to believe that these problems are necessarily "part of the job" and, consequently, are unavoidable. Not only do they threaten our lives, but they inflict tremendous harm to our national productivity.

In the same way do violence and the fear of violence damage the social fabric of the workplace, diminishing relationships that are vital to the enterprise's success. They bring about the same result as an untreated disease: the destruction of an organization's cohesiveness and vitality. We must understand that violence and the fear of violence are just as silent and insidious as many cancers. To address this we must have early warning and surveillance systems in place so that we can render the appropriate type and level of therapy.

While evaluating the scope of violence at work involves necessary limitations, any knowledge should lead us to more informed and effective courses of action. We will begin with the most dramatic type of violence, homicide.

WORKPLACE HOMICIDE
Size and Scope of the Problem

An analysis of government statistics from the Bureau of Labor Statistics (BLS) and the National Institute of Occupational Safety and Health (NIOSH) suggests that job-related homicides account for about 4 percent of all murders in the United States, a dramatic growth since the 1980's.

BLS reported that 1,063 individuals were murdered in the workplace in 1993, a 6 percent increase over the 1,004 murdered at work in 1992. Most were killed in the course of a robbery; however, increasing numbers of workers are being murdered at work as a result of workplace-directed violence. There were 149 workplace-directed murders in 1993, up 18 percent from the 126 slain at work in 1992.

BLS published its first comprehensive survey of occupational fatalities in 1993 (for the 1992 year). There is no way to gauge the comprehensiveness of the agency's data although it is likely that many job-related homicides are not revealed in this database. Other government data, though, indicate that murder on the job is growing at an alarming rate.

NIOSH tallied job-related deaths from 1980-1989 based on information from death certificates as part of the National Traumatic Occupational Fatality (NTOF) program. It found about 12 percent of work-related deaths were from homicide. BLS, which uses a variety of data sources, found that 18 percent of the workers who lost their lives in 1993 died from homicide. Part of the higher percentage attributed to BLS may be because job-related homicides grew during the 1989-1992 period while the other sources of job-related fatalities were showing a decline.

BLS also reported that 213 employees committed suicide on the job in 1993, a 16.4 percent increase over 183 in 1992. According to BLS, 21 percent of those killed on the job in 1993 died from homicide (1,063) or suicide (213). This means that more employees died from these sources than from highway fatalities (1,232). Its data indicate that employees are much more likely to be killed by homicide than by any other source except motor vehicle-related deaths. In fact, employees are about twice as likely to die from homicide as from a fall, four times more likely than from electrocution, and more than five times more likely than from an accident involving aircraft.

Neither BLS nor NIOSH data provide any insights into how many work-related homicides occur away from the workplace. Examples would include murders perpetrated by co-workers outside the premises of the employer such as fights away from the primary workplace. The National Safe

Workplace Institute has collected numerous examples of employees killing co-employees, supervisors, or managers at home or other away-from-work locations.

It is quite possible that the total number of murders perpetrated away from the workplace is quite high. According to statistics by the Federal Bureau of Investigation, 47 percent of the murders—involving more than 10,500 victims—that were committed in the U.S. in 1993 involved people who knew each other. Of this number, 2,055 involved people who were spouses or romantically involved. This means that more than 8,000 knew each other from other types of connections, including, most likely, the work environment.

For the purpose of this chapter, workplace homicide is divided into three categories delineated by the Bureau of Labor Statistics in its annual Census of Fatal Occupational Injuries (CFOI). The first CFOI was published in 1993 and included data from 1992 and 1993 which is in Table 1-1.

In this table is information on the number of individuals who were murdered in the workplace and the circumstances in which they were killed. In 1993, 106 people were murdered by co-workers or former co-workers and another 43 lost their lives in cases involving stalking by people whom they knew, usually a relative or romantically-involved friend.

TABLE 1-1

WORKPLACE MURDERS IN 1992 & 1993
CIRCUMSTANCES OF WORKPLACE HOMICIDES

	NUMBER OF HOMICIDES			
	1992		1993	
CIRCUMSTANCE				
Robberies and miscellaneous crime		822		850
Business disputes		87		106
Co-worker, former co-worker	45		59	
Customer, client, other	42		47	
Personal disputes		39		43
Relative of victim				
(e.g. husband, ex-husband, boyfriend,				
ex-boyfriend)				
Police in the line of duty		56		64
TOTAL		1,004		1,063

SOURCE: Census of Fatal Occupational Injuries, Bureau of Labor Statistics, U.S. Department of Labor, 1993 & 1994

While no one knows for sure, it is likely that the 126 people murdered in 1992—as well as the 149 slain in 1993—represent a dramatic increase from the number of people murdered in the early 1980's. The National Safe Workplace Institute, which did an exhaustive search of newspaper stories and workers' compensation records, reported that about 60 individuals were slain in workplace-directed homicides during the peak of the late 1980's and early 1990's.

ROBBERIES AND MISCELLANEOUS CRIME

This category involves violence during the course of a robbery or an attempted robbery. Victims are typically slain by gun shots, although some are stabbed and fewer still suffered death by strangulation. The victims typically work in the service sector of the economy as taxi operators, in restaurants or fast food (including delivery), convenience stores, gasoline stations, grocery stores and other service sector establishments. Data show that women, elderly workers, and teenagers are more vulnerable; those workers who handle cash in service jobs are most vulnerable. Most robberies are very late at night or early in the morning.

Probably the two largest single vocational categories of individuals slain would be taxi operators (96 were murdered in 1993) and security officers (53 slain in 1993).

LAW ENFORCEMENT

Table 1-1 shows that 63 law enforcement officers were murdered in 1993, up slightly from 1992. This number has declined sharply from the early 1980's when pre-employment screening and law enforcement training programs began to focus on more cautious techniques of criminal apprehension.

Nevertheless, law enforcement officers are still more likely to die earlier in their careers than many other occupational categories.

WORKPLACE-DIRECTED

This category involves homicide directed at current or former co-workers, supervisors or managers; by stalkers; or by clients or customers who are angry and elect to kill in the workplace. This category can also include murders by terrorists or those who commit hate crimes. Unfortunately, we know very little about murders of employees (or former employees) by people they knew from the work setting. However, it is very likely that hundreds (if not more) homicides fit this category.

The public often associates this type of homicide with the U.S. Postal Service, which experienced the murders of 34 postal workers in ten separate incidents between August, 1986 and March, 1993. Homicide by disgruntled former employees can occur months or even years after the loss of a job. For example, the Vice Chairman of a $6 billion corporation was gunned down in his suburban Philadelphia office in 1994 by an employee that was fired eight years earlier.

Another part of this group involves stalkers, individuals with misplaced affection and resulting anger. Stalkers come to the workplace searching for the intended victim because they are often barred, through legal injunctions or temporary restraining orders, from going to a victim's home, which is often much more secure than a public workplace. There were 43 employees murdered by stalkers in 1993; many more were killed in transit to or from work.

Most of the incidents in this category involve men attacking women. For every murder, there are numerous rapes and assaults that often leave victims battered and disabled. In fact a 1994 Department of Justice survey reported that 8 percent of all reported rapes took place at work. There is increasing evidence that estranged spouses, particularly men, are going to the workplace to attack their spouses, former spouses or girlfriends. More than 30 states now have anti-stalking laws which are designed to keep perpetrators from coming near potential victims. It is not yet clear what effect these laws may have on reducing violence toward women, including homicide.

Likewise, customers or clients commit a startling number of murders in the workplace. They are often demented or feel that the company has cheated them.

Finally, a small number of workplace murders involve terrorism or hate crimes. The most recent U.S. example of terrorism is the World Trade Center bombing in New York that took six lives in 1993. Some experts fear that this type of homicide may increase in the years ahead. The most significant source of terrorism is political extremists. In years past, most terrorism has been limited to the Middle East and to Europe, with scattered incidents in Japan and Asia. However, the World Trade Center bombing suggests that this pattern may be changing.

Terrorism is a unique category in that it implies random behaviors and decision-making patterns that are not evident in other types of workplace homicide and violence. If incidents of terrorism increase, there will be a stronger response by government. There will be more security cameras, monitoring equipment, and security personnel at the work site. This will make the U.S. a less open society and could inadvertently bring about increased levels of stress.

Also we now have numerous examples of hate crimes that result in workplace homicides. In the 1992 Los Angeles riots, at least three workers were gunned down in incidents not related to robbery. Another striking example occurred recently when a political extremist shot a plastic surgeon in a Chicago suburb because the physician apparently had the capacity of providing patients with Aryan features. The same perpetrator has been implicated in the murder of a San Francisco hair stylist who advertised that he would dye hair blond.

This category does not include homicides by co-employees or former employees during the course of a robbery. For example, security experts in the restaurant industry believe that many incidents of robbery-murder involve co-employees or former employees. Indeed, many fast-food outlet robbery-murder incidents that took three or more lives involved such individuals.

Workplace-directed homicides strike terror at the hearts of managers and employees across the U.S. These events are often sudden and can traumatize a workplace for months or even years. This category of homicides has grown exponentially since the mid-1980's, probably now feeding upon itself and spurring copy-cat murders. Some experts believe that this phenomenon is likely a form of mass murder-suicide since about half of the perpetrators of workplace homicide are slain by law enforcement officers or commit suicide.

WORKPLACE-DIRECTED VIOLENCE

Much of the remainder of this book will concentrate on workplace-directed violence. Actual murders, while increasing, are certainly only the tip of the iceberg of what is clearly a very serious problem for both employees and employers. There are numerous other acts, short of murder, which infect hundreds of thousands of workplaces in the U.S. at great economic and social costs to those affected. Studies and surveys are now being published which attempt to examine the scope of the problem of violence; several are highlighted in Table 1-2. None suggest the opposite—that employees are currently feeling more secure than they did previously.

TABLE 1-2

SCOPE OF WORKPLACE VIOLENCE IN THE U.S.

Department of Justice Crime Victimization Survey—(Released in 1994)

- One million crimes committed at work each year.

Northwestern National Life Insurance Survey—(for year ending June 30, 1993)

- One out of four employees was harassed, threatened, or attacked.
  - ✓ 2 million workers were physically attacked.
  - ✓ 6 million workers were threatened.
  - ✓ 16 million workers were harassed.

National Safe Workplace Institute—(for 1992)

- 111,000 incidents of workplace violence cost employers $4.2 billion.

Gallup Poll, 1994 Survey—

- Two out of three employees did not feel secure at work.

Bureau of Labor Statistics—(for 1993)

- 149 individuals slain at work as a result of anger.

Compiled by the Author.

There are significant limits on estimating the true cost of workplace violence, even in terms of actual fatalities. There are several governmental agencies whose function it is to compile statistics: the National Institute for Occupational Safety and Health (NIOSH), Centers for Disease Control; Bureau of Labor Statistics (BLS), Department of Labor; or the Federal Bureau of Investigation (FBI), U.S. Department of Justice. Unfortunately none collects truly comprehensive statistics on such fatalities. Researchers generally must rely on newspaper clipping services, employer reports, death certificates, or other data sources, all of which have severe limitations. To illustrate, NIOSH was reporting, based on its study of death certificates, that just 750 workers were murdered on-the-job each year while BLS, in 1994 reported that 1,063 were murdered at work in 1993! BLS, another Federal agency, relies on multiple sources of data and, as a result, has more comprehensive information. Historically, reports on occupational fatalities in the U.S. have been on the low side of the true number, and this could well be the case with respect to occupational homicide and violence. One reason might be that the government simply does not count work-related murders that occur away from the work setting.

DEPARTMENT OF JUSTICE DATA ON VIOLENCE

In 1994, the Department of Justice issued a study confirming that the scope of violence at work had increased alarmingly. The Department's report, released with considerable fanfare, was based on a "crime victimization" survey which involved asking victims key questions about the crime, including where it occurred. The survey, highlights of which are reported in Table 1-3, supported the judgment that workplace violence is on the rise.

Despite limitations of any study or survey, there is growing evidence that suggests that the problem of violence is on the rise. Its scope in terms of statistics and the experiences and feelings of employees and others is just one piece of the puzzle. To understand the impact of this problem, we must understand how much it costs employers, workers, and others.

ESTIMATING THE COST OF WORKPLACE VIOLENCE

Workplace violence imposes enormous costs upon employers, some of which are apparent and easy to measure. For example, if an employee is injured and away from work the employer will lose the benefits of that employee's labor and will have to pay medical costs. In addition, there are many hidden or less obvious costs: increased insurance premiums (the cost of most insurance is based, for example, on use); replacement employees; increased training and supervision; reduced productivity, etc.

TABLE 1-3
DEPARTMENT OF JUSTICE STUDY:
WORK OFTEN THE SCENE OF VIOLENCE

Key findings:

- One million crimes committed at work each year.
- 100,000 crimes (at work) involved guns.
- 16% of all assaults.
- 8% of all rapes.
- 7% of all robberies.
- 2 million personal thefts.
- 200,000 car thefts.

SOURCE: National Crime Victimization Survey, July, 1994, Department of Justice.

One way to understand the costs involved is to examine the phenomena associated with violence at work that are of concern to both employers and workers. These are discussed in Table 1-4. All of these factors impose substantial costs upon employers and employees. Ideally, it would be helpful to have specific data on each area; however, precise information is unavailable. Estimates on the numbers of incidents and the precise economic costs unfortunately must involve numerous assumptions. estimates.

One published estimate on the cost of workplace violence, made by this author in a National Safe Workplace Institute report, indicated that there are at least 111,000 serious incidents of workplace violence each year. In computing this estimate, the author used statistics gathered by the U.S. Postal Service, adjusted and then extrapolated to the larger U.S. work force. According to these numbers, the Postal Service experienced 5,000 incidents of workplace violence in 1992.[2] This information, with other data on the magnitude of the problem, gives us some sense of its scope.

TABLE 1-4
COST FACTORS ASSOCIATED WITH WORKPLACE VIOLENCE

Phenomena—

- Homicide
- Injury from battery
- Psychological trauma
- Stress-related mental disorders stemming from violence
- Assault
- Verbal abuse
- Sexual assaults

Cost factors—

- Employee replacement costs (new hiring, training, temporary employees)
- Management and supervision diversions (investigation, training)
- Increased insurance premiums
- Increased security costs
- Litigation
- Decreased productivity

SOURCE: National Safe Workplace Institute

As we have indicated, homicide—while obviously terrifying and intolerable—is just the tip of the violence iceberg. Employers who target homicide as the problem that they wish to prevent are missing very serious and potentially very costly problems. We must examine the range of injury and problems that exist to appreciate the costs that this problem is imposing on employees, employers, communities, and our nation.

Data collected by the Postal Service is probably the most comprehensive of its kind in the U.S. In 1992, the Postal Service employed more than 700,000 workers or about .6 of one percent of the civilian work force (about 115 million) in the U.S. If just 40 percent of the experience level of the Postal Service were to hold true for the U.S., then we could project about 333,000 incidents of workplace violence for the United States in 1992.

It may be that the Postal Service's workplace violence incident rate is higher than the average for the general work force in the U.S. For our purposes, we have assumed that its rate is three times higher than that for the general work force. If this is true, then the U.S. experienced 111,000 incidents of workplace violence in 1992. Unfortunately, we do not have reliable data on the severity of each of those incidents. Researchers are only now beginning to understand the impact that such events have on the lives of co-employees and others. Nevertheless, it appears quite reasonable to suggest that these events have a very serious and costly impact.

It is to the U.S. Postal Service's credit that the nation's largest civilian employer has put into place the most comprehensive reporting system on workplace violence that we are aware of in the U.S. In general, the Postal Service has given wide latitude to its postal inspectors, professionals who are charged with compiling such reports. The types of workplace violence incidents included in Postal Service reports include:

- homicides
- injuries
- property damage (arising from anger or violence)
- aggravated assault or serious verbal threats
- abusive and threatening acts
- acts of sabotage related to violence

There is a possibility that the Postal Service's statistics do not reveal the full scope of the agency's problem. Many Postal Service employees have little confidence in the Postal Inspection Service, which operates in many ways like an independent police agency. The Postal Service has operated an independent "800" hotline staffed by social workers, but has not issued a report discussing the volume of activity it receives.

NORTHWESTERN NATIONAL LIFE INSURANCE SURVEY

Also published in 1993 was a survey by the Northwestern National Life Insurance Company. In this study, Northwestern researchers surveyed a representative sample of U.S. employees to identify the amount of violence that each individual had experienced during a period of July 1, 1992 to June 30, 1993.[3] This survey revealed that one out of four employees was the victim of harassment, threats, or physical attacks during the reporting period. It estimates that there were at least two million employees physically assaulted and another six million threatened.

The Northwestern study has been useful in appreciating the scope and magnitude of the problem of workplace violence. It supported the notion that verbal abuse—harassment—can be even more destructive to employee productivity than a physical assault, as we can see in Table 1-5. Employees who are harassed, according to Northwestern's data, are more likely to take time off from work and to find their work lives disrupted than employees who are physically assaulted. This should not come as a surprise, especially to those who have examined the impact of sexual harassment on employee productivity. Harassment is typically behavior that will increase in frequency and severity with almost no end in sight unless there is intervention. On the other hand, a physical assault usually is the end of aggressive behavior because employers are often more assertive and forceful in disciplining employees who fight than those who harass.

The survey implicitly supports the view that employers should pay more attention to the problem of violence at work. It also supports the judg-

TABLE 1-5

IMPACT OF WORKPLACE VIOLENCE ON THE HEALTH & PRODUCTIVITY OF VICTIMS

	(INCIDENT TYPE & PERCENT AFFECTED)		
Effect on Worker	Attack	Threat	Harassment
Affected psychologically	79%	77%	88%
Disrupted work life	40%	36%	62%
Physically injured or sick	28%	13%	23%
No negative effect	15%	19%	7%

SOURCE: Northwestern National Life Insurance survey. Sample size: 600 full-time American workers.

ment that employers who are concerned about people, productivity, and profits should be as concerned about violence as they are about workplace injury because the result is much the same—lost wages, replacement costs, diversion of management resources, soaring insurance costs, etc.

WORKPLACE VIOLENCE AND PRODUCTIVITY

Workplace violence disrupts productivity in many important ways. Because it is homicides that grab headlines, one can easily be lulled into thinking that the probability of such an event occurring at a specific place of employment would be rather small. When employers misdiagnose the problem, they are naturally more reluctant to employ preventive strategies and programs essential to preventing violence at work.

On the other hand, providing some understanding of how violence harms the productivity of the work force will cause employers to analyze what they have to do to properly prepare for workplace violence. Ways that productivity and organizational effectiveness are harmed is shown in Table 1-7.

THE COST OF VIOLENCE AT WORK

It is difficult to formulate precise estimates on the cost of workplace violence. This is especially true because we do not have adequate data on the number of incidents, the way that specific problems (e.g. harassment) affect individual employees, or comprehensive research on how much incidents cost employers, employees, families, and other parties. Even if excellent statistics and cost data were available, it would be very difficult to measure the social costs incurred by all parties. Some questions that could be asked are:

- How much does a family really lose when a member is murdered?

- What does an employer lose when it is perceived by potential employees or by investors as being a dangerous place to work?

- How are stock values affected when a company receives negative publicity from such an event?

- What happens to the productivity of an employee when he or she is fearful of a co-worker?

TABLE 1-7

HOW WORKPLACE VIOLENCE AND CONDITIONS THAT
LEAD TO VIOLENCE HARM WORKERS AND ORGANIZATIONAL EFFECTIVENESS

Physical harm:
- Death
- Injury

Psychological:
- Trauma
- Mental Health Services
- Suicide and Suicide Prevention
- Substance Abuse
- Survivor Guilt

Property Damage

Property Theft

Productivity Impediments:
- Lower morale
- Absenteeism
- Labor-Management Conflict
- Increased turnover

Diversion of Management Resources:
- Response to crisis and problems rather than profit-making activities
- Costly litigation

Increased Security Costs

Increased Workers' Compensation Costs

Increased Personnel Costs (Employment and Training)

Source: National Safe Workplace institute

- How does one weigh the "sunk" costs of education, rearing, nurturing, etc., that go into social development?

Workplace violence places enormous burdens on the victims—employers, employees, families, friends, corporate stakeholders and others—burdens that cannot easily be measured. With these difficulties in mind, the author has tried, using assumptions about costs and incident frequency and severity, to provide a meaningful understanding of what workplace violence costs each year. To arrive at an estimate, we have divided incidents into three categories of severity and tried to estimate what an average incident costs employers, employees, families, stakeholders, and the nation. We examine each group and the elements of the cost that are involved.

1. Group A. These are the most serious incidents, posing a cost of $300,000 for each occurrence. Larger employers are more likely to spend substantially more reacting to such incidents than smaller employers. Indeed, we know of incidents that have resulted in the expenditure of millions of dollars. There could be as many as 15,000 such incidents each year. This number is based on the 149 homicides, more than 3,000 rapes, and numerous serious injuries that occur at work. One study for the Department of Labor estimated the value of the life of an employee at $7 million.

Group A incidents are likely to have many of the following costs:

- Medical and post-trauma stress treatment
- Lost wages (to workers)
- Training costs for replacement workers
- Lost productivity (disruptions in the work process)
- Property damage (plant and equipment)
- Property theft
- Increased security (physical and electronic)
- Enhanced training for supervisors and managers
- Diversion of attention of senior management to react to incident, respond to the crisis, and to plan for the future
- Investigations (including the use of outside experts, e.g. management consultants)
- Diminished image in the minds of stakeholders and customers resulting in reduced sales potential and lower stock value
- Increased legal expenditures (for lawsuits and legal defensibility measures)

2. Group B. These are medium severity incidents. We believe that these incidents cost about $20,000 for each occurrence. It is possible that there were 30,000 of these incidents each year in the mid-1990's.

Group B incidents will have many of the cost characteristics of Group A; they are just fewer in number.

3. *Group C.* These are lower severity incidents costing an average of $10,000 for each occurrence. We note that $10,000 is substantially less than the estimated cost for an occupational injury in the U.S. We suspect that there were 100,000 such incidents in 1992. Once again, Group C incidents are likely to have just a few of the characteristics of those listed for the most severe category.

Workplace violence cost estimates annually (mid-1990's):

Group A— 15,000 incidents × $300,000 = $4,500,000
Group B— 30,000 incidents × $ 30,000 = $ 900,000
Group C—100,000 incidents × $ 10,000 = $1,000,000
Annual estimated cost of violence at work = $6,400,000

We recognize that we have been arbitrary in what incidents cost. However, we have also been intentionally conservative in our estimates for each category. The costs of such incidents, even ones of an apparently superficial nature, are experienced over years in ways that may not be readily apparent. For example, the costs of incidents from Group A and B may be experienced for many years after the initial incident occurred. Many are hidden in insurance costs or other costs that employers simply are not sensitive to.

This projection of $1.45 billion is substantially higher than the $4.2 billion that was estimated in the National Safe Workplace Institute report. However, it is clear from statistics reported by the Department of Justice, the survey done by Northwestern National Life Insurance Company, and other sources of information that violence at work may be a more substantial problem than what was previously considered. More researchers should be encouraged to study and analyze this problem.

SUICIDE

Suicides in the workplace are part of a new trend that shows potential for escalation in future years. According to the Bureau of Labor Statistics, 213 employees committed suicide at work in 1993, up 16.4 percent from the previous year.[4] There are indications that males are having enormous difficulty coping with stress. Despite advances in mental health services and the prevention of suicidal behavior, the total suicide rate per 100,000 people for those of 25 to 64 years of age has fluctuated little from the late 1970's through late 1988, the last year for which data are available.

An examination of corresponding age groupings over the same period of time reveals that the total male rate of suicide was consistently recorded to be three to four times that of the total female suicide rate. It is worth noting that of all the suicides occurring in workplaces, almost every case involves a male, as is the case for workplace aggressors. As discussed further in Chapter 3, men already demonstrate a propensity to anchor their identity to their job. Thus, for those men who are suicidally at risk and disproportionately self-identified by their job, the workplace is apparently becoming a more common suicide venue.

"SAFE WORK" BOUNDARIES

No longer is worker death limited to the horror of falls, electrocution, trench cave-ins, or explosions and fires. It now includes acts of violence by other human beings from both inside and outside of the work environment. Employees, especially women who are more sensitive to abusive practices because of their experience with sexual harassment, are much less willing to tolerate menacing and aggressive behaviors. Rightfully so, people want to feel safe and secure at work.

As white and blue collar workers begin to see common ground on workplace health issues, it is likely that together they will expect more, both from employers and government. This should involve substantially more research and more educational programs, if not regulation and enforcement. Such measures, especially those pursued by enlightened and motivated employers, are the most logical course to preventing practices that make us unsafe or feel unsafe. Essentially, awareness of violence and the adoption of policies and practices will result in new boundaries for behavior—appreciation for what can and cannot be tolerated.

Workplace violence is a serious problem that warrants priority attention by employers, unions, government, researchers, and others who are dedicated to a healthy and productive work force and more productive society. Awareness of the problem will result in formulation of solutions to achieve the desired effect—workplaces free from violence and aggression.

Employers, in too many cases, have ignored measures that could have saved lives, reduced injuries, and lowered the severity and costs of workplace violence. We should carefully and thoughtfully assess the prospect of violence and what can be done to limit the effect, just as we should address other recognized occupational safety and health hazards that pose the risk of injury and illness with associated costs to employers and employees, in particular, and society in general.

2

BREAKING POINT

Career Dissonance
and the "New" Violence

The violence that we are now experiencing in our workplaces has its roots in several sources. The entertainment media, for example, have depicted the use of guns and violence in a glamorous fashion and have made criminals into heroes, turning standards upside down. We also are a society that has developed a high attachment to work. For many, success at work has become equivalent to success in life. Moreover, there has been a steady decline, especially among men, in the anchors that serve to stabilize us in life—family, church, and community, among others. When we get in trouble, we reach for these anchors to pull us through crisis. If they are not there, we will struggle and some of us will fail.

To worsen matters, we no longer equate crime with punishment, ensuring that we will be a society in which violence can be used in defense of one's needs or sense of justice. While this is true in matters of law, it is also true at work. Supervisors—if they exist at all—often no longer assert discipline in a timely and effective manner. Many workplaces are dominated by people who grew from being "Little Jerks" to "Big Jerks" and who use intimidation and fear to achieve their objectives.

In this chapter, we will concentrate on acts of violence by employees or former employees, individuals who typically have been discharged and often away from the work environment for six months or more. There are studies that suggest that current employees are responsible for less than half of the violent acts that occur in the U.S. In any event, this is a source of violence that employers have a special responsibility to address.

In the context of employee violence, workplace violence is best understood as individual, aggressive behavior. When a person acts alone, that individual's internal aspects—cognitive processes, attitudes, comprehension of the circumstances, and motives—interact with external aspects of the environment, as the individual perceives them, to lend meaning to the behavior. The perpetrator may be directed toward either self-preservation or threats of personal diminishment, or some combination of the two. In order to predict, control, and interpret incidents of workplace violence we must understand how perpetrators think and behave, the decision-making processes that they engage in, and how their thinking evolved over time.

Workplace violence reflects a wider and deeper set of problems that are growing more pervasive in our society. Witness the simple fact that the United States (and to lesser extent, Canada) are uniquely violent in the advanced industrialized world. Unless these problems are addressed at various levels—society, organization, community, and individual—the prospects for violence will remain high. While individuals must be held accountable for their actions, we cannot ignore the problems that exist in the work environment that may contribute to high levels of anger and frustration and, potentially, violence.

Many factors help us understand why we have so much violence in our society and why that violence has now entered the workplace. We can also gain some very valuable insights into why employees are now becoming violent at work. After all, it is not surprising that individuals focus anger on institutions they feel have "failed" them, especially when these institutions are so very important to them. Table 2-1 provides us with a wider context for understanding what has happened in our society and our workplaces.

To some extent, violence in the view of the perpetrator represents a choice among available alternatives. The experiences of the individual and the current social context that the perpetrator perceives are two factors which must be explored for an understanding of why violence occurs. Logically, then, in order to assess the increasingly more frequent occurrence of workplace violence—especially workplace-directed homicide—one must closely examine the environment in which such events have occurred (i.e. the workplace).How has it changed? To what extent has the perpetrator's perception of those changes motivated the behavior leading to workplace violence?

TABLE 2-1
WHY DO WE HAVE VIOLENCE IN OUR WORKPLACES?

1. Individuals are not held responsible for their actions; we do not equate crime with punishment.
2. Breakdown in stabilizing institutions—family, home, church, school, and community.
3. A sense of hopelessness generated by an inability to replace existing jobs with new positions with equal pay and benefits.
4. Glamorization of violence by the media.
5. Unwillingness by managers and supervisors to use effective discipline.

SOURCE: National Safe Workplace institute

WORKPLACE-DIRECTED VIOLENCE

Unlike robbery or commercial crime, employer-directed workplace violence belongs to a genre that almost always follows the same sequence. It is this sequence, more than any other single factor, that is consistent in acts of violence by employees or former employees. It begins with a traumatic experience that creates the perception of an unsolvable psychic state, which in turn produces extreme and chronic emotional tension or anxiety. The experience may be caused by a single major event, such as job termination, or it may be more cumulative in nature, preceded by a series of seemingly minor events, such as several reprimands, one or two negative performance reviews, etc.

Once traumatized, the individual projects all responsibility for his or her internal tension or anxiety onto the situation, in effect externalizing blame for the unsolvable psychic state. At this point, the individual's thinking turns inward, and becomes increasingly egocentric, progressing to self-protection and self-preservation as objectives, to the exclusion of all other concerns.

Within this frame of reference, the idea is conceived that a violent act is the only way out; and following a period of internal conflict, which may be prolonged, the violent act is attempted or committed. At any point in this evolution (see Table 2-2), intervention is possible, and violence precluded, but only if adequate levels of awareness and insight pre-exist, so that the warning signs flashed by the at-risk individual are recognized and responded to appropriately.

The event which begins the sequence is not always the fact of a job termination or a layoff, but how such personnel actions are implemented.

Table 2-2

Routine Sequence for Perpetrators of Employer-Directed Workplace Violence

1. Individual suffers trauma (actual or perceived) which creates extreme tension or anxiety:

   - single major event (layoff or termination)
   - cumulative minor events

2. Individual perceives that problems are essentially unsolvable.

3. Individual projects all responsibility onto the situation.

4. Individual's frame of reference becomes increasingly egocentric.

5. Self-preservation and self-protection gradually become sole objectives.

6. Violent act perceived as only way out.

7. Violent act is attempted or committed.

SOURCE: National Safe Workplace Institute

Critical factors are the perceptions of procedural justice (i.e. whether procedures are viewed as fair and equitable) and distributive justice (i.e. whether the actions are evenly distributed across the company).

Workplace violence is difficult to predict in terms of specifically which employees will commit aggressive acts. However, we can (and routinely do) identify those employees who are emotionally disturbed, heavily stressed, abusing drugs or alcohol, involved in frequent disputes with their co-workers or supervisors, routinely violating company policy or rules, harassing their co-workers sexually or otherwise, or threatening violent acts—and therefore are at risk.

EMOTIONAL FACTORS

An instance of violence then must be evaluated in terms of whether it is essentially instrumental or expressive. If it is the former, an identifiable goal of personal gain or retribution will be discernible from the facts. By contrast, the undiluted hostility of expressive violence results in revenge or destructiveness without other payoff variables apparent.

Thus, the primary motives and concerns of violent individuals must be assessed according to several more or less distinct dimensions. Because violence is always an act of social significance, the social context as it is perceived by the perpetrator, and his or her history of aggressive expression, will be focal points for thorough analysis. The risk factors which may precipitate workplace violence can be found in Table 2-3. Typically, the person has extreme stress in his or her personal and/or work life which contributes to emotional disturbance. The individual may violate company work rules or policies and begin to harass co-workers. It is highly likely that at this point threats will begin. Tragically, these individuals often fail to have a support system upon which to fall back. They then begin to think about weapons and how those weapons may be used to resolve their problems.

SOCIAL AND CULTURAL CONTROLS

All known human cultures have established verbal or written rules that regulate social behavior, and it is through such rules that violence may be discouraged or legitimized. Three control processes have been suggested that provide the conditions known to discourage violent behavior.[1] Ranked in presumed order of importance, they are:

1. An economic system that creates full or close to full employment. Because productive activity is regularly rewarded in such a system, peaceful behavior is habitual among the individuals who are part of it.

TABLE 2-3

RISK FACTORS IN INDIVIDUALS WHICH MAY PRECIPITATE WORKPLACE VIOLENCE

- Emotionally disturbed status.
- Extreme stress in personal life circumstances and/or job.
- Alcohol or drug abuse.
- Frequent disputes with supervisors.
- Routine violation of company policy or rules.
- Sexual and other harassment of co-workers.
- Threats of violence.
- Preoccupation with weapons.
- Minimal support system.

SOURCE: National Safe Workplace Violence

2. A legal system that prevents crime. Such a system emphasizes prevention heavily, but also apprehends violators swiftly and punishment follows without delay.

3. A cultural system that maintains a norm of good behavior.

Just as these control processes produce non-violent behavior as long as they are in operation, when one or more of them malfunctions or breaks down, violent behavior increases. In light of that, consider the following facts:

- The U.S. has a very high level of permanently unemployed and the largest number by far of working poor (near minimum wage) in the world. Real compensation levels have been dropping for nearly two decades for most blue collar jobs.

- The U.S. has a criminal justice system which is markedly inefficient compared to those of other modern countries. U.S. gun control laws are comparatively relaxed.

- American popular culture, especially TV, movies and the news media, glorifies violence in many ways. Not only is it glamorized, but the types of violence in the mass media are extremely damaging to young people.

Several factors unique to contemporary U.S. society have conspired increasingly in recent years to create an inherently aggressive environment. Just as more people have armed themselves with guns, so more people have "armed" their homes—with gates, iron-barred windows, attack dogs, electronic surveillance systems, burglar alarms. Many neighborhood groups have employed their own private security officers. All of these tactics, while undeniably practical and appropriate in the face of escalating crime rates, bespeak a national sense of alienation from traditional sources of public protection (i.e. law enforcement agencies) and an abandonment of the spirit of community in favor of a philosophy of "every man for himself."

Children, too, have learned to arm themselves in America more than in any other nation. It has been estimated that 20 percent of America's children have carried a gun to school at least once; and they can afford them, since a gun can be bought on the streets of most cities for less than the price of a pair of sports shoes.

VIOLENCE IN THE U.S.

It should not be surprising, then, that the risk of being murdered in the U.S. is at least seven times greater than it is in most European countries; that the majority of all murders in the U.S. are committed with firearms; or that the numbers of murders, forcible rapes and aggravated assaults committed in the U.S. increased in every year from 1980 to 1989 except in 1987. For America's young people, the homicide picture is even worse. While the murder rate for the general population has doubled since the 1960's, it has tripled among 15- to 24-year-olds.

Only automobile accidents claim more youthful lives today. But it should be noted that many auto accidents are caused by aggressive driving, often exacerbated by illegal and/or excessive alcohol consumption, and that suicide—the third leading cause of death among 15- to 24-year-olds—also is a form of violence, and has increased 400 percent during the past three decades.

All in all, data from many studies by a range of experts support the theory that violence is successfully curbed in a society in which there is full employment, an effective criminal justice system, and established mores that foster peaceful behavior.

CULTURAL DISSONANCE

It is a paradox that remarkable technological advances and increased leisure opportunities in our society have left many individuals so severely stressed. The Cold War and nuclear threat that preoccupied us for more than a generation have presumably abated for a time, but it now appears that they served one useful psychological function: they permitted us to ignore a variety of serious domestic problems that now demand our conscious attention. As a result, the respite so long anticipated has been precluded by sociocultural issues that fulminated while we were outwardly preoccupied.

So, it seems, the piper must now be paid. The economy-bolstering effects of massive military outlays expected to result in a "peace dividend" have instead required our focus to reduce the deficit created to finance them, along with a host of social, educational and infrastructural needs that apparently became acute after the dissolution of the Soviet Union. Simultaneously, budget cutbacks in the military-industrial complex have caused ripple effects that have undermined stability in the private sector to an alarming degree. All the while, a voracious media complex in search of bad guys, but bereft of active Husseins, Khaddafis and evil Kremlin potentates, has begun looking inward to apply its cynical attentions to the anguish of the victims within.

Temporarily at least, our culture seems to have forgotten the basic tenet of personal responsibility for one's own actions. Criminals function with ostensible impunity while prosocial society overestimates the probability that they will be victimized. Prisons are being built continuously by several jurisdictions (at least some of which then find they cannot afford to open and staff them) while small, well-armed gangs and religious cults alike flout the established authority of major arms of law enforcement.

In the 1990's, family disintegration has progressed to the extent that theorists now consider redefining what constitutes the desirable family unit. Even intact families as we have known them lack former supports of neighborhood and relatives. More and more, they have chosen to abdicate their traditional parental responsibilities and become tyrannized by their own offspring. Defensively, they close their eyes to illicit sex and alcohol, hoping that their child might, at least, avoid arrest. Religious institutions offer us the promise of stability in exchange for membership and financial support, and then some of their most highly regarded leaders reveal themselves to be disordered and unstable. Time and again, it seems, the very agencies we have relied upon to enforce social regulation prove themselves fallible and ineffective.

At the same time, the much cherished individual freedom, "cowboy spirit" of which Americans are so proud may contribute more than we acknowledge to the failure of our institutions to resolve conflicts. For example, those who propose restrictive laws for weapons—even assault weapons and handguns—are shouted down by indignant defenders of our Constitutional right to bear arms; and any suggestion that the glamorization of violence on prime-time television or in movie theaters should be curtailed is similarly seen as an attack on our right of free speech.

A generation ago, social theorists would have explained what is happening in America today as social disorganization, but the pervasiveness and constancy of the effects now require us to see it as more than that. Beyond the systemic imbalances implied in that concept, the extensive spread of these phenomena violates virtually every generalized expectation to which we are conditioned through socialization.

CRITICAL ANCHORS

Americans have coped with a myriad of more or less subtle stressors since the dawn of the Age of Industrialization (and even before). We have long been subjected to constraints and pressures of time management, stylistic ways of relating to one another interpersonally, a system of values that favors less productive societal members (e.g. actors, athletes, and singers) at the expense of the more productive (teachers, scientists, and parents), and culturally fostered pressures toward behavioral unwisdom through mer-chandising, etc.

Coping with the daily pressures of our lives, however, was made eas-ier in the past than in the present (and prospectively, the future) by the exis-tence of certain critical anchors in the lives of most of us. Even if stressed by financial worries, time management issues, and a host of other responsi-bilities, we had facets of our lives which could be counted on to be stable and enduring, and so offered the sense of control so essential to stress man-agement.

Only somewhat over-simplified, the critical anchor for women is the *relationship;* for men, their *chosen job* or *profession.* Both overt and covert life-stress effects are made more manageable while these anchors are in place, because they afford a sense of control that permits us to tolerate those pressures that we consider less critical. When lost or jeopardized, however, these essential life components increase vulnerability to stress.

With women, for example, economic pressures may be manageable stressors within the context of established relationships;but without the crit-ical relationship, the same pressures can easily become overwhelming. Similarly, men may tolerate various abuses so long as their self-image of bread winner is intact;but a career at risk threatens any sense of control over life events.

When these anchors fail, there are behavioral consequences, and there are notable gender differences. Moderately generalized in order to illumi-nate the issue, women seek counseling, while men become aggressive, even to the point of killing. And as women have gained ground in their struggle for equality in the workplace, often to the perceived disadvantage of men, there has been a marked increase in assaultive crime by males on females, reflecting the destruction of a secondary anchor that men see as a challenge to their authority and potency. Even so, it held to moderate levels while the jobs picture was positive. But layoffs, cutbacks, and the downsizing of cor-porations in recent years have threatened this most critical male anchor.

The prediction, then, is that assaultive crime by males on females will increase even more dramatically as jobs continue to diminish, and there will be a concomitant rise in crimes against figures perceived to have authority over the career control mechanisms of hiring and firing, i.e. management.

This is the essence of *career dissonance:* the anchors that men have clung to in order to cope with life's stressors are often no longer present for many men nor for an increasing number of women. The incongruity is enhanced by the realization that the long-held, generalized expectation that loyalty, diligence and hard work would be rewarded with job stability and security is of a relationship which no longer holds.

With honest self-appraisal, virtually every man in our culture will recognize the function of his job as a primary anchor, and understand his potential for lashing out if it fails him. Predictably, management will be his typical first target of choice, since the authority vested therein is the parental symbol of his child-like ego involvement with the corporate enterprise.

As documented in the statistics provided in other sections of this book, incidents of workplace violence and workplace-directed homicide are already frequent enough, and sufficiently widespread across all types of industries, as well as among workers of every status, that there can be no question that this societal behavior is not an aberration but an established trend.

Unless fundamental change is swiftly wrought in economic, social and criminal justice policy, that trend is likely to continue; and if it is allowed to continue, to become a threat more serious to our survival as a nation than all the Khadaffis, Husseins and evil Kremlin potentates combined.

CHAPTER

3

DYING JOBS

Stress in an Era
of Uncertainty

Until recently, American employers have been expected to follow a path of efficiency and business competitiveness coupled with a commitment to employees—line, staff, and management. As U.S. business prospered, employers offered an increasing benefits packages. "Good" employers would offer health insurance, increased wages, paid vacations, pension plans and, most important, job security. What has evolved through the years between employers and employees has constituted a social contract. In fact, many people were basically told to expect lifetime employment "unless they screwed up." Corporate America, powered by the most productive industrial base in the world, could afford to be generous.

Today, the circumstances are by no means the same. A 1994 *Fortune* magazine cover screamed "The End of Jobs." The feature story gave us the bad news:jobs often constitute a poor way of organizing work. We have now entered a period of radical change, perhaps the most dynamic period since the Industrial Revolution. In this new world, job security is very much up for discussion as U.S. employers embrace new corporate structures and face realities that change moment to moment. It would be easy to blame the death of jobs on the rise of Wall Street and financial markets as a dominant influence on the corporate suite. However, the reality is more likely as

Fortune portrayed it: jobs were an artificial creation that no longer have the same logic or necessity in the contemporary business world. Businesses are finding that one of the most crucial challenges is the intelligent organization of work and the tasks that need to be done. Jobs as such represent a less efficient way to organize work. As we realize that the situation and circumstances we face are not a trend or fashion but a revolution in the way economic life is organized, then we can begin to comprehend what business and work will be like in the 21st century and beyond.

All parts of the corporation are now expendable. Indeed, corporations themselves are expendable. "Re-engineering" has entered the lexicon of American business. A host of factors—not just financial performance—now defines and determines the value of the Modern Corporation and your position within its structure. Just a generation ago, most (if not all) high school graduates envisioned an adult life where they would have a single employer. Then, just a few years ago, labor experts claimed that the typical American would change careers three times during the course of his or her career. This reality, too, has now changed. To switch jobs three times during the course of a work career would seem "stable" for many people. Now, more than ever, we as individuals are having to live with change. We need to learn how to prepare, anticipate, adjust, and adapt. With these demands comes ever growing pressure, stress that tests our capacity to function in this new world.

THE RAPID PACE OF CHANGE

In this new world in which we live, the pace of change is very rapid. Dozens of corporations—new, old, service, and industrial—are striving to reduce production cycles and new product engineering time. Tom Peters, the guru of Management Consulting, states in his seminars that crazy times call for crazy organizations. "Radical" and "revolution" are key words in his vocabulary. He insists that organizations that don't think in those terms are likely to be swallowed up by the competition, including by businesses much smaller than the targeted prey. The pace of change, while challenging to some, is intimidating to others.

In this chapter, we will examine organizational cultures and how change is affecting the lives and well-being of employees. We will try to document the scope and magnitude of the organizational change. We will consider specific examples of what organizations are doing to prepare their employees for the change that is all but inevitable. We will examine how organizations can become inferior places to work and how internal stress can create aggressive and even violent employees. This does not mean that we should excuse violent behaviors in employees or others. Indeed, we need to hold individuals accountable for their actions under any circumstances. But a stressed environment can be a hostile environment. If this is the case in your organization, your business will suffer consequences that could and should have been avoided.

CHANGING THE WAY ORGANIZATIONS WORK

The current passion of management consulting, re-engineering corporate structures and processes, is forcing massive changes in the way organizations work. The logic of re-engineering is to squeeze as much cost out of the system as possible by reducing time for product development and manufacturing cycles. To the extent possible, layers in the organization are contracted, reducing redundancy. In this new world, processes that don't contribute directly to the bottom line are often in jeopardy. They include most of the human resource services and even functions like product development, research and development. Virtually everything in the corporation can be short-changed in the interest of high short-term profits and enhanced stock values. In this "brave new world" of financial management, those who survive the fiscal ax are declared "superior" and capable of doing the work of many. Never mind the historic bonds that once tied the managers and the managed in a concept called "comity." This new world asks the "fit," those who hang on to survive, to assume ever-growing burdens.

We have yet to fully appreciate that this new world has come with hidden costs that could eventually destroy the social fabric of many corporations. Levels of stress in a re-engineered corporation governed by financial management are overwhelming. It is no surprise that corporate mental health costs are soaring. Suicides at work are on the rise—213 employees killed themselves at work in 1993 according to the Bureau of Labor Statistics. In this new world, some individuals actually absorb substantially more work. Still others, including those who may lose their jobs, have been placed in ambiguous roles that in many ways are equally stressful. Often new pressures force people to choose between family and job—a choice that should not have to be made if at all possible. Some of the role-related stressors, as identified by industrial psychologists, are given in Table 3-1.

Table 3-1

Some Role-Related Stressors Found in the Workplace

- Job Overload—

  Demands that exceed the capability of the individual.

- Job Underload—

  Demands that do not challenge the individual either qualitatively or quantitatively.

- Role ambiguity—

  Job tasks are not clearly defined.

- Role conflict—

  The expected behavior for one role directly conflicts with another concurrent role (e.g. watching your child's soccer game versus working overtime, i.e., good parenting versus good employee).

SOURCE: National Safe Workplace Institute

The true level of damage to the mental health of those who work in such corporations cannot be accurately measured. Those who are forced into "early retirement" or into a "buy out" do not show up neatly in government statistics. The costs are as much social as economic. After all, how much value can be placed on a career for a person who has by any historic measurement been productive? The breaking of social contracts between employers and employees is now commonplace. Nevertheless, for those who lose their jobs the problem is especially real. For some individuals, job loss has become part of their lives. Some professional managers have now lost three or four jobs due to restructuring. Government statistics show that as many as four million former middle-managers are now unemployed or significantly under-employed as "free lancers" or consultants without real portfolios. This number will surely grow in the months and years ahead as businesses continue to push for "leaner" organizational structures.

Then, of course, we have the survivors. The survivors often do not have time for mental health services, vacations, time with family, educational or professional development, etc. Some survivors don't even have time to be sick. These people are the walking wounded of the downsizing wars. In many ways, these men and women are time bombs ready to be exploded. The rapid, even brutal, pace that characterizes their lives is often buried under waves of palliatives designed to mask the real experience. The macho among these survivors will always ignore inner cries for help. For them, heart attacks and strokes are preferable to the use of mental health services.

UNDERSTANDING CHANGING BUSINESS CONDITIONS

Reducing the number of employees by downsizing and layoffs is not an altogether new phenomenon. However, what is new and different is the inability of workers to replace their wages if they lose their jobs. In the 1960's and 1970's, more than 80 percent of workers who lost their jobs were able to find positions with comparable wages. In the 1980-1985 period, that figure declined to 50 percent. In the late 1980's, just 25 percent, or one out of four workers was able to find a new job with wages and benefits comparable to the previous position. By the 1990's, more than nine out of ten Americans who lost their jobs could expect to have severe difficulty finding comparable new employment.

Consider another set of data on this same matter. Research by Isabel Sawhill, previously at the Urban Institute, a Washington-based think tank, reported that U.S. family income grew 20 percent (adjusted for inflation) between 1968 and 1977. The increase was consistent for both blue- and white-collar workers. During the next decade, from 1978 to 1987, average family income rose 17 percent, but this time those with only a high school diploma suffered a four percent loss while income of college graduates grew by 48 percent.

Clearly, increased cost-reducing efforts, regardless of the reason, have caused more companies to look at their employees as variables instead of traditionally fixed costs. This has directly affected millions of American workers through such measures as large and permanent lay-offs, plant closings and plant relocations to areas where it is simply less expensive to do business. The result is rising stress and frustration in the workplace, which may lead to an increase in the already epidemic levels of stress and potentially, violence.

A GROWING HOPELESSNESS

The experience of displaced workers casts a very disturbing trend. Seen as a special subset of the larger group of the unemployed, displaced workers are those who have lost jobs due to plant or company closings or moves, slack work (lowered product and labor demand), or the abolishment of their positions or shifts.[1] The early 1980's represented a discouraging period for workers largely as a result of the lingering ills of the late 1970's and the dual recessions of 1980 and 1981-1982. However, even in the subsequent economic growth of the first half of the 1980's, roughly 4.3 million workers were displaced, representing structural adjustment outside of the influence of a struggling economy. The five- year period from 1987-1992 was even worse, as 5.6 million were reported as displaced.[2] (It is important to note that displacement numbers only represent those who have lost jobs held for at least three years. Those who lost jobs of less tenure would swell the 1987-1992 number by an additional 9.7 million.[3]) While this rise reflects a natural occurrence due to the recession of 1991, the fact that the economy is still weak is not heartening.

Historically, the fastest growing cause of displaced workers in a recessionary period is the lack of demand for a certain product or service. In the most recent recession this held true. Unfortunately, for many workers, there have been gradual increases in plant closings, relocations and position or shift cuts since the mid 1980's, even in the face of economic growth.[4] Those who survive one downsizing may find that they have difficulty in the future. In a 1993 survey, the American Management Association reported that 60 to 65 percent of businesses that downsize are likely to do so again within 18 months.

Breaking the data into different components shows other interesting results and trends. While men used to be much more likely to be displaced than women, that is no longer the case. Now as more women have entered the labor force, more are being displaced. Also, job displacement has entered the service sector which is where the majority of women work. White collar workers, once seemingly immune to large scale reductions of the labor force, are joining the ranks of the unemployed. This new trend does not appear to be temporary; a poll in Fortune magazine showed that most Fortune 500 CEOs plan to keep management ranks at present or reduced levels in the near future.[5]

The work force is changing dramatically on a national scale. Most Americans understand the changes in the job market, either from knowing someone who has been displaced or by having lost their own jobs. The names of specific companies engaged in downsizing and numbers to be laid off are familiar to everyone because they are constantly reported by the media. The cuts at General Electric, IBM, General Motors, Ford, and AT&T are all familiar, as are the reasons that accompany such work force reductions.

What has become more troubling and tougher for most to understand, though, is the spread of downsizing to companies that are not in financial straits, such as Proctor & Gamble, Apple Computer, and American Express, to name just a few. While IBM's immense layoffs, as well as those of most downsizing corporations in the recent past, were due to declining profits in the face of changing product trends and fierce competition, companies with the same benevolent reputations toward employees as IBM have begun to make cuts even in years of record earnings. For example, Proctor & Gamble recently announced that it would eliminate 13,000 jobs, even though it has not yet felt the crunch of competition. Chairman Edwin L. Artzt cited that the cuts were needed to prepare for the competitive 1990's. It is likely that this policy will continue. With millions of American workers displaced and laid off, and the number growing daily regardless of economic circumstances, the question is "What happens to them?"

FOLLOWING AMERICA'S DISPLACED WORKERS

The restructuring of Corporate America has placed immense strains on the larger job market. Jobs are no longer for life. When a job is lost, it becomes increasingly difficult to replace it with one of equal pay or status. Of the 5.6 million who were displaced within the five-year period ending in 1992, over one third (34.2 percent) had not found jobs when that survey occurred.[6] This number was considerably higher than the number of those still displaced in a January, 1990 survey, a fact owing to the stagnation of the economy since that year. Of the workers who were reemployed in full-time positions, nearly half were forced to work for wages or salaries less than on their previous job, demonstrating a disheartening and consistent rise over the past four survey periods.[7]

Similarly, many new jobs that workers find lack job security. Estimates show that in the period from 1980-1988, there was a 175 percent rise in the number of temporary status workers and a 21 percent rise in part-time workers.[8] Unfortunately, most of these jobs do not include health and benefits packages. If they do, such packages involve greatly reduced benefits. New jobs found by displaced workers underline the hopelessness that is increasingly pervasive in the U.S. today. Basically, new jobs simply are not as attractive as old jobs. Pay and benefits are reduced, and often good jobs require one to relocate at substantial distances. Table 3-2 illustrates the characteristics of new jobs.

Table 3-2

Characteristics of New Jobs Found By Displaced Workers

- Temporary or part-time.
- Less pay than previous job.
- Much-reduced sense of job security.
- Benefits are either nonexistent or greatly reduced.
- Relocation at great distances often required.

SOURCE: Based on data from the Bureau of Labor Statistics and National Planning Association.

Apart from the numbers are insights as to how displaced workers regain jobs and try to make a living. In the traditional white collar sector, made up of professionals, administrators, technicians and others, high displacement is relatively new. Many with advanced educations, who have been previously immune to layoffs are now turning en masse to jobs in consulting, temporary positions, and other forms of self-employment.[9] Often, in their quest to maintain former wage and status levels, they engage in two or all three of these. Regardless of the new occupation or exact mix of occupations, displaced white collar workers face increased work and stress levels and still suffer wage and status losses.

Manufacturing employees have faced falling wages because of a variety of factors including competition with lower paid workers in other countries. Those that have become displaced have headed largely for the service sector. While it is no secret that this sector has boomed, pay and benefits are rarely comparable to that of former production positions. Thus, like white collar workers, the blue collar segment of the work force has seen a rise in temporary employment as well as the numbers of those maintaining two or more jobs. The result can be high levels of frustration and stress.

For employees, high job performance which adds value to a company is not enough in today's fierce job market and in the face of layoffs and plant relocations. For those who maintain jobs or become reemployed, the tenuous position that so many are pushed into causes stress levels to rise along with hours worked, while wages and benefits often decline. For some, the pressure can manifest itself in violent behaviors which, if not prevented, can cause deaths, reduced employee morale and lower productivity. In short, everyone loses. Fortunately, even though downsizing and layoffs continue, many companies have the foresight to enact programs which, if implemented well, can greatly reduce the increasing risk of workplace violence.

THE CONNECTION BETWEEN STRESS AND AGGRESSION

There is little doubt that the changing economic circumstances create a feeling of hopelessness and frustration among a large segment of the work force. As people become stressed, their physical condition actually changes, sometimes with destructive results. Stress at work, stemming from fear of job loss or survivor guilt, can spill into home life—and vice versa. The conditions that exist in many workplaces have been counteracted, to a certain degree, by the growing use of corporate wellness programs and other initiatives. But the damage is profound and growing, affecting many workers in ways that will not be totally appreciated for many years . Suicide at work, unheard of just a decade ago, now is growing at an exponential rate. There were 215 suicides at work in 1993 and labor experts fear that this number will grow for years to come.

For some families, the restructuring of American business has been a common event. Individuals feel like pawns in a chess game of management consultants and board rooms, with little power and influence of their own. As one individual said, "To be downsized out of a job once is bad enough. Two times is a disaster and three times is a tragedy." This person could be speaking for tens of thousands of families across America where husband and wife have now lost their jobs twice or more.

There is a growing body of literature in industrial psychology that demonstrates that work and non-work (or home life) roles are mutually dependent. Conflicts between work and family roles are heightened by the following:

- Long, irregular work hours.
- Exposure to ambiguous tasks or roles.
- Presence of conflict-producing work experiences.
- Presence of work demands that threaten to exceed employee's capabilities.

Industrial psychologists have discovered through research that any role pressure that increases time demands or work stress is capable of producing conflict between work and family roles. As our organizations struggle to meet the challenges of radically changing markets and new technology, the burdens of that struggle fall on individuals. While many can take the pressure and adjust, some cannot. These individuals will carry the often explosive pressures home with them. Tension and stress grows between couples, spilling over onto children and even extended family members. The converse is also true. If employees have trouble at home, they carry those problems into the workplace. A vicious cycle is created—pressure from home to work and work to home.

For too many individuals, there is a consequence of the build-up of stress. Research has demonstrated that stress will produce biological changes, impacting how we think and behave. Unless these individuals are identified and early interventions are provided, there can be serious results. Some individuals will inevitably become aggressive, even lethal toward those around them. They will strike back at the environment—the workplace—that has created the problems that they are experiencing.

THE SHUN PRINCIPLE

Organizations and their subunits can be very cruel. A postal worker in Denver wrote a powerful letter describing what he termed the "shun" principle. This was, as he described, the manner in which organizations, such as the Postal Service, shun, ostracize and eventually banish unwanted or unpopular members. These dislocated individuals often evolve into resentful and angry people, some of whom will emerge from isolation and strike back at those who created the harm in the first place.

TABLE 3-3
THE CONNECTION BETWEEN STRESS AND AGGRESSION

Stress and Aggression—

> The experience of work stressors is directly related to aggressive behaviors such as sabotage, interpersonal aggression, and hostility.

Convergence of Models—

> Within the frustration/aggression model, work stressors tend to impede goal attainment, leading to frustration, which may lead to aggressive behavior.

SOURCE: P. Chen and P. Spector, 1992, Journal of Industrial Psychology.

We all have seen examples of the shun principle at work in our lives. Groups—work or social—often tend to isolate unpopular members. We send them signals designed to diminish their roles in the group. By doing so, we often diminish their dignity and sense of self-worth. We may not think that what we have done is serious, but often the hurt is deep in the minds of those whom we are trying to shun. What is clear is that many violent people often have a background of being shunned and isolated by peer groups at work and in their communities. At some point, many of those shunned will retaliate in an aggressive way. When we see this behavior at work in our organizations, we should think carefully about the damage that we may be doing. We need to be concerned that the messages we are sending may be poorly received and that anger and hostility may be internalized, only to emerge later. We must remember that we are dealing with perceptions, not reality. How we see something is not necessarily how others will see the same thing.

Employees are becoming more stressed in the 1990's for another important reason as well. The support systems—family, church, and community—simply are not what they once were. When individuals become worried or fearful, they are not able to turn as readily to the institutions and resources that in previous generations were so important. Instead of being able to talk out a problem, they internalize it and over time, the stress alters their thinking process. In today's world many men feel a sense of failure when they compare the chaos, failure and uncertainty in their lives with conditions that characterized the careers of their fathers. The response will sometimes be violence and aggression, toward people and property, often with very destructive results.

IDENTIFYING "SICK" ORGANIZATIONS

We tend to blame individuals for violence. Without question, we must hold individuals accountable for their behavior. If we can blame our behavior on anything but ourselves, who is to be held responsible? Nonetheless we should be aware of the fact that there are "sick" organizations. The U.S. Postal Service, for example, is poorly managed and the results are evident in the fact that 34 individuals have been murdered in 10 separate incidents in just eight years. The Postal Service's own employee opinion surveys show that a significant percentage of the organization's 700,000 employees are very unhappy with working conditions and management styles. The consequences are equally clear. Not only are employees violent and aggressive toward each other, but they are abusive toward property and the mail that they are pledged to deliver. Stories about letter carriers burning and stashing mail, drivers inexplicably damaging trucks, and other acts of property damage and sabotage have flooded the news.

There are many other "Postal Services" in corporate America and government. These extremely stressed institutions are "sick" and expose employees to "disease" that is damaging, potentially life-threatening. In theory, we ought to be able to identify them through some of the characteristics in Table 3-4 and begin the process of making them well. In fact, if we are to retrace our steps from lethal attacks and visit the organizational cultures that previously "housed" perpetrators, we can find many characteristics that should be red flags to management that styles and conditions should change.

The notion of the "sick" workplace has other important aspects as well. Individuals employed in a sick work environment may well attempt to attribute their acts to a "hostile" workplace. Already lawyers are asserting the "hostile work environment" doctrine in lawsuits. Numerous cases involving abusive law practices, stress claims, sexual harassment, etc., have already established this doctrine as a basis to rationalize behavior. There is substantial evidence that lethal perpetrators often come from such environments.

CONFRONTING THE NEW REALITY

The changing way that we do business in the United States adversely affects the employment status of millions of American workers of all types. Many

TABLE 3-4
CHARACTERISTICS OF "SICK" WORKPLACES

- Chronic labor/management disputes.
- Frequent grievances filed by employees.
- Extraordinary number of injury claims, especially psychological (occupational stress).
- Understaffing and/or excessive demands for overtime.
- High number of stressed personnel.
- Authoritarian management approach.

SOURCE: National Safe Workplace Institute

people are losing their jobs and finding it increasingly difficult to replace them because of a combination of factors. Employees are being forced to work in conditions of greater uncertainty, working in temporary jobs or in environments of little job security. The trend or new reality does not appear to be slowing down, as corporations continue to restructure to accommodate emerging demands and new markets. Because of the world in which we live, it is entirely reasonable to expect rising frustration in the workplace which may escalate to violent outbreaks by employees and by former employees who feel betrayed by their employers.

It is crucial that organizations continue to identify individuals who are experiencing excessive stress and pursue early interventions. It is equally crucial that organizations attempt to identify internal problems or deficiencies that may contribute to a hostile work environment. We live in difficult times. But we need not bury our heads in the sand to conditions that can be corrected.

This chapter is not meant to wind back the clock of time. That is impossible. We need to confront reality and strive to make our workplaces dynamic. But we also need to make them as caring—as possible. This is a radically and rapidly changing world, imposing dramatic change on the best prepared among us. It is probably now more important than ever, that management understand and appreciate the levels of stress that exist. By working hard to alleviate the pressures appropriately, management will have taken important steps to develop a quality work force that will be the hallmark of business in the 21st century and beyond.

4

GAINING CONTROL

A Model for Confronting Workplace Violence

There is a need for a model that will help individuals and organizations understand the steps that should be taken to curb the epidemic of workplace violence that is now menacing the United states. The value of such a model is that it should provide a clear path away from ignorance into the kind of knowledge and insight that leads to true prevention. The one presented in this chapter is based on many years of research and thought into how business enterprises can best approach violence and aggression. Because this thinking has been tempered by the reality that businesses exist to make money and not to conduct sociological research, a responsible model must be organized in such a way where the benefits ultimately outweigh the costs.

The model presented in this chapter should meet that test. It involves six specific steps; one containing any fewer would be incomplete and could expose the enterprise to substantially weakened program effectiveness.

IDENTIFYING YOUR WEAK SPOTS

You must begin with an organizational assessment which involves a number of components. Its goal is to compile as much usable information as

Table 4-1

A Model for Identifying and Curbing Workplace Violence

1. Identify vulnerabilities.

2. Develop early intervention systems.

3. Prepare a threat protocol.

4. Establish method for assessing threats.

5. Organize to manage complex threats.

6. Develop feedback mechanisms to assess performance.

SOURCE: National Safe Workplace Institute

possible about the company's existing performance in addressing violence and internal stressors or pressures. Crucial to this first step is a systematic and thorough approach to understanding the concerns of employees. Experience is that line-level or craft employees often have endured a much higher level of anxiety about violence and aggression than have senior managers who are often far-removed from the "line" environment where such behaviors are much more likely to exist.

Many organizations survey their employees routinely and follow up such surveys with interviews or focus groups in order to obtain more detailed information and a greater comprehension of the data. That is precisely the approach that is suggested here as a key part of the organizational assessment. Examples of some of many questions that may be included are:

- Have you experienced verbal abuse while an employee of this company?

- Have you experienced a threat of physical violence while an employee of this company?

- Have you experienced a physical assault or attack while an employee of this company?

- Are you concerned about violence on the job? What is the source of that concern? Do you believe that such a possibility represents a high, medium or low-level risk?

- What do you think of the company's security? Do you trust security to respond effectively in the case of violence?

Also essential in such an assessment phase is a review of past experiences and how effective the organization was in responding to those problems. This review will often overlap an assessment of the organization's security policies and procedures because security officers historically have been responsible for addressing most types of violence (e.g. employee fights or threats to the organization from outside).

Finally, the assessment phase should include a careful review of the team orientation of individuals likely to be involved in the management of complex threats. An individual with a poor concept of team will probably be ineffective in this role. Those involved in threat management must be capable of working as part of a team since this type of approach is so crucial to managing such situations. Threat assessment and management will be covered more fully in the next chapter.

If done properly, the comprehensive assessment suggested in this chapter will provide clues about development of a violence prevention program for your organization. There is no one-size-fits-all approach to workplace violence prevention. How you proceed must be carefully customized and tuned to meet your organization's particular requirements.

STRIKING EARLY AGAINST WORKPLACE VIOLENCE

Early intervention is a key to keeping your organization healthy and avoiding the problem of workplace violence. Steps are identified in Table 4-3. An early intervention system must begin by choosing new employees care-

TABLE 4-2

TECHNIQUES FOR IDENTIFYING AND ASSESSING VULNERABILITIES TO WORKPLACE VIOLENCE

1. Survey employees to learn of their experiences and concerns.

2. Use focus groups and interviews to develop detailed insights.

3. Conduct security assessment.

4. Review past incidents of violence and how successfully they were managed.

5. Evaluate knowledge and team orientation of key managers.

SOURCE: National Safe Workplace Institute

Table 4-3

Early Intervention Mechanisms for Identifying Workplace Violence

- Behavioral Observation Programs

  Behavioral Observation Programs (BOPs) are paper-and-pencil forms that are used to document employee behaviors for a certain period of time (e.g. quarter year). BOPs should be used to evaluate behavior over time to help identify patterns relating to reliability, productivity, cooperation, etc.

  Managers must ensure that BOPs are used uniformly throughout the organization to ensure consistency and to minimize bias.

- Incident Documentation Forms

  This is a standard form used to document incidents of threat and aggression. Standard questions: Who? What? When? Where? and How? should be addressed in this form to ensure comprehensiveness of information. The preparation of such forms should be carefully reviewed by legal counsel for purposes of legal defensibility.

- Supervisor Selection and Training

  Employers should subject supervisor applicants to a comprehensive selection process that includes interviews by trained psychologists that can determine a person's fitness to manage others. Likewise, supervisors should be given training in issues such as sexual harassment and diversity before being deployed in a position of responsibility.

- Applicant Selection

  Employers should carefully evaluate an applicant's suitability prior to employment. This evaluation should involve careful review of a person's job application, including careful scrutiny of employment gaps, interviews (by trained interviewers) to determine suitability, and psychometric testing to evaluate their psychological status. The purpose of this screening is to avoid hiring someone who is likely to become a problem later in his or her work experience.

SOURCE: National Safe Workplace Institute

fully. Some corporations are now centralizing the process of employee selection to ensure that applicants are scrutinized uniformly. Such reviews give careful attention to employment gaps and checking an applicant's employment history. Businesses that use such techniques report that they are reducing turnover and losses to employee theft while maximizing productivity.

There are two key strategies for enhancing employee selection:

- Using trained interviewers to carefully screen applicants and their employment history prior to offering employment.

- Using psychometric testing to objectively learn about an applicant's psychological composition and suitability.

Both steps outlined above must be done with great care. There are a number of laws, including the Fair Employment Act and the Americans with Disabilities Act, that regulate or potentially regulate how employees are chosen. Clearly, an employer must demonstrate the relevance of any procedure that is used to the job for which the person has applied. However, there is every reason to believe that such procedures, if used consistently among all applicants, can withstand legal scrutiny. Employers can assert, within certain parameters, that processes that help the company avoid selecting job applicants with aggressive personality characteristics are crucial to maintaining a healthy and productive work environment.

Certainly it follows that supervisors should also be carefully chosen and provided with substantial training on how to effectively manage employees. This matter is covered specifically in a later chapter.

WRITING AN EFFECTIVE PROTOCOL

Every organization should have a clear statement against violence, even if that statement simply says the "This organization will not tolerate violence and aggression, either from within or from outside this organization." Such a policy must be made known to all employees and reinforced in internal communications such as newsletters, posters, etc.

Naturally, most organizations think that they have existing policies and procedures addressing the issue of violence. Actually, most existing policy statements fall short of the mark. For example, many admonish or punish employees (rightfully) for fighting but fail to address abusive acts or threats. Most fail to address violence from outside the organization (e.g. stalkers or customers) even though these are very serious problems.

An adequate protocol should address numerous issues, including those in Table 4-4 which are addressed elsewhere in this book but warrant repeating here. First, a protocol should identify unacceptable types of behavior as well as appropriate sanctions for that behavior such as termination of employment, if necessary. Second, the protocol should address the training needs of different levels of personnel within the organization. Clearly, a "threat management and violence prevention coordinator" must be trained in a different manner than a line supervisor (although much of that training will overlap). Unless the organization is prepared to train and equip personnel to meet its needs, it will fall short of obtaining its objectives.

TABLE 4-4

KEY ELEMENTS IN A WORKPLACE VIOLENCE PREVENTION PROTOCOL

- Clearly articulated statement demonstrating the organization's commitment against violence and abusive behaviors.
- Policies and procedures for documenting and punishing threats and abusive behaviors.
- Identification of training requirements for different levels of the organization.
- Procedures for organizing a team to manage complex threats.

SOURCE: National Safe Workplace Institute

Finally, the organization should establish teams, committees, or task forces to address complex threats. In most organizations such a team will seldom meet because most threats and issues can be addressed by a single manager or small group of people who receive information and make preliminary decisions. However, there could easily be situations and circumstances that require a much more sophisticated response. In those cases, individuals of varying perspectives and expertise should be brought together to respond. How teams are organized and work is addressed elsewhere in this book.

EARNING OUR WINGS AND PROVING IT

There are many good ideas that businesses should consider implementing to help improve employee performance and morale. But we cannot lose sight of the fact that businesses exist to earn profits and, as a result, programs and policies must be rationalized within that context. Violence prevention policies and programs should be carefully evaluated in order to determine their effectiveness to the organization Some methods for conducting an appropriate evaluation are identified in Table 4-5.

Perhaps the most definitive method for obtaining feedback is to compare data from employee surveys, although other methods are appropriate. Essentially what you want to determine is whether or not your program is effective. Presumably this could be demonstrated in reduced levels of stress and fewer incidents of violence. Every organization is unique and you must customize your particular system for evaluating effectiveness. To some extent, you will find increased attendance and productivity, less tension between supervisors and line/craft employees, and fewer internal examples of stress (e.g. fewer workers' compensation stress claims, fewer Equal Employment Opportunity Commission complaints).

ONE SIZE DOES NOT FIT ALL

There are no magic buttons to push in order to prevent workplace violence— it takes considerable effort, imagination and persuasion. While this chapter has provided a model, you must customize and modify it to fit your organization's unique needs. This requires a keen understanding of your organization, its culture, work force, stakeholders, and pressures. You must also have imagination in identifying exactly how to construct the programs and policies that will work best within your organization's limitations.

Finally, you must be persuasive. There will always be those who will insist that violence is foreign to your organization and that " it can't happen here." This is only natural, because many managers deny pressures and threats that have existed for a long time. You must persuade them that violence prevention is well worth the cost and that the techniques implied in this model will save the business money while improving employee performance and productivity.

Unfortunately there could easily be pressure to avoid certain steps or to take short cuts. The model provided in this chapter is designed to be comprehensive and to establish standards by which to evaluate performance. Therefore you should strive to take a comprehensive approach in order to ensure success.

TABLE 4-5
METHODS FOR OBTAINING FEEDBACK ON PROGRAM EFFECTIVENESS

- De-brief and evaluate after serious incidents of violence.
- Obtain feedback from employees and stakeholders on program effectiveness.
- Examine levels of stress within the organization.
- Evaluate knowledge and competence of key program participants.

SOURCE: National Safe Workplace Institute

5

CURBING THE EPIDEMIC

First Steps
in Violence Prevention

Violence prevention should be a part of any organization's business plans because it is a means to enhance organizational effectiveness and profitability. Such prevention policies and procedures are necessary to ensure a healthy work environment that is a legal obligation under the Occupational Safety and Health Act of 1970 and a moral obligation as well. As we push toward the end of the 20th century, businesses are learning that the quality and health of the work environment produce a competitive edge for increased profits, and for obtaining and retaining the human resources essential to finding the outer limits of the organization's potential.

It is not enough to wait for something to happen.Employers should aggressively pursue the types of options outlined in this book. The time to begin is now. This chapter is meant to stimulate creative and productive thought rather than to define the limits of what can be done.

WHAT DO YOU NEED TO DO?

The first step toward a violence-free work environment is to assess your organization's requirements. Unfortunately, this step is often overlooked when organizations rush to develop programs and fail to establish a good baseline from which to build and operate. A sound needs assessment should be tailored to meet the unique and special requirements of your work environment. Don't be fooled by the thought that you can develop an effective program simply by duplicating what has been done elsewhere. Your unique situation and circumstances will be different.

Most organizations in the U.S. today do not have a proactive or hands-on approach to workplace violence. The response to this crisis is often splintered. Until now, most employers have been content to depend on existing human resource or security policies and programs to cope with workplace violence. By any measure it poses challenges that will test most employers well beyond their existing capacity to respond. Most employers have just not identified it as a separate issue that warrants special focus. In some cases, one part (e.g. human resources) of an organization will have a far different response than another part (e.g. security). Sound policy development will lead to coordination of the many different actors within the organization.

Examples of workplace violence and typical responses are outlined in Table 5-1. What this table shows is that organizations are very reactive, that they fail to do a good job anticipating violence. The nature of the crisis suggests that prevention is almost always better than intervention, a response when that situation has grown very severe. Also, under the status quo there

TABLE 5-1
TYPICALLY USED POLICIES AGAINST EMPLOYEE VIOLENCE

LEVEL OR TYPE OF VIOLENCE	*RESPONSE*
• Murder or physical abuse.	• Phone local law enforcement.
• Threats of violence	• Perhaps involvement of security personnel.
	• Application of personnel procedures
• Abusive acts or signs of stress	• Employee assistance programs or existing mental health services.
• Property damage or sabotage	• Surveillance cameras, electronic monitoring.
• Verbal abuse	• Disciplinary action, including suspension or discharge.

SOURCE: National Safe Workplace Institute

is no certainty that responses will be coordinated and that appropriate investigative procedures will be followed to ensure adequate and proper decisions.

These reactive strategies will no longer suffice for the 1990's and beyond. Contemporary business leaders must be concerned about intruder threats as well as threats from within the work environment. Included in the myriad of possibilities are stalkers, angry customers, suppliers, former employees, and terrorists. Moreover, visible corporations (national or local) may spur violence from severely deranged individuals.

Workplace violence really constitutes a corporate crisis, because these incidents usually:

- Involve threatened or actual loss of life or property
- Create severe danger for the corporation or subdivision undergoes severe danger
- Disrupt fulfillment of some or all essential functions
- Exceed authority and resources of immediate supervisors to respond

During the remainder of this chapter, we will examine a menu of measures that an employer can take to address workplace violence. We thereby hope to empower employers in addressing often long neglected problems. Surprisingly, there is much that each employer can do, even without the assistance of consultants and other outsiders.

SHIFTING TO PROACTION
Rationales

Litigation and government regulation are providing the impetus for many businesses to pursue strategies for workplace violence prevention. There now have been successful lawsuits by plaintiffs in several states and the Occupational Safety and Health Administration has issued a number of citations. Rationales for programs are presented in Table 5-2.

Once a rationale is established, senior managers must understand the need to shift the business to a proactive mode. Effective policy must begin with senior management assuming an active role in the development and communication of general policies and procedures. Without clear support from above, there is little chance that a coherent violence prevention policy and program will be planned and implemented. Once senior managers understand and support the need for a violence prevention program, development of policy can flow in a logical and prudent fashion.

Table 5-2

Employer Rationales for Workplace Violence Prevention Programs

- Legal

  Case law has established that an employer must respond to threats in a reasonable and prudent fashion. Doctrines of foreseeability, negligent security, hiring, supervision, etc., have potential application.

- Regulatory

  The Occupational Safety and Health Act of 1970—Section 5(a), the general duty clause, means that an employer must act in a reasonable and prudent fashion to address "recognized hazards." OSHA has issued several citations arising from workplace violence.

- Good Business

  An inferior work environment will encourage good employees to leave and deter good applicants from applying. A violent work environment will harm productivity and damage profitability.

Crucial to understanding your organization's unique requirements is a needs assessment which will involve understanding the fears and experiences of your employee population, as well as your organization's past experiences with workplace violence. These steps are outlined in Table 5-3. Once it has been completed, then the organization can begin to focus on the steps that are crucial to putting a sound program together.

By discussing some of the points in Table 5-3, the reader will begin to understand how to properly conduct a thorough assessment. Key points:

Attitude/Climate Surveys

Our work shows that line employees are much more aware of violence than middle and senior managers. This is true because line employees tend to be the organization's interface with the outside. To learn what employees think, we suggest that a survey be conducted asking crucial questions. We have found that (1) employees often see violence as a problem that is increasing and (2) that potential violence is often a more serious problem than other safety and health concerns. A number of national surveys have shown that most employees see violence as a serious problem that is neglected by management.

While surveys are useful instruments in identifying the scope of the problem, focus groups as the next step can be useful in identifying the intensity of the beliefs and feelings that exist. They can also flesh out the data for the elaboration that is often lacking in mere numbers.

Evaluation/Assessments

Employers may consider contracting with consultants and experts for evaluations that are truly independent and free of bias. It is only natural that existing personnel will have a stake in the status quo and will be reluctant to evaluate critically programs that they or colleagues have managed. While you may wish to go outside for an evaluation, you will want to aggressively manage your consultant. This may be necessary because of the unique culture of your organization or because your organization may possess characteristics and nuances that are difficult to comprehend.

No organizational assessment can be truly complete unless there is a thorough review of past incidents of violence in the workplace. It is surprising how even small organizations have had numerous incidents in the

TABLE 5-3

STEPS IN UNDERSTANDING WORKPLACE VIOLENCE & ESTABLISHING A PREVENTION STRATEGY

1. *Needs assessment* of the employer's unique requirements.

2. *Attitude/climate surveys* followed *by focus groups* with employees and others to identify problems, issues, etc., that may currently exist.

3. *Evaluation* of:

   existing programs, policies, and personnel.

   past incidents and threats of violence.

   role of the existing personnel in investigating and designing preventive measures involving workplace violence or threats of violence.

   security policies, procedures, and physical security systems to determine whether existing policies and systems are well-suited to controlling violence at facilities.

4. *Briefings, reports, and memoranda* to provide background on issues, management considerations, need for policy, etc.

5. *Review of what is known* about occupational stress and workplace violence within the work environment and what is being done to address those conditions.

SOURCE: National Safe Workplace Institute

past. Such a review should focus on how effective your organization was in addressing the problems that you experienced. You will also, of course, want to think about your successes in managing such incidents. Questions that can be asked in such an assessment include:

- What could management have foreseen about the situation?
- Was there a pattern in an individual's background that could have tipped off management about the prospect for violence?
- How well did key players (e.g. security, human resources) manage the crisis of violence that occurred?
- Were there steps that could have been handled more effectively or efficiently?
- When did management know about the violence or prospect for violence? What did it do about the situation?

Executive Level/Senior Manager Briefings

The growing body of knowledge and literature on workplace violence issues includes information of very unequal quality. For example, there are a number of videos—some poor, others excellent—that can be used to increase awareness and empower employees. Senior managers should learn what they can about this important subject in order to understand all aspects of what is required by the workplace violence challenge. Outside experts are available for high-level briefings and workshops.

In truth, most organizations currently have a violence program. Typically, it is an executive protection program designed to help senior managers face the vast array of threats generated against their lives and well-being. Corporate boards have supported such programs because they know that an insecure executive is a non-productive corporate officer. The same rationale holds true for other parts of the organization. If employers want to have effective and productive organizations, they must think of violence prevention in a more realistic fashion.

EVALUATION OF PHYSICAL SECURITY AND ACCESS AUTHORIZATION PROGRAM

Employers should periodically evaluate physical security systems and access authorization programs. They must pay as much attention to the human dimensions of this problem as the physical. Witness the February, 1988 example of the ESL tragedy in Sunnyvale, California. A fired computer technician evaded ESL's elaborate security system and murdered seven and injured twelve company employees.

Special security requirements should be constantly reevaluated. For example, senior managers may require special security when threatened with retaliatory acts by former employees, or females may have special needs when threatened in a domestic dispute. In some instances, the preventive response may be as simple as relocating a threatened employee within the office complex.

The Cummins Engine Company in Columbus, Indiana provides an excellent example of corporate policy geared to prevention. Developed jointly by human resources and security professionals, it establishes guidelines for interpersonal conduct. It stresses respect for others regardless of their gender, age, race, national origin, religion or position in the corporation. The company's commitment to the policy and willingness to respond without delay to charges of intimidation or harassment are unequivocally stated.

Employees are provided with a flow chart which illustrates the process for making and handling complaints. According to corporate security director J. Branch Walton, there was an increase in complaints following the program's initiation in 1991, followed by a significant decrease within the next year.

COMMUNICATING A WORKPLACE VIOLENCE POLICY

Most organizations will want to consider a positive strategy for communicating a workplace violence policy in order to avoid alarming employees, stockholders, or others with a stake in the organization. A wise course may be to acknowledge the high levels of violence that exist in our society while pledging to prevent that violence from spilling into the work environment. For openers, employers should assert that violence of any sort is contrary to business purpose. Employees must understand that management has or is putting into place a strong violence prevention policy.

Whatever policy is developed must be supported through *reinforced communication* on a periodic basis to continuously regenerate its impact. Senior managers must articulate the organization's policy on a periodic basis so that employees understand the high priority that they give to violence prevention. Some of the ways for such communication include statements in corporate newsletters, posters on bulletin boards, statements to employee meetings, newsletters and customized communications.

Senior managers' role in violence prevention is critical and must be periodically reinforced. If employees perceive that such a program lacks top management priority, then they will have less confidence in the program and will be reluctant to offer their support. Likewise, a sound program will require a modest budget, particularly for training and outside consultants. Once a program is established, managers must ensure that sufficient program funding exists and is continued on an appropriate basis.

ENCOURAGING EMPLOYEES TO REPORT THREATS

There must be a place where threats and other such information can be reported. If employees are skeptical about management and its intentions (a normal situation in many organizations because of layoffs), then employees may be reluctant to fully participate in a program. Communication from management about the violence prevention program and its reporting procedures is critical to instill employee confidence in the mechanism where threat information is received. If they do not perceive that mechanism as neutral, effective, and able to treat information in a confidential fashion, then they will probably ignore the system and the policy will lose its effectiveness.

Traditionally, employees must have designated personnel (e.g. security or human resources) who are qualified to receive and act upon threats. They may or may not be appropriate, depending on how these personnel are perceived. The option of an independent 800 hotline or even a telephone answering service for confidential reporting can be considered. The use of an outside service raises many questions. Operators must be able to distinguish routine information from that which requires an immediate response. For emergencies, operators must be able to immediately contact key personnel within your organization. Each and every option has shortcomings and must be examined critically. Table 5-4 has been designed to highlight the basic options that most organizations have in examining where threats should be reported; it certainly is not all-inclusive. Any option that is considered should be carefully and thoughtfully scrutinized.

EARLY DETECTION PROGRAMS

Ideally, an organization is best served when problems are identified and addressed as early as possible. As discussed earlier, aggressive or aberrant

TABLE 5-4
ANALYSIS OF OPTIONS FOR THREAT REPORTING

OPTIONS	POSSIBLE IMPLICATIONS
• Human resources	1. Could confuse employees during period of layoffs or other Staff changes.
	2. Employees usually have confidence in HR.
• Security	1. Probably best equipped to deal with serious threats and dangers to the organization.
	2. May be seen as organization's "Police."
• Independent hotlines or answering service	1. May be seen as neutral or confidential.
	2. Critical time may be lost in reporting threats to designated Personnel.

SOURCE: National Safe Workplace Institute

behaviors should raise red flags and trigger appropriate interventions. There are three behavioral tools that employers can use that will help serve as early warning systems for violence and other risk factors. These tools are pre-employment psychological screening, post-employment behavioral observation, and dangerousness assessments.

Workplace violence programs can start before employees are hired. Hiring decisions are important, especially because of the negligent hiring doctrine that is emerging in tort law. For jobs with public responsibilities some employers have tried using psychological screening programs to help identify risk factors that may be of concern, including a propensity toward violence. Such screens are usually not used to deny individuals employment, but to help identify characteristics and risk factors that can be monitored and considered in supervision strategies. Effective screening methods have existed for decades but they have not been effectively used, even in high-risk industries. Unfortunately, there is some debate concerning the value of such information over a period of time.

Paper-and-pencil testing must be consistent with the Americans with Disabilities Act of 1990 and the Civil Rights Act of 1991. Typically, the strategy is to validate a test specifically for the position or category/family of positions. However, where human reliability is critical to public health and safety, an exclusionary screening program may be implemented. Here the emphasis is upon screening out at-risk persons as opposed to a model for predicting job compatibility and success. Thus, one must carefully analyze the needs of the organization, its obligation toward employees, and social consequences to determine whether a strict validation model should be implemented or exclusionary screening be conducted on a post-offer basis.

A very important strategy involves post-employment Behavioral Observation Programs (BOP), designed for use by supervisors with regard to existing employees. In its common usage, a paper-and-pencil form is completed by the supervisor, noting job-related behavioral changes such as changes in job performance and interpersonal relations in the workplace. Ideally, the forms should be sent to an independent agency which maintains records and ensures that information is used in an objective and systematic way for the benefit of both the organization and the individual. A number of programs in a variety of industries have been used for many years. The net effect of these programs has been a significant increase in interaction among employees and supervisors which has led to effective referrals for employee assistance and set the occasion for professional intervention. The program receives positive recognition as individuals receive counseling or rehabilitation and then re-enter the workplace as effective team members.

The third tool is dangerousness assessment which is a formalized psychological evaluation to determine if a person represents a clear and imminent threat to those around him or her. Such an examination must be conducted by a licensed psychologist or psychiatrist who is trained and experienced in such assessments. Most mental health providers do not have this capability.

These three strategies are described in Table 5-5 below.

TABLE 5-5
STRATEGIES TO IDENTIFY RISK FACTORS

- *Pre-employment psychological screening.* Paper-and-pencil test that a job applicant takes prior to employment which is designed to reveal risk factors and/or predict effectiveness. In general, tests should be validated to ensure appropriateness for the jobs being offered.

- *Post-employment behavioral observation.* A rating form used by supervisors to document behavioral patterns and changes that may be used for counseling, employee assistance or professional evaluation of threat (dangerousness assessment).

- *Dangerousness assessments.* A psychological evaluation of a person to determine if he or she represents a clear and immediate threat to others. Such evaluations recommend specific interviews or follow-up for management.

SOURCE: National Safe Workplace Institute

MANAGERS AND SUPERVISORS THE FRONT-LINE DEFENSE

Senior managers by definition have broad administrative responsibilities and, as a result, are crucial actors in violence prevention. Managers and supervisors are on the firing line in addressing violence; because they interface with employees and are often present in the workplaces, they serve as a bridge between different parts of the organization. They are, in essence, management's "eyes and ears" and are in the best position to meaningfully and effectively execute policies and procedures. Chapter 9 addresses in detail the role that managers and front-line supervisors play in violence prevention.

POST-INCIDENT AND TRAUMA DEBRIEFINGS

Many employers have already developed contingency plans for certain emergencies such as fires, natural disasters, sniper attacks, etc. Prudent employers may wish to plan also for the worst case of workplace violence in order to be fully prepared. This implies that employers will have thought through the scenarios so that they know exactly how they will respond to a serious incident, which could include any of the following:

- Injuries or death.
- Death of an employee (e.g. heart attack).
- Extreme aggression (aggravated assault that stops short of injury).
- Property damage.

When such incidents occur, employers should contract with post-trauma consultants that will act to restore stability and morale to all employees in the workplace. With respect to post-trauma care, there are a small number of such highly qualified care consultants in the U.S. A growing number of Employee Assistance Program personnel are engaging in this work or can recommend specialists.

FAIRNESS
One Step Toward Prevention

There is little question that most perpetrators have a strong sense of anger and injustice toward their work environment. They feel that managers or co-workers, both, or even the entire company system have conspired to infringe on their rights as workers. More often than not, investigations have shown that companies have had uneven and imbalanced policies that, intentionally or otherwise, have proved to be biased. By following simple rules to make procedures and policies as bias-free and as objective as possible, you can go a long way toward fairness, thereby eliminating a problem that may trigger a potentially violent individual.

Program development must be appropriate. Ideally, those involved in policy and program development should include craft, line or staff employees—whatever is natural based on the structure of the organization (e.g. unionized, management system, type of industry).

TRANSFORMING INTENTIONS INTO REALITY

After completing an assessment of your organization, you will begin the challenging process of transforming intentions into reality. Key considerations in developing your program include:

- *Be inclusive.* Programs that exclude craft workers, support staff, and others will lack credibility. Think about putting together a team that will make sure that you are including the most comprehensive perspective.

- *Meet your needs.* Think about your organization—not the ideas of some expert-in putting together your program. Experts have insights and ideas and should be seen as resources, not decision-makers. You make the decisions—make this *your* program. With these thoughts in mind, let's turn to the key points in translating thoughts into action.

First, you should consider stating your policy clearly and effectively: "This company will not tolerate violence or any other practice that abuses the dignity of our employees or stakeholders." A clear policy statement that is publicized in posters, in internal newsletters, and in comments by senior management will communicate your company's position loud and clear. Naturally you will want to take steps to ensure that your policy is not stated in such a fashion that will alarm employees, their families, or stakeholders. You also have to be sensitive to how and when the policy is stated.

There are other steps that you may wish to consider, including early intervention mechanisms such as behavioral observation systems, training programs for supervisors, and other protocols and procedures for managing threats. These topics will be handled in more detail in subsequent chapters.

TABLE 5-6

WHERE THE RUBBER HITS THE ROAD— TRANSFORMING INTENTIONS INTO REALITY

1. Articulate anti-violence policy.

2. Establish a reporting mechanism.

3. Implement early intervention mechanisms:

   • supervisor training

   • behavioral observation programs

4. Ensure that supervisors are focus point for prevention.

5. Establish a procedure for policy and threat management.

SOURCE: National Safe Workplace Institute Peer Review

PEER REVIEW
An Early Intervention System for Employees and Employers

This chapter would not be complete without a brief discussion of the concept of peer review. Typically, employees are confused and want answers following a serious incident of violence. But those same co-workers who feel bewildered about a worker's violent acts could have played a key role in preventing the tragedy had a company peer review program been in place.

Peer review for all employees may be one of the most effective outlets for resolving grievances since it relies greatly on peers' judgments to address and help resolve issues.

Generally conducted by panels of employees and managers, a peer panel is established as company policy and panelists are trained to deal with workplace issues in determining the fairness with which company policies or rules were applied. The worker-turned-violent perpetrator sometimes contends that management applied policy or treatment inconsistently, leaving him feeling desperate and with no where to turn.

During the early stages of an employee's problems, in which he shows signs of aggression toward co-workers or management, he may be served with written warnings and disciplinary actions. As a recourse, the employee can turn to a peer review panel to intervene with management to consider his disputes.

The panelists are charged with confidentiality and review issues generally in the disciplinary stages of a worker's dispute. Like with a jury, the worker may be able to "strike" (or disallow) certain peer review panel members. Management cannot overrule a peer panel decision.

"If a worker is dismissed, a peer panel reviewing the case might decide that the worker was dismissed wrongfully," said J. Steven Warren, an attorney with the Greenville, S.C., firm of Jackson, Lewis, Schnitzler and Krupman. "The peer panel might reinstate the worker, but with conditions such as requiring that the worker enlist in the employee assistance programs or therapy," Warren continued. "Workers say that knowing that peer review is available gives them greater job security. Workers feel they are being treated fairly, and tend not to resort to legal action or violent acts, for that matter."

Peer review, said Warren, also helps an employer avoid costly litigation, regulatory agency complaints, or other outside intervention that can result from a grievant worker's act, Warren said. This is because peer review shows juries, regulatory agencies (e.g. Equal Employment Opportunity Commission), and plaintiff's lawyers that the employer applied more than reasonable care in trying to address a problem.

"If an employee becomes violent, workers' compensation will generally pay for the injured, but you may have family members trying to sue a company," Warren explained. "If peer review had been used as a remedy to a worker's complaints, a lawyer may see a plaintiff has no case, and OSHA (Occupational Safety and Health Administration), EEOC, and a jury will recognize that a company was not negligent since it attempted to address the issue through peer review."

Companies that do not employ peer review contend that it limits management's power. They fear both the results of a peer panel's decision and the perception of wrong-doing.

Without programs such as peer review or employee assistance, the worker who perceives that management is "out to get him" often feels that he has no recourse, Warren said. He feels that management has responded poorly to his concerns, such as in denial of a promotion or raise, improper work conditions, or co-worker disputes.

"Perception is reality to most workers," Warren said. "We see as many cases based on perception of wrong-doing as we do in real wrong-doing by employers."

Experts who study the growing trend of workplace violence say that warning signs are visible long before an act occurs. Unfortunately, many managers do not pursue early interventions effectively. The result is a violent act: either a physical assault, destruction of company property, or sabotage of production processes.

Harvey Caras, president of Caras Associates in Columbia, Maryland, developed the peer review panel process 12 years ago while he was a human resources manager for General Electric. He feels that the use of peers in conflict resolution can be a powerful tool. "Peers have tremendous influence, and peer review panels make very good judgments regarding worker issues." In a survey Caras conducted of his 300 corporate clients, 143 responded that peer reviews have improved the consistency of policy and practice application by 92 percent. He added that no outside agency has ever overruled a peer review decision among any of his clients; moreover, supervisor effectiveness has been improved by 82 percent. The survey also showed that employee morale had improved by 88 percent since the implementation of peer review.

The survey did not include data relating to acts of violence among companies with peer review, but Caras said its likelihood is reduced since peer review helps to eliminate the notion of unfairness, bias and ultimate control by management. Issues that can be covered by peer review are illustrated in Table 5-7.

TABLE 5-7

GRIEVANCES CONSIDERED BY PEER REVIEW PANELS

There are no set limits to the issues that can be considered for a peer review panel. They are as varied as the work force, but may include:

- promotion/performance review
- drug test results
- disciplinary actions
- overtime disputes or abuses
- sexual harassment
- race, sex, age, religion or disability discrimination
- safety issues
- job assignments

SOURCE: National Safe Workplace Institute

COOPERATION AND COMMUNICATION

Establishing Teams to Address Threats

Violence knows no bounds. The brutal and seemingly irrational violence that was once confined to urban gang warfare now rears its ugly head in all aspects of our lives. Some signs: a U.S. President declares that we now have a generation of teenagers that is better armed than the police; Hollywood celebrities and Olympic athletes are attacked and maimed in public view; a six-year-old Chicago boy is caught carrying a pistol to school in a struggle to protect his lunch money; four teenage girls are gunned-down in a late-night robbery and shooting in an Austin yogurt shop, their bodies torched beyond recognition by the perpetrator to hide any evidence.

The inevitable reality is that individuals are acting out violently at every age, in all social and economic strata—and in the work environment as well with an alarming frequency. The list of U.S. employers who have experienced lethal violence is growing ever longer: the U.S. Postal Service, General Dynamics, IBM, Honeywell, 3M, Homedco, Merrill Lynch, Kraft General Foods, General Motors, and scores of others. Violence strikes large and small employers alike;companies that are either benevolent or authoritarian in management styles—neither is truly immune. Even those employers with an outstanding people management records face violence or its threat under many different circumstances: from current or former employees, customers, intruders, stalkers or individuals involved in domestic disputes, and others with real or perceived grievances who decide to strike out against an organization.

While it is difficult to predict the precise time when violence may strike an organization, there are steps that employers and workers can and should take to prepare for such a possibility. They can begin by understanding that most violent incidents follow recognized threats, and that the reasonable and prudent course of action is to adequately prepare for violence as a life-threatening hazard that can be minimized or even, with proper preparation and action, be prevented. Employers must realize that violence is a hazard much like other safety or health hazards in the workplace. If they fail to act in a prudent fashion, they can face the likelihood of regulatory sanctions from safety officials, lawsuits from those who are injured, and, perhaps most important, loss of faith by once-trusting employees.

In this chapter, we will discuss the idea of building threat management teams. Some organizations have crisis management teams that may assume this responsibility. In many organizations, though, senior managers will want to have a process involving the complementary skills of different individuals to manage threats. That is what this chapter is about.

REASONS FOR A THREAT MANAGEMENT POLICY

There are many rationales for formulating a "threat management" policy. Ideally, employers should have the goal of work environments that are free from harm. For those who are not so motivated, there is increasing evidence that regulation and the real possibility of lawsuits will require employers to develop policy for addressing the possibility of violence. Murder is now the second leading killer of U.S. employees with more than 1,064 slain in 1993 alone. Of that number, 149 were slain by co-employees, former employees, and stalkers.

In a move consistent with the thrust of existing Federal job-safety law and regulation, the U.S. Occupational Safety and Health Administration (OSHA) has now issued numerous citations to employers penalizing them for failing to protect employees in a range of circumstances. And they are likely to impose more in coming years. . An analogous situation would be when a construction company fails to shore a freshly dug trench. Even though there is a low probability that the walls of a construction trench will collapse and harm workers, a failure to shore the trench is viewed by the law as a very serious violation of the Occupational Safety and Health Act of

1970. Inevitably, then, employers who fail to respond to such threats of violence are exposing themselves to governmental liability and regulatory sanctions.

Perhaps more significant are the lawsuits that will emerge as an even more compelling factor in the development of workplace violence prevention policy. Employers and their insurers have already spent tens of millions of dollars in defending or settling such lawsuits in Florida, Michigan, and Texas. It is likely that millions more will be awarded in the future in cases where employers have failed to act prudently to protect their employees from such possibilities.

Development and operation of threat management teams will be the focus of this chapter, after a review of policy issues. Threat management teams are where the "rubber hits the road" when it comes to workplace violence. Threat management teams are now the centerpiece for violence prevention strategies by organizations as diverse as Kraft General Foods, County Government in San Diego, and the Postal Service's Denver District. Many more businesses and government agencies are considering the use of such teams as they formulate a response to America's violence epidemic. As we will see later in this chapter, the use of such teams reflects the complexity of some threats and the need to have a "team" response. Teams may not be appropriate for every organization and certainly don't need to be convened every time a threat exists. Indeed, learning when to convene a team is an important step in the process of developing a sound violence prevention strategy. Prematurely convening a threat management team will frustrate some members and discredit the process.

Ideally, employers will take a bottom-up approach in building threat management policy. While virtually all employees—including senior managers—have seen and experienced the anger and hostility that can easily spill over into physical violence in the work environment, line-level employees often have greater experience of considerable violence and feel that they have a lot to lose from the lack of a sound program. Early involvement of rank-and-file workers will help ensure employee acceptance of policy and greater cooperation and communication because all employees intuitively understand that they have a stake in the success of such policy.

RECOGNIZED HAZARDS

What is a recognized hazard? What steps can employers take to reduce the chance that a "recognized hazard" will harm an employee? These questions must be understood as part of the process of developing a threat management policy. Threats and behaviors should be the focus of an employer's attention and the focus in threat management, not whether someone fits into a profile based on the acts of past perpetrators. How to distinguish threats and behaviors is carefully examined in Chapter 7.

The most serious and frustrating situations that can be considered by an organization come from outside, especially from former employees or stalkers (individuals who are romantically obsessed). External sources of violence are hard to manage because of two reasons. First, the perpetrators are beyond the control of the organization and, as a result, it is far less likely that good information will be available. To successfully manage a threat, an organization must have access to *accurate information in a timely fashion*.

Second, threat management of individuals from outside the organization often must involve cooperation from law enforcement. Law enforcement is often reluctant to cooperate unless there is convincing evidence that a law has been broken because, by their nature, they are reactive rather than proactive . However, if a law enforcement agency joins with the organization in the threat management process, the tools for violence prevention increase exponentially. For example, most law enforcement agencies have the legal power to detain individuals until they can be properly evaluated for dangerousness.

INVESTIGATING INCIDENTS

All threats and bizarre behaviors should be investigated by individuals who have been trained for such a purpose. Many security or human resource departments in large organizations have trained such investigators on staff who can enhance the investigative process. However, individuals can be trained in a short period of time to undertake the crucial aspects of investigation. Indeed, many training videos and manuals are available that are designed to instruct sound investigative skills and techniques.

When it comes to violent behaviors, investigations can be supported through the involvement of licensed psychologists working in tandem with a company official who coordinates threat management. Involvement in most cases will normally conclude with one of several options: referral to the employee assistance program; reassignment of the target to another job within the company; requesting a fitness for duty evaluation; placing the individual on medical and therapeutic leave; another course of non-punitive discipline; or, if necessary, termination. The important consideration is that threats must be taken seriously, appropriately investigated, and followed through to a logical conclusion that ensures the safety and security of the work environment.

There are a number of key considerations in investigating threats that will be examined later in this chapter and in Chapter 7, which presents a detailed overview of managing serious threats. For information on how to best pursue the management of threats, please refer to that portion of this book. To some extent, there is overlap between these two chapters. Often, the threat management team will scrutinize many of the same pieces of information considered by the investigator and coordinator (who are often the same person). Such duplication is inevitable.

STEPS IN THREAT POLICY DEVELOPMENT

Table 6-1 provides six essential steps in the development of a Threat Management Policy. Because threats should ideally be addressed by a team approach involving individuals from different parts of the organization, senior management must support policy to ensure cooperation and cohesion. Otherwise, the involvement of key team members and outside specialists runs the high risk of becoming limited, reducing the chances for successful management.

The entire organization must recognize that threat situations may represent a threat to the lives of individuals. Nothing less than a cohesive approach, with sufficient support, is crucial to a positive outcome. Some organizations are implementing rules that make it a rules violation for failure to report threats in a timely fashion, reinforcing the need and facilitating the process for individuals who otherwise may be reluctant to reveal such information.

Many organizations are naturally and understandably reluctant to promulgate rules. In some cases, their attorneys have said that management cannot address problems they "don't know about." This point suggests that managers take an ostrich approach to violence. In reality, managers often know about violent behaviors or the threat of violence and simply have failed to act. The very *foreseeability* of events by a limited cadre of managers is likely to establish liability.

Still other managements don't want to burden what they feel is an already burdened organization. The reality is that it is the essence of management's responsibility to provide a safe and healthy work environment that is free from violence, threats, menacing behaviors, and other problems.

FIRST STEPS IN THREAT MANAGEMENT

Table 6-1 outlines the first steps to establishing a threat management policy. In most organizations where such a policy exists, it has been established by a committee of individuals working together to ensure that the organization has the most sensible strategy possible to prevent violence. In essence, the issues identified in Table 6-1 will help set an agenda for violence prevention. While it is essential that top management support the overall program, it is also crucial that key parts of the organization, with different perspectives and talents, participate in policy and team development so that everyone buys into what is going on and formulates a better balanced program and policy.

SCOPE OF ACTIVITIES AND OPERATIONS

The scope of activities and operations involving large complex organizations is enormous. The Denver Postal District, which has 12,000 employees in both Colorado and Wyoming, established a violence prevention program that was overwhelmed the first few months it was in operation with reports of threats and related behaviors. It has spent considerable time and resources in determining how to best organize and expand its services. This group wisely targeted the Denver metropolitan area, a manageable geographic area, for the first stage of its program.

Table 6-1
Steps in Establishing a Threat Management Policy

1. Outline the scope of activities and operations covered by the policy.

2. Identify a location for reporting threats.

3. Identify individuals who will be a part of the threat management team.

4. Choose a team/violence prevention coordinator.

5. Establish the criteria for convening the threat team.

6. Set training criteria for team members.

SOURCE: National Safe Workplace Institute

Organizations need to debate how far-flung their teams will be. In most cases, it is desirable to have teams localized so that they can respond quickly and efficiently. An example of what not to do is the Postal Service which established a national response team that originates from Washington. Such an approach makes little sense in addressing the complex requirements of its more than 700,000 employees. On the other hand, some organizations may function well with a headquarters-based team. DuPont, the chemical giant, essentially has a strategy similar to that of the Postal Service, utilizing the services and talents of employees in its Wilmington, Delaware, headquarters.

IDENTIFY A LOCATION FOR REPORTING THREATS

Identifying a place to receive threats is far more complex than what one might expect. Generally security departments are the most logical places to receive reported threats since they are usually the best equipped to deal with menacing individuals.

However, in organizations where security officers are off-duty or retired law enforcement officers or contract employees, some employees may be reluctant to report if they feel that the department lacks the sophistication to properly and adequately address problems

There are a number of other possibilities about where a threat- reporting center can be established in the organization, including human resources, the legal department, etc. Or you can use a toll-free number, an answering service, or other outside agency. Toll-free hotlines are becoming especially popular with many corporations. There are many advantages in going outside the organization, but the most important is that you are ensuring independence. This may increase the confidence that employees (and others) have in reporting threats. If this is the case, you may simply want to piggyback threat reporting into an existing employee hotline or contract with a vendor that provides such service.

Once a policy has been articulated, it must be reinforced throughout all levels of the organization. This can be through employee newsletters, training sessions and meetings, and other normal channels of company communications. Likewise, policy should be unequivocal in its content. There should be no doubt in the minds of those who read or hear the policy as to its goals or purpose. Furthermore, once a policy has been articulated, management must be ready to receive and act appropriately upon the information about threats, in order to make such a policy real and fully appreciated by workers and others who have a stake in a safe and secure work environment.

You will probably receive more reports of threats or abusive practices from family members and friends than from your employees. This information is very difficult to evaluate and must be done so with care. Because victims are often embarrassed, they are reluctant to come forward. But family members who see the recipient's acute stress and who are concerned about the individual's safety, are more inclined to act to ensure that proper steps are taken to protect that individual. .

THREAT MANAGEMENT TEAMS

Many organizations are turning to teams to manage threats and acts of violence. A team response implies that different skills are necessary for such a process. As we will see later, a team approach can potentially involve a significant number of individuals with varying but complementary perspectives. Ideally most threats will not require such a complex response but can be met through the decisions of the team leader or other official. Unfortunately, some situations will require a response involving multiple talents. As a result, key individuals must be trained and prepared to swing into action with very little notice. The ability of these specialists to work together as a cohesive unit can spell the difference between the success and failure of a company surviving everything from a low-level crisis to a catastrophic event.

When organizing for threat management, planners in large organizations may wish to consider a policy-making committee that formulates policies and serves as a consultant to more decentralized teams. In some instances, decentralized threat teams may be small, involving just two or three individuals. If small teams are used, they must focus on completing their investigation and making referrals as promptly as possible. They must recognize that their size and limited local resources impose limitations in complex situations. Ideally, such teams will include a member of management as well as a line worker. Team members should be widely perceived as unbiased in order to ensure that their response is viewed as credible and independent.

Whatever the method selected, the organization must have an approach and policy in place and have involved personnel well prepared for the possibility long before violence strikes. The training for operational teams includes skill building in areas such as mediation, conflict resolution, listening, investigation techniques, diversity awareness, and role-playing.

TABLE 6-2

THREAT MANAGEMENT TEAM MEMBERS

- Coordinator

  Duties:

  ✓ Takes information on threats; conducts investigation; and determines when to convene team.

  ✓ Coordinates team member activities.

  ✓ Lead contact with experts and consultants.

- Human Resources/Employee Assistance Program

- Clinical Psychologist (Consultant)

- Safety and Health Specialist

- Security Officer

- Attorney (Employment Law)

- Facilities Management Specialist

- Public Relations Specialist

SOURCE: National Safe Workplace Institute

Role-playing is especially important so that team members can understand the specific circumstances that they are likely to face.

The composition of teams, as shown in Table 6-2, should include individuals from within the company (e.g. security, human resource, legal, mental health professionals, safety, medical) and external consultants (e.g. psychologist, security specialist).

The development of an employee violence policy should flow from cooperation between management and workers. For a policy to have broad acceptance, it is important to involve managers and workers jointly on a committee that will work with those staff specialists who have primary policy development and execution responsibilities.

For large corporations that operate in several locations, senior management will likely organize Threat Management Teams on the basis of geographical territory. Because of demographics and other characteristics, certain regions may be given priority for the placement of teams. For example, a locale with chronic labor-management difficulties in an economically stressed region may be given priority over an area that appears problem-free.

CHOOSING A COORDINATOR

For a number of reasons, teams must have individuals who coordinate team activities. The term "coordinator" is chosen with care as opposed to "chairperson" or something equivalent. The idea behind coordinator is because that is essentially what the function is—coordinating the activities of numerous parties in a fashion that will produce the desired results. Coordinators are often individuals who work well with others and who have good judgment and reasonable investigative skills. They must be able to transcend the boundaries of the organization and obtain information that is crucial to making sound judgments.

A threat coordinator, the individual who manages this information, plays a key role in an effective violence prevention program. It is the coordinator who must make a crucial determination on how far a matter should be investigated. Obviously few employers can afford the luxury of assigning a team to every situation. In many cases, the coordinator alone will be able to manage an issue through to an appropriate conclusion. In cases where the problem is more complex or intractable, the coordinator will have to employ further resources, up to and including an entire team.

In most organizations, a coordinator will have job tasks that involve responsibilities beyond threat coordination and management. A coordinator will generally be a security or human resources professional who is assigned these additional responsibilities. However, regardless of that person's position in the organization, it is crucial that threat management be the coordinator's priority. To be competent in this area, he or she must receive substantial training in interviewing, incident documentation, and other skills essential to this important role. At the inception of a new program, it is quite possible that the coordinator will depend heavily on an outside consultant for assistance until he or she becomes confident in the execution of the many job responsibilities.

Ultimately, a coordinator should be designated and assigned the task of coordinating company policies, programs, and procedures in order to obtain a good overview. Since there are a number of responsibilities inherent in violence prevention, it is important that someone have a good feel for the organization's total violence-prevention mission.

Most important, the coordinator should also have the critical role of determining when threat management teams should be convened. This is a very important responsibility for a number of reasons. First, team members will have other responsibilities. They do not want to feel that they are wasting their time with tasks that could and should be handled by the coordinator or a subgroup of the threat management team. Second, what is known about group dynamics suggests that teams with more than four individuals are likely to have difficulty making decisions in an efficient and effective manner.

In some cases, the coordinator may wish to meet with a few team members rather than with the entire group, especially in situations that do not involve comprehensive or detailed management. This experience will help all members understand the process of team management and build trust between members. At the same time, this tactic will avoid the problems inherent of large groups meeting to address complex problems.

An individual charged with coordinating such threat management faces an enormous and complex challenge, even in small- and medium-sized organizations. To the extent possible, the coordinator should have access to outside consultants and other resources in order to approach the job in an efficient, professional, and effective fashion. Within a few months, the coordinator and key team members should be able to function cohesively.

CRITERIA FOR CONVENING THE THREAT TEAM

In general, the team must be convened when it has become apparent when the coordinator can not meet the challenge alone. In fact, there are some circumstances when the convening of the team should almost automatically occur. An example would involve a situation when a potential perpetrator, perhaps a former employee, has made a series of threats that suggest that he or she is about to take violent action. Of course, there are situations when the team leader may conclude that only specific team members are required to form a response. For example, the team leader may simply require the assistance of an attorney in seeking a restraining order.

In most cases, the coordinator will be able to conclude a response without involvement of other team members. However, he or she should maintain a log book, available to all team members, carefully detailing reports and the response that was made. The coordinator should de-brief team members on a periodic basis to illustrate the types of problems he or she is encountering as well as the responses being implemented against specific threats.

There are three factors that coordinators should always be alert to in managing a specific threat. These are: (1) presence of weapons in the possession of the perpetrator; (2) increased frequency of hostile or aggressive behavior or threats by the perpetrator; and (3) a perception that the perpetrator has little or nothing to lose by being violent. These three conditions, if they exist, suggest that there is a very real possibility of violence. Under these conditions, the organization needs to take concerted action to protect people and property against the increased likelihood of aggressive acts. Many of these processes and tasks are more carefully reviewed in Chapter 7.

TRAINING CRITERIA FOR TEAM MEMBERS

Several techniques should be taught to threat management team members. Most of these skills can be learned through video learning programs supplemented by instructional manuals, or, if necessary, from training by outside organizations such as the American Society for Training and Development.

Specific skills that team members should be exposed to include interviewing, conflict resolution, human reliability and stress, domestic violence, diversity, and incident documentation. There is no reason why a well-trained coordinator cannot put together an in-house training program consisting almost exclusively of video learning and instructional materials.

CORPORATE CRISIS MANAGEMENT

Many Fortune 500 corporations have crisis management committees already in place that may take up workplace violence as a subset of their responsibilities. Normally, they are involved in issues such as natural disasters (e.g. earthquakes or hurricanes) or product tampering. The response to threats and violence involves many of the same skills that are used to resolve other corporate crises. However, it is only prudent that these committees carefully examine the issues that are unique to workplace violence and that they consider adding appropriate personnel to their committees or creating a separate threat management team.

Table 6-2 provides the model composition for a Threat Management Team. In actual practice, each employer should conduct a needs assessment as a first step to determine his or her specific requirements. There is no right or wrong composition for teams. The right mix of skills and experiences is far more important than simply filling a slot. The reality in most small groups is that certain individuals will likely emerge as more assertive, given the challenge, the circumstances, or the personalities involved.

USE OF RESTRAINING ORDERS

Some experts have recommended employers to be reluctant in seeking protective or restraining orders. Opponents of restraining orders suggest that seeking such interventions may trigger a violent reaction by the target. There is no evidence to indicate that this is true. If a restraining order is appropriate, then it should be pursued. Indeed, emergency health care provides us with an analogy. We go to the hospital when we are seriously ill, even though there is a chance that we may die. The same is true with restraining orders. We use them because we are seeking relief from a threatening situation. That is a logical step. Furthermore, employers may wish to consider the alternative. If they fail to seek a restraining order, they may be exposed in a lawsuit for negligence if people, in the eyes of a jury, are needlessly injured.

A survey taken by the National Safe Workplace Institute in 1994 indicated that most corporate security directors have little confidence in the capability of law enforcement to enforce restraining orders. Naturally this confidence seems to vary widely from jurisdiction to jurisdiction. Law enforcement that has the legal authority and resources to detain people deemed to be dangerous to the public appears to be more effective in enforcing such orders. In fact, San Diego County, which can detain aggressors in cases of domestic violence, has been able to reduce its domestic homicide rate as a result of such efforts. The Charlotte Police Department is also now pursuing such an approach.

BALANCING RIGHTS
Perpetrator v. Organization

There should always be concern about the rights of individuals, including those of potential perpetrators. It is too easy to focus just on the needs of the organization. Complex situations demand a cautious approach. In general, a coordinator or a team must engage in a balancing act. Laws protecting an individual's privacy must be carefully considered in mapping out approaches in difficult cases. Also, labeling someone can create the possibility of slander which could result in a significant lawsuit. Nevertheless, a situation that could explode and result in the deaths of numerous individuals must be a foremost consideration. In complex situations, the balancing act can be made more manageable by including attorneys and others who understand the ramifications of an inappropriate or illegal decision or approach.

We have covered a lot of ground in this chapter. We have examined how to put together a team to manage threats while emphasizing that a coordinator is probably going to handle the vast majority of threat situations. This chapter should help you understand how to manage threats properly and systematically. However, there is no substitute for thoughtful action by people closest to the situation—men and women in the work environment who should participate in violence prevention activities.

CHAPTER

7

THE TURNING POINT

Assessing and Managing Threats

While it is difficult to predict the precise time when violence may strike, there are steps that employers and workers can take to prepare for such a possibility and to effectively manage a crisis once it occurs. Employers and employees alike can begin by understanding that most incidents of violence follow recognized threats. The reasonable and prudent course of action is to adequately prepare for violence as a life-threatening hazard that can be minimized or even, with proper preparation, be prevented. Employers must realize that violence is a hazard much like other safety hazards in the workplace. They must also recognize and accept the reality that law requires and good management dictates a response to a recognized threat that will reduce the possibility of physical harm to the employer's workers.

As we saw in Chapter 6, the complexity of some threats reflects the need to have a "team" response. This chapter takes this thinking a step further by highlighting proper procedures to be followed when threats of violence and actual incidents occur. This chapter does not attempt to address "team dynamics" as much as the process and mechanics of threat management.

In dealing with threatening behaviors, we must understand that we are dealing as much with an art as we are a science. Nonetheless, it is crucial that we have practical processes for handling threats because failure to respond poses far greater risks and problems. This chapter presents useful pieces of information that we have woven together to understand threats and how people act out violently in a work environment. Nevertheless we must recognize that situations differ and the circumstances and personalities vary.

All threats and bizarre behaviors should be investigated by trained professionals. Investigations can be supplemented by licensed psychologists or professional investigators working together with a company team coordinator. In most cases, threats can be brought to an effective conclusion without substantial damage to the organization or its members.

Generally, we must think of threats coming from two different sources: existing employees and intruders. Normally, management's involvement with an existing employee can end with his or her referral to the employee assistance program or mental health treatment facility, reassignment to another position, placing the individual on medical leave, or other courses of non-punitive discipline. In some cases, termination may be necessary. The important consideration is that threats must be taken seriously, appropriately investigated, and followed through to a logical conclusion that ensures the safety and security of the work environment.

Threats from an intruder (e.g. former employee, stalker, or other third party) typically pose greater risks and complexity. While employers can exercise some control over employees, intruders have freedom of movement and rights that make them difficult to contain. Nevertheless, there are steps that will be discussed in this chapter to be taken when threats are known by appropriate personnel. But before we begin, we should examine exactly what we mean by threats. Once we have proper definitions, we can devise sensible responses that will protect lives and property.

THREATS

A person who makes threats to an employer or to a worker represents a *recognized hazard* that must be addressed in an effective and timely manner. Even though most threats will not result in violence, management must respond as if violence were a real possibility. Threats and their three different types-direct, conditional, and veiled—as well as behavior should be the focus of the first step of the threat management process.

Management of threats from outside the organization involves far more sophisticated skills and sources of information than is required for those from an existing employee population. If a former employee or stalker is involved, getting information may be difficult. However, there are almost always sources of information, including some directly from the perpetrator. We must carefully analyze such information.

There are three primary types of threats. Each of these is defined below and a series of possible responses is identified.

1. Direct threats. These involve clear and explicit communications such as "I am going to kill you." They distinctly indicate that the perpetrator intends to do bodily harm.

RESPONSES TO DIRECT THREATS

Direct threats almost always involve laws being broken. If strong evidence exists, such as statements from multiple witnesses, many prosecutors will be willing to pursue criminal charges or seek restraining orders. If an employee has made a direct threat against another employee, he or she should be immediately discharged. Such a policy can be described as a zero-threat-tolerance policy.

Even in cases where a direct threat has been made and documented, you should investigate the circumstances behind the threat. You want to ensure that the perpetrator was not functioning in a hostile environment such as one which may involve an abusive supervisor, work team practices that ostracize an individual because of personality factors or perceptions, racism, sexism, or a host of other factors. If you investigate and find that such conditions existed, then it may wish to take disciplinary or remedial action against those responsible. However, it is unlikely that they will want to restore the threat perpetrator to duty.

2. Conditional threats. Such threats involve a condition. An example: "If you report me, I will get even with you and you will sorry."

POSSIBLE RESPONSES TO CONDITIONAL THREATS

Conditional threats are more difficult to assess than direct threats. There has to be a determined effort to understand the circumstances in which the threat was made and what the perpetrator actually meant by the threat. These situations necessarily involve investigation and judgment. If it is determined that violence or intimidation was intended by the perpetrator to be the result, then discipline is appropriate. Proper documentation is crucial in any event to legitimatize removal if a pattern of such threats exists over time.

3. Veiled threats. A veiled threat usually involves body language or behaviors that leave little doubt in the mind of the victim that the perpetrator intends harm.

POSSIBLE RESPONSES TO VEILED THREATS

A veiled threat must be analyzed and documented with care. The important question is whether or not reasonable people would agree that a threat was actually made. The perpetrator will usually insist that he or she did not intend harm even though the behavior was very disruptive and threatening to the victim. While such behavior or communication may be tolerated once, proper documentation will enable management to respond more severely if the pattern persists or repeats itself.

AGGRESSIVE OR BIZARRE BEHAVIOR

Research clearly demonstrates that the perpetrators of violence sometimes do not make threats that we would typically associate with anger or frustration. Instead, they are likely to engage in bizarre behavior. They are likely to do things that are uncharacteristic but clearly abnormal, even to the untrained observer. For example, one perpetrator left brown paper bags of

TABLE 7-1
WAYS TO DISTINGUISH TYPES OF THREATS & AGGRESSIVE BEHAVIORS

Types of Threats—

- Direct ... "I'm going to kill you."

- Conditional ... "If you report me, I will hurt you."

- Veiled ... Body language, subtle threat messages.

Aggressive Behaviors, Frequency & Severity—

- Aberrational ... A "bad day" that is unusual for individual.

- Periodic anger ... Typically apologetic following outburst.

- Endemic ... Part of a person's behavioral pattern.

SOURCE: National Safe Workplace Institute

kittens or puppies on the locking dock where he worked. Another perpetrator would come to work wearing underwear on his head.

Often, individuals make comments of a bizarre nature or challenge the boundaries of their supervisors and managers. When a worker engages in such behavior, the possibility of violence must be considered. Like threats, behaviors—especially those that involve aggression—should be documented and reviewed. We will attempt to identify patterns that will help us understand differences in behavior. We also must ascertain the frequency and severity of the behavior in terms of its impact on the organization and its members.

1. *Aberrational.* Aberrational aggression essentially involves an apparently spontaneous outburst. In examining such an event, we must determine if the behavior is part of a pattern. Ultimately, we should try to reach a conclusion about whether or not a person was simply having a bad day. Most organizations will be reluctant to have policies that severely penalize someone for behavior that is clearly out of character.

2. *Periodic or intermittent.* With periodic aggression or behavior, a pattern is emerging. Without question we must begin to seek interventions by trained mental health professionals. This is especially true if the behavior is harming others or reducing organizational productivity and effectiveness.

3. *Endemic.* Endemic aggression or behavior has become a part of the person's everyday personality. If the person is being aggressive, then management must take prompt action—usually termination.

PUTTING BEHAVIOR IN A CONTEXT

Behavior typically occurs in a context, not in a vacuum. As human beings, we tend to have a method to our madness—a reason why we do things the way we do them. Employers need to be aware of deviations from trends and patterns as a possible warning sign that trouble may lie ahead.

In other sections, we have discussed early warning mechanisms, including behavioral observation systems which provide a reasonably objective way to measure and evaluate behavior over time. Employers implementing early warning mechanisms will have systems that will provide a foundation from which to evaluate more extreme behaviors. Unfortunately, information usually does not exist to provide a good baseline from which to evaluate perpetrator behavior. In those situations, with or without such a foundation, decisions must be made in a prompt and efficient fashion.

COORDINATING THREAT MANAGEMENT

There are proper ways to investigate and manage threats. Once the information is received, it must be carefully evaluated. For the purpose of this discussion, we will call the primary threat manager a "coordinator." Ideally, a coordinator will receive information from a reporting center (e.g. hotline) within hours of the report and conduct a preliminary investigation. The coordinator will be able to handle most cases, but should defer to a threat management team (please see chapter 6) in cases where there is reason to do so.

The first issue the coordinator must attempt to evaluate is the immediacy of the threat: is danger imminent? If the danger is imminent, then prompt defensive action must occur (please see last part of this chapter). If there is no sense of urgency, then there should be a systematic attempt to carefully and thoughtfully weigh the nature of the threat against the person's likely capacity to carry out acts of physical violence. The ultimate goal is to protect people and property. The sequence of steps that the coordinator should follow can be found in Table 7-2. Again, this table is meant as a gen-

TABLE 7-2
STEPS IN INVESTIGATING THREATS OF WORKPLACE VIOLENCE

---

1. Consider the source (inside or outside the organization)—the source of a threat will help determine basic strategy.

   For existing employees—

   Evaluate options for managing threats from existing employees. Ideally, any person who has made threats should be suspended pending an investigation.

2. Analyze the immediacy of the situation. Is danger imminent?

3. Analyze the threat—explicit nature of the behavior or communication.

4. Weigh threat against "stabilizers."

5. If there is a significant prospect that a threat can be transformed into reality, consider options for managing a crisis.

SOURCE: National Safe Workplace Institute

eral guideline for action. There will always be exceptions when this sequence should be changed or different steps added.

IDENTIFYING POTENTIALLY DANGEROUS INDIVIDUALS

No one can say with any degree of certainty who will kill and who will not. Competent, licensed psychologists and psychiatrists have failed to diagnose individuals as dangerous even though that same person committed a lethal act just a few days later.

Indeed, the process of identifying dangerous individuals poses enormous risks and uncertainties for those involved in the threat management process. Undue emphasis on profiling can be harmful for numerous reasons. For openers, many individuals within a large corporation are likely to have some or even many of the characteristics of past perpetrators. As a result, these individuals fit a profile.

This tendency on the part of some employers to compare the behavioral characteristics and features of those with whom threats have been attributed with the personal characteristics of those individuals who previously committed acts of violence can severely damage the reputations of otherwise innocent individuals. Unjustly blamed individuals may then wish to pursue defamation lawsuits. Moreover, an undue focus on certain types of individuals rather than on behaviors can divert attention from other individuals who pose more serious threats. The use of profiles should be limited to psychiatrists or licensed clinical psychologists; even then profile data should be used only in the later stages of a threat evaluation process.

Perhaps a more systematic and objective way to make decisions has to do with the sequence in behavior by someone making threats. Research by the National Safe Workplace Institute confirms the notion that there is a sequence in the behavioral steps perpetrators of violence. Generally, the individual will deteriorate over time, becoming isolated from others as he or she grapples with frustration and a sense of failure. Often, the process begins when the individual suffers from a significant traumatic event or the cumulation of many smaller traumas. As shown in Table 7-3, the individual begins to perceive that his situation is unsolvable and places all blame on the situation, rather than on himself or herself. Gradually, the individual concludes that violence is the only way out.

Those who have responsibility for threat management should place more emphasis on behavior, its patterns and its sequence, than on other factors. The actual act of making a threat or bizarre patterns of behavior should

TABLE 7-3
ROUTINE SEQUENCE—VIOLENCE PERPETRATORS

1. Individual suffers trauma which creates extreme tension or anxiety:
   - single major event (layoff or termination; actual perceived) or
   - cumulative minor events
2. Individual perceives that problems are essentially unsolvable.
3. Individual projects all responsibility onto the situation.
4. Individual's frame of reference becomes increasingly egocentric.
5. Self-preservation and self-protection gradually become sole objectives.
6. Violent act perceived as only way out.
7. Violent act is attempted or committed.

SOURCE: National Safe Workplace Institute

be the trigger for further investigation and possible action. Investigating an individual simply because that person has been angry and fits a statistical profile not only runs certain risks that are detrimental to corporate and individual welfare but are likely a waste of time and resources.

TIMING IN EFFECTIVE THREAT MANAGEMENT

When a threat has been posed, it is crucial that the organization move quickly and efficiently to protect people and property. Table 7-4 identifies essential factors in timely intervention in workplace violence. This table should serve as a checklist for the threat coordinator and team members in planning their decisions. It is important to plan in a thoughtful and systematic fashion so that all bases are covered.

One of the most important factors in gauging the danger in a given situation is the presence of weapons. Perpetrators with weapons pose a much higher degree of risk than those without. Sometimes individuals have only recently acquired weapons for the purpose of conducting lethal acts in the workplace.

As part of the assessment process, you must consider not only the presence of weapons but the capacity of an individual to use force. Indeed individuals have often used other methods to kill people at work. While guns are the preferred method, perpetrators have used guns and other forms of lethal force, including strangulation. During this period, prior incidents of violence and disregard for established authority become very important in threat assessment process. If a person has exercised violence in the past, then we must assume the potential for violence in the future.

POTENTIAL INHIBITORS

Experience shows that there are numerous inhibitors likely to diminish the possibility that an individual may become violent. For example, a person who is financially secure with a stable family and community life is less likely to commit violence than an individual with nothing to lose. Conversely, a person who does not have a family life and who is badly in debt may be more inclined to become violent.

A capable threat manager will develop an inhibitor or anchor profile for each individual who is a source for threats. Data on a person's finances, health, family and community life, supervisory relationships, and other pertinent factors can be obtained from co-workers or public sources without violating an individual's right to privacy. While such information may not be conclusive, it will help determine what steps may be prudent in a particu-

TABLE 7-4
ESSENTIAL FACTORS IN TIMELY INTERVENTION

1. Timely intervention.
2. Proper referral.
3. Weighing threat behavior versus capacity to be violent.
   - Possession of firearms or weapons?
   - Perception of what the individual has to lose.
   - Presence of anchors.
4. Proper use of options ...
5. Effective coordination and use of internal and external resources.

SOURCE: National Safe Workplace Institute

lar situation. A list of the anchors that may inhibit violence is shown in Table 7-5. While this Table is valid, you should not think about this information rigidly. Some factors not on this list may be as important, while it is highly possible that one or two anchors (e.g. religious) may be disproportionately significant.

DEALING WITH A PERPETRATOR FOLLOWING AN INVESTIGATION

There are many options available when a worker has made threats or engaged in low-level acts of violence. Managers must be aware of these options in order to make decisions resulting in "win-win" choices that will eventually protect the interest of both the employer and individual worker alike. These rational decisions should achieve a favorable result and must withstand scrutiny over time. Proper planning will result in appropriate action that will help limit and control damage.

If an employee is the source of a threat, it may be necessary to undertake a professional evaluation by a licensed mental health professional. This

TABLE 7-5
ANCHORS THAT MAY INHIBIT VIOLENCE

- Secure family life—spouse, children, other relatives.
- Reasonably rational, somewhat future-oriented.
- Stable finances—good credit rating; savings; reasonable debt load.
- Drug & alcohol-free—no drug use or alcohol abuse.
- Community ties—involved in community; may own home.
- Outside interests—hobbies, sports (e.g. bowling).
- Religious life—involved in church.
- Friendships—externally driven, concerned about others.
- Good work history—continuous employment.
- Character—no real pattern of criminal conduct.
- Emotionally stable—steady personality.

SOURCE: National Dafe Workplace Institute

should involve a "fitness for duty" or "dangerousness assessment" by a licensed psychologist who is trained to conduct such assessments. Employers have a number of options after such an evaluation is conducted. Unfortunately, experience demonstrates that many of these options are simply not considered when considering appropriate action.

The options that exist for managers when the individual is not an employee are far more limited. Nevertheless, there are some, especially when the perpetrator is a former employee or known to management. In such situations, all possible information should be obtained to determine what steps are necessary to ensure that the employer has taken prudent action. Substantial data on employment histories, financial and credit information, criminal records, etc., can be obtained through various sources.

Unfortunately, some circumstances are difficult to foresee and intercept. Some threats, especially those not properly understood or addressed, will flare up in acts of violence. These may involve physical injury or even death, property damage, disruption of business activity, and other harmful acts.

TABLE 7-6
OPTIONS AFTER EVALUATION OF AN EMPLOYEE WHO HAS MADE THREATS

1. Take no action.

2. Take usual disciplinary procedures.

3. Give the individual opportunity to resign with prejudice.

4. Recommend voluntary counseling.

5. Recommend mandatory counseling with treatment monitoring.

6. Refer for fitness-for-duty evaluation.

7. Place individual on medical leave. Reevaluate after treatment.

8. Seek temporary or permanent restraining order.

9. Involve law enforcement and seek to charge suspect with criminal acts.

10. Notify targets of threats to protect themselves.

11. Provide security for specific individuals on worksite or during interviews.

SOURCE: National Safe Workplace Institute

When violence occurs, a number of steps must be taken for the employer to assert control of the work environment (see Table 7-7). Hopefully, an employer will have properly planned for such a crisis so that key individuals, such as threat management team members know their individual and collective roles. Acts of violence nearly always result in laws being broken, either in terms of injury to individuals or in terms of damage to the employer's property. Ultimately, violence becomes a legal issue, with necessary law enforcement consequences.

Effective managers, however, should be able to control and manage most incidents to a logical conclusion that does not involve action by law enforcement. When law enforcement becomes involved, employers run the risk of losing control of the work environment. By definition, their decisions and performance in preventing violence have failed.

Employers must be prepared to address crucial issues that inevitably arise during serious incidents. Typically a violent act that is underway will ultimately require involvement by law enforcement. Nonetheless, there are many steps that prepared employers should consider in developing plans. For example, employers should have identified a licensed clinical psychol-

TABLE 7-7

CRITICAL INCIDENT MANAGEMENT STEPS

Steps in managing a critical incident:

1. Control and secure the workplace; contact law enforcement.

   ✓ Account for all personnel.

   ✓ Ensure employee, customer, and public safety.

   ✓ Evacuate all individuals.

2. Provide law enforcement with as much information as possible.

   ✓ Perpetrator data.

   ✓ Facilities information.

3. Caution in making statements to the press.

4. Plan for post-trauma care.

5. Conduct investigations and post-incident analysis.

6. Conduct debriefings of relevant personnel.

SOURCE: *National Safe Workplace Institute*

ogist who can debrief "survivors" of violent events or even those who have experienced serious threats. Such measures have been proven crucial in terms of identifying workers and others who will require long-term care while returning others to full productivity. Many law enforcement agencies routinely contract with such professionals to debrief officers after fatal accidents, shootings, violent acts, and other events that may disrupt an officer's psychological well-being.

A NOTE ABOUT PLANNING

Employers are using role-playing and other techniques to prepare for critical incidents. There is a considerable advantage in a complete preparation for the worst possible case in that it can minimize the damage from the crisis when it does take place and facilitate a smoother transition to normalcy following the event. Most incidents are unlikely to develop to a "worst possible case" level; nevertheless, team members and other threat managers who are prepared are likely, when confronted with challenge, to perform their tasks successfully.

The National Safe Workplace Institute will begin a certified threat manager program beginning in 1995. The Charlotte-based NSWI is now seeking accreditation from the appropriate Federal agencies for this certification. Participation in this or similar programs will provide employers with the assurance that they are building appropriate capacity to manage threats internally.

DEFENSES AGAINST VIOLENT INTRUDERS

Threats are sometimes made against individuals. A primary example of such a circumstance would involve a person who is stalking his or her spouse. When individual employees are threatened there are prudent ways to defend them against the possibility of violence. Sometimes, organizations will hire investigators to track the moves of the perpetrator. They also will employ bodyguards to protect those who have been threatened. These decisions are very expensive and may have questionable effectiveness. The Secret Service employs literally hundreds of individuals to protect the President *on a daily basis,* when there are no unusual threats. Deployment of a bodyguard may give the target a greater sense of security but will probably have minimal effect against a truly determined perpetrator.

Chapter 8 examines steps that can help protect individuals who have been threatened and the best approaches for defending against a violent intruder. If a perpetrator knows a person's whereabouts and schedule, then the element of confusion may serve as an effective means of protection, particularly in situations involving threats by stalkers.

THE RISE OF PSYCHO-TERRORISM

During the past few years, there have been cases where individuals—usually fired employees or angry customers—have exercised what can best be described as psycho-terrorism.

Psycho-terrorists are individuals who prey upon the fears of managers trying to cope with the unknown. They often are very intelligent and creative individuals who understand the line between behavior that is legally permissible and that which is not. Their goal is to terrorize the organization without bringing undo legal attention upon themselves.

One such documented case involves John Kliebert, a fired Kidder, Peabody bond salesman. *The Wall Street Journal* published a front-page exposé on April 29, 1994 on Mr. Kliebert's psycho-terrorist campaign against his former employer. Key features of this story are highlighted in Table 7-8.

Two facts are beyond dispute. Mr. Kliebert certainly captured Kidder, Peabody's attention. According to sources, Kidder, Peabody spent $1 million during the course of ten months for psychiatric assessments and for investigative reports about Mr. Kliebert. After nearly a year, beleaguered Kidder, Peabody called off its full-court press.

There are two fundamental questions that should be considered in light of this example—which, by all accounts, is fairly common in American business. The first question is how to consider whether or not a person is really capable of murder or physical violence and, if not, what should be done about threats made by such individuals. Certainly, there are threat management and security firms working hand-in-glove with mental health providers who will insist that individuals like Kliebert be investigated and *monitored* on a daily basis.

In reality, Kidder's reaction to Kliebert was overkill. Clearly, Kidder was following what had been described as a prudent course. However, there is little evidence that Kliebert had the emotional state of mind (e.g., present-time oriented, isolated, and irrational) to suggest he was about to kill anyone. For example, workplace murderers don't go on vacations to plan how they will kill someone.

Table 7-8

The Saga of John Kliebert—
A Fired Kidder, Peabody Bond Salesman

Behaviors of Mr. Kliebert, 41-years-old (as of April 29, 1994):

- Threatened former boss of Kidder's headquarters, saying that "his shirt would look good with a red splotch in the chest area."

- Phoned threats, promising to "get even" with four coworkers.

- Sent long-stem roses and faxes to secretaries in the bond trading area.

- Employed an attorney who apparently advised him on behavioral issues.

- Threatened to expose a scandal at the firm's Board meeting (but didn't).

Response by Kidder and Law Enforcement:

- Spent more than $1 million on private investigators, who even followed him on a vacation to the Caribbean.

- Had Kliebert arrested on third-degree menacing charges, a misdemeanor. Charges were dropped when he agreed to see a therapist and honor a court order.

SOURCE: The Wall Street Journal, April 29, 1994, page one

There is a way to deal with psycho-terrorists. A possible course of action in the Kliebert case would have been to brief appropriate Kidder personnel on Kliebert's state of mind and the likelihood that he would not be violent. Second, Kidder may have wished to investigate Kliebert on a periodic basis to evaluate whether his emotional state of mind had changed. Third, they could have protected targets of Kidder's wrath (see Table 7-7). It is possible that Kidder's overreaction was precisely what Mr. Kliebert wanted. In fact, it is highly possible that Kliebert may have played a key role in providing details of what was going on to the *Journal.*

Threat management is a complex but reasonably logical process. Ideally, management will involve workers from all levels of the organization in policy development in order to ensure that such a policy is well received and credibly implemented. The foundation for any policy must be a reporting system that is comprehensive, encouraging threat information from both internal and external sources. If threat managers are properly trained, well-prepared, and blessed with adequate leadership and support, most challenges can be successfully managed. Senior management must be committed to effective threat management, and policies, to be credible, must be effectively communicated to both employees and stakeholders.

Ultimately, management must face the reality that violence may occur, and that appropriate policies must be in place to ensure a safe and secure outcome under the circumstances. Like other processes, threat management can be done poorly. As we have noted, failure can be costly in terms of financial and human resources.

8

TENSE SITUATIONS

Dealing with Dangerous Employees

It is inevitable that managers will have to deal with employees that they think are potentially dangerous. We live in a world where violence is a common phenomenon, one that is found more frequently inside our workplaces. We must know how to handle the possibility that one of our employees may be dangerous. When no laws have been broken, we can't call the police. These are situations where managers are terribly alone and must make decisions that are difficult.

This chapter will address how to deal with potentially dangerous employees. The decisions to be faced are made difficult by fear, superstition, peer anxiety, and by law. Often a manager feels paralyzed and is confused about how to address the situation. The challenge, while difficult, is not impossible.

After a short but crucial digression, we will scrutinize the role that Employee Assistance Programs (EAPs) play in employee mental health issues in general and in workplace violence in particular. EAPs are now in a state of flux and their role in workplace violence, while important, will change. Later in this chapter, we will examine the issue of mandatory psychological evaluations for troubled employees. This is a sensitive topic that must be addressed with care.

We will then look at how we can enhance the odds that the termination of a frightening individual can be done non-violently.

We must realize the individuals who are psychologically disturbed or dangerous often rely on fear as a means to get what they want. Often, they desperately want to hold their jobs and will use aggression as a tool against those who threaten them.

This discussion is particularly important —and poignant— because employers should have little difficulty managing difficult employees. In an ideal world, employers should be able to refer troubled or difficult employees to mental health providers or, if necessary, terminate their employment. However, we don't live in an ideal world. Employers don't always act in a careful and thoughtful fashion. There are often mental roadblocks or barriers to achieving successful outcomes.

BARRIERS TO SOUND DECISIONS

Employees who engage in behaviors that might suggest the possibility of violence pose clear dangers for employers. For their own benefit such employees should participate in well-tested psychological evaluations generally called fitness-for-duty evaluations or dangerousness assessments.

In spite of the risks, employers are reluctant to persuade or order employees to participate in such evaluations, let alone mandate clinical exams. There are many reasons for this reluctance; some have a more factual foundation than others. Some are known and must be addressed in order to rationally and thoughtfully consider the option of mandating psychological examinations. In general there are at least five reasons for this employer reluctance. We shall discuss each individually.

REFERRAL CRITERIA

There are legitimate questions about what behaviors or conditions should result in an evaluation. Because employers want to be consistent, they feel that they must have criteria which can be adequately understood by managers and others who must play an important role in the decision-making process. In reality there are objective criteria that can be used to make a rational and legally defensible referral decision. Ideally, employers should develop guidelines in conjunction with licensed mental health professionals or their Employee Assistance Program (EAP). Possibilities that can be included are *aggressive acts* (e.g. shoving, pushing), *conditional or veiled threats,* or *prolonged or aggravated hostility/anger.*

There should be very few circumstances when hitting, fighting, or direct threats are allowed. One exception may be where a work unit has *informally* accommodated a person's abnormal behavior. Under such circumstances, legal sanctions under the Americans with Disabilities Act may require the employer to *formally* accommodate the employee. This exception will be very rare.

General guidelines are required. Discretion must rest with the manager or other appropriate official to make referrals. Managers who have carefully observed employees over a long period of time may have intuitive feelings or anxieties about employees that should be considered in making a referral decision.

FEAR OF VIOLENCE

Sometimes even the suggestion that an employee become involved in a clinical examination may make him or her more violent. In these circumstances—which are very common—managers often feel paralyzed by employees with aggressive behavior. They blindly hope that the person will improve and in the interim they remain afraid to make recommendations.

Prolonged fear of aggressive employees is a condition that should never exist in an organization. It should be obvious that interventions are crucial and that ignoring such behavior will only make it worse. But scores of organizations have turned the other cheek in the face of such abuse. This tragic reality has been revealed in statements made to law enforcement officials following lethal or violent events in the workplace. In very few cases have co-employees been surprised by a person's behavior. Yet during this period of fear and intimidation employers remained reluctant to suggest medical treatment.

POSSIBLE LEGAL EXPOSURE

Some managers and some legal counsel believe that employers lack the right to mandate that employees participate in psychological evaluations. They cite the Americans with Disabilities Act (ADA), legal doctrines relating to employee rights, privacy defamation, etc.

Legal liability is a legitimate concern when it comes to such referrals. Any action that alters an employee's duties could be subjected to legal review. Legal concerns begin with referral (e.g., ADA, defamation), continue during the course of treatment (e.g., defamation), through a return to work (e.g., defamation, discrimination).

However, there is also every reason to believe that employers are safe-ly within their legal rights (and their moral obligation) to have a policy of mandatory referral. Legal liability must be addressed in two ways. First, there must be carefully defined procedures to address each of these processes: (a) referral, (b) treatment and (c) return to work. With careful procedures the employer can protect both corporate and employee/patient interests. Second, someone, most likely a licenses medical practitioner, is usually the best manager of how these concerns are addressed by on-site personnel and others within the organization. By involving such a profes-sional, the organization is demonstrating care in how it achieves a safe workplace while ensuring that employees are treated in a medically sound and confidential fashion.

Employers must keep in mind their foremost responsibility to maintain a safe workplace. While this does not mean that they can trample the rights of an individual, it does mean that there are larger obligations that justify measures designed to safeguard people and property.

RETURN TO WORK

Employers may be worried about what to do with employees who must be re-entered into the work force after a medical leave for mental health rea-sons. Co-employees who are anxious about an employee returning to work may refuse to accept him or her in the workplace.

Managers should anticipate such a reaction. The best remedy is a scheduled de-briefing for the person's co-employees prior to his or her return to work. This will reduce the anxiety or even hostility that some employees may harbor.

BIAS AGAINST PSYCHOLOGICAL METHODS

Managers often do not understand the methods that are involved in or the need for such evaluations. Some are skeptical or even cynical about the entire mental health profession. To develop this point even further, there is very little evidence that either managers or employees have a reasonable understanding for employee mental issues. Only a small percentage of employees use mental health resources even when they are available at not cost. This lack of appreciation greatly handicaps the possibility for diagno-sis and treatment.

This bias that exists toward the mental health profession is a difficult issue that will be addressed over time. Fidelity must seek counsel and involve mental health providers in a manner that showcases their capability and potential contributions to Fidelity and its business practices. Through such interactions Fidelity managers are likely to have more appreciation for the role of the mental health professional.

EMPLOYEE ASSISTANCE PROGRAMS

For the past three decades Employee Assistance Programs (EAP) have played prominent roles in employee mental health care. In most cases, employers contract with an outside service provider; employees are then allowed a certain number of visits (four to eight) before the employer will terminate reimbursement or payment of benefits.

Employee EAP participation in most corporations is very low. Women are generally more likely to use such services than men. In most businesses, about 2 percent of the employee population can be expected to participate in EAP services, although in some professions, such as law enforcement, participation rates may run as high as 20 percent.

Historically, EAPs have made important contributions to employers through alcohol and drug treatment programs. These services will remain important as long as these problems exist. In fact, some EAPs are expanding their roles to provide employers with more services, including violence prevention. The U.S. Postal Service, for example, has appointed EAP coordinators in each Postal District (covering about 10,000 employees) who will act as mental health consultants to management.[1]

Certain limitations of EAPs, however, are coming to light. Some managers are inclined to refer employees who have possible psychological problems. This approach involves risks that are just now being more fully appreciated. One major risk is that some EAP professionals may not be qualified to diagnose violence and aggression. It is possible that employees may become even more angry and abusive than if they were in an appropriate treatment regime.

Also many EAP professionals are not licensed psychologists or psychiatrists. As a result, the methods that they use to evaluate an employee may not be medically sound in the eyes of the law, irrespective of the EAP professional's competence and experience. Use of methods considered unscientific or professionals who lack capability to use methods that are consistent with ADA requirements may expose an employer to ADA sanctions. These methods would include use of psychometric tests and diagnostic techniques usually undertaken by licensed professionals (e.g. psychologists or psychiatrists). To avoid the possibility that inappropriate evaluations or services may be provided, it is advisable that proper clinical evaluations consistent with ADA requirements be utilized.

It would seem, therefore, that while EAPs play an important role in meeting employee mental health needs, their role with respect to employees who are potentially violent may become more limited because of the ADA. According to a staff attorney with the Equal Employment Opportunity Commission (EEOC), an employer can remove a potentially dangerous employee and have that employee's behavior diagnosed if the employer has consistent policies for removal and if the provider who undertakes the diagnosis uses medical methods. This requirement suggests that EAPs, under certain circumstances, may be an inappropriate source to which you should refer troubled employees.

Nevertheless, there are many ways in which EAPs can contribute positively to violence prevention in American businesses. The role they play should be carefully thought through in order to achieve maximum effectiveness. Some ideas for how EAPs can contribute are included in Table 8-1.

MANDATING EXAMS OF EMPLOYEES

The issue of mandating psychological evaluation of employees who are potentially violent is a matter increasingly on the minds of managers.

TABLE 8-1
ROLE OF EMPLOYEE ASSISTANCE PROGRAM PROFESSIONALS IN PREVENTING VIOLENCE

- Train supervisors and managers on issues of employee reliability.
- Identify abusive supervisors and managers.
- Help high-risk individuals cope with job loss.
- Show how internal stressors contribute to aggression and violence.
- Establish strategies to contain domestic violence spillover.
- Participate in violence prevention/ intervention teams.
- Assist in managing relationships with outside service providers.
- Conduct critical incident stress debriefings.

SOURCE: National Safe Workplace Institute

Unfortunately, many employees who are asked to participate voluntarily in such evaluations refuse. This failure to cooperate may leave an employer with no option but to mandate an evaluation as a condition for continued employment.

American corporations are now giving long-overdue attention to the matter of mandatory referrals as part of their strategy of violence prevention. Employers should adopt a policy of mandating referral of employees who have exhibited behavior indicating the strong possibility of violence or aggression. The development of such a policy is both the most appropriate method for addressing employees with aggressive behavior and may be the only legally defensible method. In addition, employers should engage a licensed medical consultant to help develop guidelines under which a mandatory referral can be made.

Enlightened employers do not require the specter of regulatory intervention or imminent injury to formulate policies and procedures that have the promise of preventing injuries in the workplace each year. They realize that preventive strategies are more effective than crisis-oriented responses. When it comes to violence, employers realize that there are many reasons why they must take action when an employee has exhibited behavior which suggests the possibility of aggression or has engaged in threats or threatening acts. These behaviors or acts clearly represent risks of injury to employees and, possibly, customers, risks which are intolerable.

The issue of violent employees has concerned employers and the mental health profession for many years. For example, law enforcement agencies have long recognized that job-related stress can cause aggressive behavior by certain employees. As a result, the law enforcement community, working with the mental health profession, has developed what is commonly called fitness-for-duty examinations or dangerousness assessments. Administered by either licensed clinical psychologists or psychiatrists, they can determine if a person represents a danger to self, co-employees, or the public. These examinations have been used all during this century, even more since World War II.

In more recent years an increasing number of employers have utilized these clinical methods for evaluating their employees. Public utilities that operate nuclear installations are obliged by statute to psychologically screen all hires prior to employment, and they have the legal right to impose fitness-for-duty examinations whenever circumstances or conditions dictate the necessity. The Federal Government does not require that employees undergo such examinations but its agencies have the right to terminate employees who are unwilling to participate. This right was established during administrative reviews of personnel actions by the U.S. Office of Personnel Management.

The fact that employees who are requested to participate in such evaluations do not always wish to do so is understandable for several reasons. First, the employee may be mentally incapacitated and unable to appreciate the need for such an examination. Second, the employee may harbor an intense anger that may lead to violent acts and may not want his or her employer to take actions which prevent expression of hostility. Third, many employers do not trust managers or their employers to safeguard such information. There are no known studies which report the percentage of employees who decline such evaluations, but the number is likely to be substantial. This reality makes it necessary for employers to consider how to manage the delicate but critical task of ensuring that the employee does not represent a risk to himself or herself, co-employees or the public.

Employees who are experiencing emotional problems or psychological disorders represent a real risk to themselves and may inadvertently expose co-employees to substantial problems. For example, if an employee has become depressed, other employees may be compelled to absorb work that is not being completed. Also, if that person commits suicide at work, the resulting trauma to co-employees can be severe. This is a possibility that cannot be overlooked. In fact, there is a greater likelihood of employees committing suicide at work than of being murdered by an angry party. The Bureau of Labor Statistics reported that in 1993, 213 employees committed suicide at work, up 16.4 percent from the previous year (183).[2] This very limited information suggests that suicide at work is a growing problem.

INCIDENT AND BEHAVIOR DOCUMENTATION

Prudence suggests that employers document more comprehensively any behaviors and threats that are of concern to them and to co-employees. This is both sound administrative procedure and essential in the case of litigation or if other problems occur.

Ideally, managers should document unacceptable behaviors and communications as quickly as possible and have such documents reviewed by a human resources manager early in the process in order to ensure that information is being properly and adequately recorded.

REFERRAL COORDINATION

Employers may wish to consider the use of a medical professional, ideally a psychiatrist or licenses clinical psychologist, to coordinate referral of employees for "fitness-for-duty" examinations. This is especially true for organizations that have numerous locations across the U.S.

The idea of centralizing the referral process is sound both professionally and legally. First, it is important to work with people who have experience in the field of dangerousness assessment and who can identify qualified professionals at other locations that are remote from corporate headquarters. The referral staff can consult with the employer about the appropriateness of referral and, perhaps, help monitor clinical treatment of the employee. Such staff can also help to develop guidelines on when to refer an employee for evaluation. They can help as well to create incidental documentation procedures and to evaluate when proper documentation has been prepared. Legally it is important that medical methods be used to meet ADA standards. Also, this staff may be helpful in managing the sensitive process of the return to work.

PREDICTING VIOLENCE

Despite the fact that the mental health profession strives to improve methods and procedures, that is evidence that fitness-for-duty evaluations have occasionally failed to predict dangerousness in employees. Nevertheless, such methods have been successful more often than not. The use of scientific and medical methods is still the most appropriate means available to an employer for identifying, with as much validity as possible, potentially dangerous employees.

Finally, we should consider what happens to employees after they have been evaluated. Once again, this is the most rational and thoughtful way of understanding the consequences of a mandatory referral policy. As one can see from the following table, management has many options that it can consider. Obviously, these options should be considered in consultation with a professional mental health provider, human resources managers, security, and other appropriate individuals.

In this chapter we have evaluated the issue of mandating psychological evaluation of employees who have exhibited aggressive behaviors or

Table 8-2

Options After Evaluation of a Potentially Dangerous Employee

- Mandatory counseling with treatment monitoring.
- Give individual opportunity to resign without prejudice.
- Use disciplinary procedures.
- Recommend voluntary counseling.
- Obtain restraining order.
- Notify law enforcement agencies and/or criminally charge suspect.
- Warn targets of threats.
- Provide security for specific individuals on worksite or during interviews.
- Take no action.

SOURCE: National Safe Workplace Institute

who otherwise warrant psychological examination. Employers have the authority to adopt a policy that would allow them to mandate (if necessary) psychological evaluation of such employees. Referring an employee for an examination by a mental health professional is a more appropriate course for cases of a serious nature than to mandate EAP services or to ignore the problem altogether.

Managers need to know more about employee mental health issues and when interventions are necessary. Lack of information contributes to inappropriate and uninformed decisions. There are other recommendations that employers should consider as part of a program to mandate psychological evaluation of employees. These include:

1. Development of *consistent guidelines* to determine when an employee should have a fitness-for-duty evaluation.

2. Development of monitoring procedures, using the resources and capabilities of outside medical experts, to ensure that diagnostic procedures and clinical treatment are appropriate.

3. Assurance that managers, as part of human resource training, receive information on the need to refer potentially dangerous employees for medical evaluation.

AT SPECIAL RISK

Women in the Workplace

During a one-week period in late 1991, women in Atlanta and in the Queens borough of New York City were gunned down in murders linked by a common thread: both were killed by former employees. The Queens woman was a supervisor with the Social Security Administration, the huge Federal bureaucracy that administers pension claims for senior and disabled citizens. A 26-year-old male she had previously managed killed her. He also stole a car, later smashed into a police car, injuring two officers. In Atlanta, a man murdered his boss after he was fired from her manicuring boutique. The killer also wounded the woman's husband and brother before killing himself.

These murders, involving women from different occupations in different regions of the country, illustrate a disturbing trend: women are being murdered at work with increasing frequency. While only one out of five people murdered at work is a woman, more women who die on the job will die from homicide than from any other cause. In the U.S., slightly more than 10 percent of the men killed at work are murdered; for women the statistic exceeds 40 percent. Men are more likely to die from electrocution, the crushing blows of heavy equipment, or from industrial accidents; women are more likely to die from workplace homicide.

Recently, the National Institute for Occupational Safety and Health (NIOSH) of the Centers for Disease Control identified workplace homicide as a serious national public health problem. NIOSH researchers reported that 42 percent of the women and 12 percent of the men who died from injuries sustained in U.S. workplaces during a six-year period had died as a result of homicide. This report, along with other documentation, is helping to persuade Federal and state regulators to contemplate investigating employers for tolerating high levels of risks.

For both women and men, the risk of workplace homicide is just the tip of the iceberg. While the evidence does not support the contention that women are more at risk of homicide in the workplace than men, it is possible and even likely that women suffer disproportionately more from non-homicidal forms of violence than do men. Women are beaten, stabbed, raped, and intimidated or harassed at the work place every day. Indeed, a Department of Justice survey showed that one out of ten rapes occurs at work. Other forms of violence against women have followed them to work.

All available information suggests that women are much more likely than men to suffer from battery at work and an overwhelming percentage of sexual harassment claims come from females. A 1994 National Safe Workplace Institute survey of corporate security directors suggests that domestic violence is following women into the workplace and that more than nine out of ten corporate security chiefs now see such violence as a high priority. The crisis that women face must not be seen as purely the result of more women in the work force

There are many ways that women are injured and abused in the workplace. Some forms of injury and abuse suffered by women are found in Table 9-1.

The 1994 NSWI survey showed that a significant percentage of corporate security directors had personal knowledge of at least three serious incidents of stalking in their workplace. While many acknowledged situations where women stalked men (e.g. left abusive phone messages), those surveyed said that they had far more experience with women being stalked by men.

Women are victims at work in much the same ways that men are. They are murdered, beaten, and abused. Studies suggest that women may be victimized because they appear vulnerable or weaker than males. The threats can come from inside the workplace or from outside.

The most severe form of violence —homicide—is likely to come from outside, either committed during robberies or by stalkers. There are numerous physical security measures that can be taken to protect employees from robberies. These include the presence of security cameras, drop safes, and

TABLE 9-1

EXAMPLES OF INJURY AND ABUSE SUFFERED BY WOMEN AS A RESULT OF WORKPLACE VIOLENCE

- Homicide
- Rape
- Physical beatings (battery)
- Sexual assault and abuse
- Strangulation
- Gun shot wounds
- Stabbing
- Psychological trauma
- Sexual harassment
- Verbal abuse

SOURCE: National Safe Workplace Institute

better lighting, among others. Steps can be taken to protect women from stalkers as well. Table 9-2 presents some examples that companies could use to protect women in especially serious situations. It is important to note that most of these steps involve little or no expenditure. For example, providing protective services simply means having security officers alter their patrols to focus on the area where a potential victim works. This may help deter an attacker and will probably give the employee a greater sense of security.

Management will not know about threats unless it encourages employees to report concerns and fears. Managers need to understand that it is often difficult and embarrassing to report such information. Nonetheless, they need to emphasize that such reports may save a life and prevent a serious incident from occurring.

More research needs to be done to measure and understand the magnitude of the violence against women in the work environment. We especially need data on the spillover of domestic violence into the workplace (and from the workplace to home). However, the need for more data does not prevent us from reviewing two major reasons why women are at special risk of violence in the workplace.

TABLE 9-2

STEPS THAT COMPANIES CAN TAKE
TO PROTECT EMPLOYEES FROM STALKERS

Management must understand that it is in the company's interest to provide a safe and secure environment—and that a stalker is a direct threat to the employee and the company. Steps that can be taken to protect employees include:

- Establish a policy providing protective services (e.g. security or human resources) to stalked employees.
- Relocate work station of threatened employee to a location unknown to the stalker.
- Alter employee's work schedule to confuse stalker.
- Provide photographs of stalker to receptionists, security officers, and other relevant personnel.
- Encourage law enforcement to enforce restraining order.
- Provide employee with time off if threat is acute.
- Place silent alarms or buzzers at employee's work station.
- Deploy security camera near entrances to employee's work area.

SOURCE: National Safe Workplace Institute

ECONOMIC FACTORS

The differences in causes of death in the workplace reflect sex segregation and stratification in our work force and economy, the changing roles of men and women in the economy, and the changing structures of American families. Both the number and percentage of women who work outside the home have increased steadily throughout this century. More women work for pay now than ever before, and the numbers are likely to continue to increase.

At the same time, divorce rates are high, and single parenthood—overwhelmingly, single motherhood—continues to increase. Because of the stratification of the economy, many women are relegated to low-wage service or clerical jobs. Many of these jobs place women on the front lines, where workplace security measures are inadequate or nonexistent. Thus, although women's income is often crucial for the bare economic survival of families, the jobs most readily available to many women continue to be in the low-wage sectors. As cost-of-living increases continue to exceed growth in real wages, a woman's financial contribution becomes crucial to the basic subsistence of her family. Therefore, when violence does strike women, it is likely to devastate the financial as well as the emotional well-being of their families. The social and hidden costs of violence, especially murder, against women in the workplace cannot be measured easily. These costs cannot be relegated to the short run but often occur over the course of generations.

The proliferation of establishments that accommodate society's demand for convenience at all hours is continuing to increase. Such convenience frequently comes at a price, however, as employers and owners sacrifice the security and safety of their employees. Anybody—man or woman—is susceptible to crimes when left alone at late hours without adequate security precautions and provisions. In short, then, the very jobs many women are most likely to be able to get are precisely the jobs that hold great risks and offer little security and no compensation for the high risks.

In addition, employees in these positions often are less likely to have the power to be able to persuade employers to pay attention to threats. An employee who expresses concern with the possibility of violence may find management unwilling to act. In some cases, employees who have reported threats have been fired so the employer doesn't have to deal with those threats—or the person making the complaints. Overall, the incentive for women to report threats diminishes as the probability of a positive response is low and the potential for a retaliatory discharge exists. And, in turn, the employer's ability to monitor a threat and prevent the occurrence of violence decreases as a direct result of an employer's unwillingness to address safety issues.

A second economic factor is highlighted by the advancement of women in the work force. Some men may resent women who are promoted to supervisory positions, especially men who believe that they, not the women, deserved the promotion. One of the recent U.S. Postal Service murders illustrates this pattern of behavior. In May 1993, Larry Jasion, a postal employee, entered his Dearborn, Michigan office and shot three people, killing one. According to the Postal Inspector, Jasion had specifically expressed his displeasure at being passed up for a promotion that went to a female employee. Jasion had filed a complaint with the Equal Employment Opportunity Commission (EEOC) alleging gender discrimination that was rejected about six weeks prior to the shooting.

As our economy remains uncertain, men who feel insecure about their own jobs may feel threatened when women with whom they work are promoted. Even profitable companies are cutting back their work forces. Employees with inadequate or insufficient anchors in their lives may become increasingly frightened, frustrated, and resentful. These feelings will continue to manifest themselves in violent acts unless employers and society as a whole take steps to prevent such acts. As noted in other chapters in this book, men are more likely than women to have inadequate support systems and to turn to violence when they feel threatened. And men will often commit that violence against women, for a variety of reasons.

In summary, women are at risk from economic factors in two ways. First, many women are relegated to low-wage, high-risk positions. Men are also at risk in these positions. The risks are related to the position, not to the sex of its occupant. Because women fill these positions disproportionately, the risks they face are also disproportionate. Although women have made significant gains in advancing in the workplace in the last century, a substantial number of positions are still sex-segregated. Women are still stuck into low-paying clerical positions. Employers who are already insensitive to security and safety issues may be even more insensitive to complaints when women voice them.

Second, women who do gain promotions may incur the resentment of men who feel they were passed over or who simply do not like having a female supervisor. In an economy where workers' jobs are insecure and where layoffs or cutbacks are increasingly common, workers without social supports or anchors may become violent. Men are more likely to become violent than women, and, as women do get promotions, that violence may be directed against them in the workplace.

VIOLENCE AND HARASSMENT

Women are at special risk in the workplace in a second way: women are much more likely than men to be the victims of sexual harassment. The overwhelming majority of incidents of harassment are committed by men and directed at women. This harassment presents two kinds of problems.

- First, such harassment is itself a form of violence. Employees have the right to a safe and secure workplace; that is, a workplace where they are not subject to unwanted advances or implied or actual threats related to those advances. Verbal intimidation and sexual harassment inflict psychological and emotional harm that can have long-term negative repercussions for victims. This psychological harm is often equally or more disabling than the harm resulting from physical assaults.

- Second, sexual harassment is often a precursor to battery, rape or murder in the workplace. After sexually harassing postal worker Kim Springer for months, co-worker Mark Richard Hilbun, 38, was discharged from his job as a postal worker at a small postal facility 50 miles southeast of downtown Los Angeles. Hilbun was discharged for unreasonably interfering with Springer's work performance and creating an intimidating, hostile, and offensive working environment.

Springer—or any employee—should not have to be constantly on guard against having a fellow worker fondle her knee, kiss her on the neck, or seek to kiss her on the lips. No one should be required to submit to a gauntlet of sexual abuse in return for the privilege of being allowed to work and make a living. In addition to making sexual advances, Hilbun made threats to Springer and wrote a series of violent, sexually explicit notes. This behavior continued even after Hilbun was discharged from the U.S. Postal Service. The intensity of Hilbun's threats was so great that Springer was forced to take a week off from work. The final note by Hilbun read, "I love you. I'm going to kill us both and take us both to hell." Then, on Springer's first day back to work, May 6, 1993, Hilbun walked into his former post office and opened fire, killing a letter carrier and wounding a clerk.

In another 1993 incident, a gunman entered the offices of his Sunnyvale, California employer and began shooting with both a hunting rifle and shotgun, killing seven people and injuring five others. The gunman was an ex-employee who had sexually harassed a co-worker with whom he had become romantically obsessed. He had sent his co-employee notes that something bad might happen if she did not reciprocate. When she continued to refuse his advances, he took violent action. This example illustrates the disturbing trend that sexual harassment is often followed by a more destructive act of violence against the employee being harassed.

Addressing sexual harassment with a serious commitment can prevent workplace violence from occurring. An employer's sexual harassment policy should describe conduct that constitutes harassment and include a forceful statement that such conduct is tolerated neither by the company nor by state or federal law. The employee's right to complain about sexual harassment without fear of retaliation should be explained in the policy, and a provision should be included to guarantee that an employee does not have to complain directly to the harasser. The policy should have a grievance procedure that the recipient of the harassment can follow and sexual harassment hotlines for emergency situations. Such hotlines are now required by law in at least 30 states.

Employers must learn to take all threats to employee safety seriously and take action to deal with those threats. They must recognize that gender-based threats of violence *are* real threats: sexual harassment, resentment, and anger may be only preludes to physical violence or even murder. Companies should establish programs which focus on early intervention so that such threats can be addressed before violence occurs. These programs should encourage all employees—men and women-to report threats and preserve the rights of everybody involved, including the accused.

10

ON THE FRONT-LINES

The Role of Supervisors and Managers in Violence Prevention

A key group in any organization—public or private, large or small—is comprised of supervisors and front-line managers, the individuals who are the bridge between management and line or craft employees. Supervisors and first-tier managers can do a lot to improve and enhance the performance, productivity, and efficiency of employees. If these key forces are insufficient in terms of numbers, training, or ability, then work force management problems will increase. In designing programs to prevent workplace violence, management should focus on the role of supervisors and front-line managers, making sure that they are fully adequate for the task at hand.

In this chapter, we will try to understand the role that supervisors and front-line managers can play in preventing violence; examine the training requirements that are essential for developing these key players in the organization; and present both the do's and don'ts that are critical for them in combating workplace violence.

Unfortunately, supervisors and managers are frequently the *source* of the problem, not the solution because they are too often thoughtlessly chosen and, worse yet, poorly trained for the mission at hand. In implementing a workplace violence program, it is crucial that careful consideration be given to how line-level employees see supervisors and front-line managers.

If any supervisors are found wanting, then steps should be taken to correct any deficiencies.

In most cases, supervisors and front-line managers understand how they serve as a bridge in the organization. Many of their functions are identified in Table 10-1. In this simple depiction, supervisors not only act as the eyes and ears of management, but also as barometers. In weather forecasting, barometers measure barometric pressure which often signals a change in weather. As barometers for management, supervisors and front-line managers can provide useful information on the pressures that exist in the organization. The importance of these tasks should not be underappreciated by a management focused on preventing violence in the work environment. In fact, it is quite possible that violence prevention training for supervisors may someday be mandated, just as sexual harassment training is now mandated for supervisors and managers in many states.

WHEN SUPERVISORS GO "BAD"

There is no reason to assume that all supervisors are truly up to the task at hand. Tragically, there are many poor supervisors in American business. Worse yet, there are far too many who are abusive and authoritarian toward the employees that they are entrusted to manage. If supervisors or front-line managers are guilty of such behavior, then they should be removed from the job. Countless companies have been successfully sued for creating a hostile environment because of the actions of supervisors who have not been properly selected or trained. You should work to ensure that your company does not have such a problem.

TABLE 10-1
ROLE OF SUPERVISORS IN ADDRESSING WORKPLACE VIOLENCE

- Observation—eyes of management.
- Listeners—ears of management.
- Mediation—resolve low-level disputes.
- Communication—messengers for management.
- Barometers—reading pressures that exist in the work environment.

SOURCE: National Safe Workplace Institute

Two keys to good supervision involve thoughtful selection criteria and good training. These both go together. If you don't choose supervisors well, it will be difficult to train them properly. Numerous employers are now using psychologists and sophisticated testing instruments to more carefully select supervisors for the key roles that they play. However, still more must be done in the vast majority of companies to ensure that they are properly and adequately trained for the challenge at hand. In an era of growing violence and increased sensitivity toward harassment and abusive behaviors, employers simply cannot afford to have supervisors who are not up to the job.

Table 10-2 identifies some of the many important training needs that exist for supervisors. It is difficult to choose a single skill or training need that is more important than any other. But if one has to be chosen, it would be training that helps a supervisor understand how to recognize employee reliability problems. If problems can be identified early before they become too acute, then there is a possibility that the underlying factors can be constructively addressed and the employee restored to full productivity.

A second skills priority would be in the area of incident documentation—helping supervisors understand how to accurately and properly record incidents of abusive behaviors, harassment, threats, or actual assaults.

TABLE 10-2
TRAINING NEEDS FOR MANAGERS AND SUPERVISORS

TRAINING NEED	DESCRIPTION
Fitness-for-duty	Training in recognition and response to circumstances involving fitness-for-duty and incidents which could result in high stress levels or violence.
Employee reliability	Workshops and training in skills development related to employee reliability and potentially aggressive acts.
Behavioral observation	Systems to monitor employee behavioral changes as part of a progressive, non-punitive process.
Incident documentation	Proper documenting of threats in accordance with policy and legal requirements.
Interpersonal skills	Critical incident management; people or communication skills; conflict resolution; stress management; and substance abuse recognition.

SOURCE: National Safe Workplace Institute

Employers need to have information that is accurate, complete, and, above all, consistent between supervisors. While we have identified two priority concerns for supervisor training, all of the areas in Table 10-2 are important and should be carefully considered. Again, to emphasize the point, supervisors and junior managers serve as a bridge and to work effectively they must be equipped for the mission at hand. If they are unable to properly undertake this role, they will be ineffective or possibly counterproductive.

Many supervisors are in desperate need of interpersonal skill building, especially in an era where they are expected to supervise even greater numbers of workers. In many organizations, supervisors who previously managed 10 or fewer employees now find themselves responsible for 25 or even more workers. It only stands to reason that a person cannot spend as much time communicating with 25 workers (on a per-employee basis) as he or she did with 10. As a result, pressures will likely grow with adverse results. This makes interpersonal skill building even more important than ever before.

THE DO'S AND DON'TS OF SUCCESSFUL SUPERVISION

There are several do's and don'ts that are crucial to proper workplace violence prevention strategies. Table 10-3 illustrates some of the positive issues that supervisors should concentrate on doing as part of their job. These may seem to be common sense but they are roles that can be overlooked in the real world where decisions must be made quickly and where there are many difficult challenges and tasks facing supervisors and managers. Indeed, many organizations have restructured in recent years, increasing the ratio of workers to supervisors. These new management systems are creating many new challenges for supervisors and increasing communication burdens.

Also, it is clear from reviewing many examples of acute workplace violence (e.g. homicides) that supervisors had inadequate guidance on making appropriate decisions. You cannot assume that supervisors will automatically know what to do. Rather, the proper mission of the supervisor should be constantly reinforced through appropriate training and internal communications.

INVESTIGATING INCIDENTS OF THREATS OR VIOLENCE

Supervisors are likely to play a key role in conducting preliminary investigations of threats or violence. Generally speaking, employees who engage

Table 10-3

What Supervisors *Should Do* in the Effort to Prevent Violence

- Be consistent in treatment of employees.
- Immediately intervene when threats occur:
  - ✓ Counsel employee that threats will *not* be tolerated.
  - ✓ Seek the employee's side of the story.
  - ✓ If appropriate, refer to counseling.
- Report threats immediately to appropriate management.
- Know what options are available.
- Realize that some employees will test "boundaries."

SOURCE: National Safe Workplace Institute

in such behavior should be suspended pending investigation. If an incident occurs that meets the criteria of a threat or act of violence, a supervisor should immediately conduct a preliminary review until a trained professional takes over this role. In many ways, this role is similar to a traffic officer who first happens upon the scene of a serious accident. The officer will take notes and document the incident as carefully as possible before a trained expert takes over. In general, the supervisor should ask basic questions: who? what? when? where? and how? in the course of such an inquiry. It is important that supervisors hear both sides of the story so that the investigation be as thorough as possible.

Table 10-4 warns of tactics that supervisors and junior managers should avoid using. Again, these are mistakes that supervisors have made in the past that they should have been able to avoid, if properly trained and prepared for their roles in violence prevention. Perhaps the most critical mistake that a supervisor can make is to try to psychoanalyze employees or compare them with a "perpetrator profile" or other statistical information. Such strategies, improperly used, may be very unfair to the employee and potentially could result in the employer being sued for defamation. Likewise, case histories show that supervisors have made threats that were entirely inappropriate and even illegal. They must know their options and be able to exercise their authority in a proper fashion.

Finally, it is vital that supervisors do not meet alone with dangerous employees. If the supervisor is concerned that an employee may be dangerous, he or she should ask for appropriate protection from security. Caution should be the watchword in such a situation.

TABLE 10-4
WHAT SUPERVISORS *SHOULD NOT* DO

- Don't psychoanalyze employees.
- Don't meet with dangerous employees alone.
- Don't make threats (e.g. "You will go to jail if you don't cooperate.").

SOURCE: National Safe Workplace Institute

In mapping out a workplace violence prevention program, one simply cannot stress enough the importance of good supervision. Too often in the past employers have been sloppy in selecting supervisors and even more haphazard in training these key personnel. To be effective in violence prevention, an organization must recognize how critical supervisors are as the front-line defense.

11

PRE-EMPLOYMENT SCREENING

Don't Hire Your Mistakes

One of the cardinal rules for an organization is to employ individuals who have adequate skills and who fit the organization's culture. The opposite is also true: an organization should avoid hiring a "mistake." Yet organizations make this painful and costly error over and over again. Hiring professionals are frequently pressured to fill vacant or new positions considered crucial to business productivity. Pressures from production or the intuitive feelings that hiring officers have about an applicant often overtake good sense and sound hiring practices. Employment decisions, even as important and as costly as they are or can be, are frequently made with few controls.

This chapter will focus on safeguards that can be used in the hiring process to help us achieve violence-free work environments. This chapter is not meant to cover all aspects of the hiring process, a subject best covered by book-length material. Instead, this chapter will focus on how to avoid hiring employees who are likely to be especially aggressive or even violent. We will also take a look at supervisor selection. An abusive supervisor will contribute to stress which often leads to aggressive behaviors. If you would like to read more about the hiring process in general, please consult organizations such as the Society for Human Resource Management or the American Management Association.

There are compelling reasons why an organization dedicated to a violence-free work environment should pay attention to the hiring process. Substantial evidence suggests that individuals with a history of violence and aggression are likely to repeat past behaviors. As a result, we should attempt to screen out potentially aggressive or violent individuals during the hiring process. Some social scientists have suggested that there is a lack of empirical evidence to support screening-out policies (especially psychometric testing). While that may be true, we know from our study of lethal perpetrators that indeed the most violent among them generally had a history of violence.

Even though we may lack empirical data on this question of pre-employment screening, there are compelling legal reasons why employers should be cautious about hiring individuals with violent histories. This concern flows from what attorneys call the negligent hiring doctrine. According to this doctrine, employers can ultimately be held responsible for damage done by the employee if there are clear indications that those behaviors or attitudes should have been discovered during the hiring process.

THE IMPORTANCE OF BACKGROUND INFORMATION

It is often difficult to obtain background information on individuals with histories of violence. There are privacy and other laws that impose some limits on the information that you can expect to obtain from previous employers, educational institutions, and law enforcement authorities. However, these obstacles should not prevent you from attempting to gather information from plenty of other sources that are not blocked by such legal restrictions.

Employment officials should be familiar with the laws and regulations that govern the hiring process where they operate. A competent attorney who specializes in employment law should review your hiring practices to ensure that they are legally sound. In larger cities and states, you might be able to obtain guidance on employment practices through trade or professional associations. Moreover, your local library may have legal or employment practice books that will cover these issues.

The overall record of violent perpetrators suggests that individuals with such experiences are more likely to become violent again. While a person may outgrow a problem and deserve a new chance, there is still a reasonable possibility that the applicant will emerge again as a violent and abusive individual. In the 1990's, it is important that you examine work histories and other background information with care, recognizing the laws and standards that protect the rights and interests of applicants.

One key step that virtually any organization can take in the hiring process is to look for a history of violence in a person's background (see Table 11-1). Evidence of any of the behaviors in this table should be a red flag. Numerous incidents of such violence, especially in the recent past, should be carefully considered before an offer of employment is made— particularly when the vacant position involves meeting with the public or sensitive exposure to large numbers of employees.

Just because a person has been violent does not mean that we should automatically disqualify him or her as a potential employee. We should allow people a chance to learn from their mistakes. After all, very few of us are perfect. If the number of violent events in a person's past is small, then the hiring officer should try to identify ways that the applicant may have corrected the problem or been rehabilitated. Corrective measures would include education or training programs, psychological therapy, or success-

TABLE 11-1

EVIDENCE OF VIOLENCE SOMETIMES FOUND IN APPLICANT BACKGROUNDS

- Arrest records for violent crimes:
  - ✓ Homicide or manslaughter
  - ✓ Rape
  - ✓ Battery
  - ✓ Assault
  - ✓ Property damage
- History of abuse toward women or animals.
- Fighting at previous jobs.
- Violent arguments with superiors or co-workers.
- History of disciplinary problems in previous employment.
- Less than honorable discharge from the armed services.
- Abusive or disruptive behaviors toward law enforcement or authority figures.
- Discipline problems in school record (if available).

SOURCE: National Safe Workplace Institute

ful involvement in community or religious programs. In circumstances where an applicant tries to recover from a violent past, you may wish to talk to program managers or therapists who are familiar with the individual and any behavior change.

It is also important to note that there are occasionally physiological reasons why a person is violent. In rare cases individuals have become violent as a result of a vitamin B deficiency or other nutrition-related abnormalities. There is little doubt, however, that almost all cases of violence are a function of behavior and choices that perpetrators comprehend.

You must assume that the applicant's potential co-workers—your employees—are going to learn of the applicant's history of violence. Because evidence is that violent individuals are likely to repeat their past, this knowledge will be unsettling, depending on the nature of the information. Hiring officers should be ready to explain their decisions to people who are likely to fear that they will suffer violent consequences in the future.

If you still believe that there are compelling qualities about the applicant after considering these steps, then you may move ahead with a job offer. But you must be prepared to rationalize your decision to employees and to your organization's stakeholders (individuals with an interest in the organization). You may also wish to consider how your hiring decision may look to a jury in a court of law, should the employee become dangerously violent again.

Time may cure some problems. It is much easier to discount a violent experience twenty years in the past than such an experience two months earlier. If you discover evidence of violence in a person's distant past, then look for information that the individual has changed. This is especially true for individuals who were aggressive or violent as adolescents. Numerous studies show that young people, especially males, react in ways that may be uncharacteristic for that individual because of peer pressure. People can and do change, and we should be prepared to give them a chance unless we, as a society, wish to punish individuals permanently for their mistakes. The crucial element here is to be diligent, to carefully consider what you learn during the hiring process, and to document what you find in a thorough fashion.

If information about violence or aggressive acts was readily available to the hiring officer and was not sought or considered, then an employer would be especially vulnerable to a lawsuit. However, the negligent hiring doctrine would probably not apply if the hiring officer examined this information and found that remedial actions mitigated the experience of violence. Few courts are likely to punish employers who are willing to provide an applicant a second chance. However, hiring officers must be prepared to demonstrate what they felt had been done to mitigate the evidence of violence or abuse. It is simply not enough to say that they *felt* that the person had matured or become less violent.

WHY GOOD HIRING ISN'T ALWAYS EASY

One of the goals in an employment application procedure should be to screen out individuals who have violent histories, which is, of course, much easier said than done. Unfortunately, human resource managers feel that they must hire off the street to obtain the required personnel to maintain or re-establish levels of productivity. To resist such impulses, some companies, such as Circuit City, have centralized all hiring decisions. Circuit City found that sales goals were getting in the way of good hiring decisions and the company subsequently centralized all employment decisions in its Richmond, Virginia headquarters. It claims that the benefits of a sound practice far outweigh the costs. In addition to improved morale and productivity, Circuit City claims to have reduced employee theft and drug use because of its careful hiring policies.

Circuit City is clearly an exception. Far too many employers give applicants a superficial once-over when they hire. Over the long run such decisions result in mistakes, often bad mistakes. While the job-hungry applicants appreciate a new job for a short time, the luster of new employment wears off quickly. An aggressive individual is likely to become frustrated and angry, engaging in abusive acts against co-employees or superiors. The cycle of violence and aggression is repeated. There is even a distinct possibility that the level of violence and aggression may increase in the new job, as the stakes and pressures associated with successful employment increase.

THE TOUGH SUPERVISOR STRATEGY

Some personnel directors convince themselves that a difficult person can be effectively managed by a tough supervisor. Unfortunately, this is often wishful thinking. Things don't always turn out the way we want them to turn out. Supervisors and employees are transferred to different divisions or change shifts. Then management discovers it has a serious problem that is costing the organization through lost productivity and diminished morale, or worse.

The weight of bad hiring decisions can be heavy. Undoing poor decisions can be expensive both in terms of dollars and morale. Bad employees are often entitled to severance pay or are protected by laws or grievance procedures. Even short-term employees can command severance and some will even file a lawsuit if they feel that they have been wronged. Also, aggressive employees can become disgruntled former employees. They often strike back at the work environment with a vengeance, wreaking havoc months after they are terminated.

Perhaps one way around pressures to employ "off the street" is to establish the standard that the current or new jobs simply will not be filled for a minimum of two or three weeks. This will give the hiring manager time to do the job properly, to avoid the serious mistakes that will plague a company down the road. By establishing this waiting period for filling new jobs or vacancies, unrealistic or unreasonable expectations are changed among managers in production or operations. You have a chance to avoid making a costly mistake and they, in the long run, will have better and more productive employees.

AVOIDING BAD HIRING DECISIONS

The remainder of this chapter will focus on screening personnel applications and interviewing procedures used to identify individuals prone to violence. We will explore how to get the type of information that is required for an *informed* employment decision. Not only should there be careful scrutiny of available records, but you may wish to consider the use of psychometric tests which will help you understand the psychological composition of the individual and how likely he or she is to succeed in the organization.

Psychometric tests should be administered with care. As an employer, you must be able to demonstrate that these tests have some relationship to the type of job that is being offered as well as the skills that are necessary for that position. If the employee is likely to have substantial public contact, it is easy to explain the need for psychometric testing. The further removed from the public the employee is, the more difficult such testing is to justify. You should consult with a local licensed clinical psychologist and attorney familiar with Federal and state employment and discrimination laws where you operate. Contrary to what you may think, such testing is reasonably priced and results can often be obtained in a matter of two or three hours, if not less. It is likely the cost of such tests will be further reduced in the future as the expenses of computers and telecommunications are further reduced through technological advances and increased competition.

The most important information that an employer should try to obtain is the applicant's criminal record, if any. Unfortunately, this information is often unavailable, especially for younger individuals whose records as adolescents are typically protected by law. Other sources of information that you may wish to consider in making a sound employment decision include employment/work records, military histories, as well as credit and driving records (see Table 11-2).

To obtain proper information, you have to ask for it. The personnel application form that you use should be designed to provide you with comprehensive information on an applicant's background. *You should require that the form be completed in its entirety.* Once you receive the form, then you can begin the task of determining what additional information you can learn from other official sources. Through a careful examination you may be able to identify information that should cause you concern. These are red flags that should, at the very least, result in caution in the employment process; some are listed in Table 11-3.

TABLE 11-2

RECORDS AND SOURCES OF INFORMATION
THAT CAN BE REVIEWED IN A HIRING DECISION

- Criminal records.
- Credit and financial reports.
- Military discharge information.
- Motor vehicle record.
- Education records (verify degrees).

SOURCE: National Safe Workplace Institute

Table 11-3
"Red Flags" Sometimes Found in Job Applications

- Long, unexplained time gaps on employment record.
- Confusing or unclear job histories.
- Extensive use of personal references when substantial employment history exists.
- Inability to provide references that can verify employment.
- Unexplained reasons for moving long geographical distances or out-of-state.

SOURCE: National Safe Workplace Institute

Many troubled job candidates assume that you will be less than diligent in reviewing their application. They assume this because that is their experience. If you want to hear some horror stories, call a competent employment attorney who can share with you tales of how hiring officials have employed people with deficient qualifications or even when the information provided in the application could not be substantiated. Every crucial piece of information in the application must be carefully scrutinized and verified to the best of your ability. If you cannot authenticate the information, then you should delay the employment decision until you have adequate information. You do not have to be paranoid to be effective in this process, simply thorough.

THE INTERVIEW PROCESS
How to Do it Right

There are numerous Federal and state laws that determine how you can conduct an interview. You should consult your employment attorney to be certain that you are complying with all applicable laws. Unfortunately, many laws make the hiring process tedious, awkward, and even difficult, but not impossible.

A good starting point to keep in mind is that there are no laws that *make* you employ a person. It goes without saying that you cannot discriminate based on age, race, color or creed. Now there are further requirements: the Americans with Disabilities Act mandates that you must reasonably accommodate individuals with disabilities.

In conducting an interview, it often helps to think like a psychologist. This is the time when you are trying to learn about behaviors that might indicate undue aggression or abuse. The need for such information will increase if there are indications that an individual has had a violent past.

Possible questions that you may wish to consider asking an applicant:

- In what ways are you hard to get along with or aggressive with others?
- How do you deal with disappointments?
- How do you express anger or hostility?
- How do you deal with difficult people?
- How did you feel about your managers or supervisors where you previously worked?
- What do you do when you disagree with another person?
- What kinds of situations or circumstances frustrate or anger you?

There are no perfect questions. You should improvise as you complete the interviewing process, trusting your instincts. The purpose of the interview is to learn, to the best of your ability, how individuals deal with conflict, frustration, anger, disappointment, etc. If you feel troubled by the applicant's responses, then you may wish to be cautious in making a hiring decision. If a person has a good record and doesn't demonstrate a troubled personality, then you may wish to move ahead with other parts of the hiring process.

SELECTING SUPERVISORS
Finding Those Who Can Manage

This is a critical function, especially during a period when supervisors and front-line managers are expected to do far more with less. Many employers traditionally have paid little attention to this important role. They too often select supervisors based on personalities, tenure or other factors. They may be right, but they also may be wrong. When bad decisions get made, line employees often pay a price. There are countless stories of supervisors and front-line managers abusing employees with disastrous consequences for the organization such as reduced morale and productivity and even lawsuits for creating a hostile environment.

Because supervisors are a bridge between management and craft or line workers, they should be chosen with care. Nucor Steel, a fast-growing steelmaker headquartered in Charlotte, North Carolina, takes extraordinary care in selecting supervisors. It subjects all supervisor candidates to psychometric testing and psychological interviews conducted either in Charlotte or Chicago. Since both cities are geographically long distant from Nucor's far-flung production facilities, applicants must travel to the interviews and test sites at substantial expense to Nucor. Nonetheless, senior management believes that the results have been well worth the price. They think of this expense as an investment in good management, and they are right. They believe that the quality of the new supervisors is good and that productivity—and profits—are enhanced as a result of this investment in supervisor selection.

An employer can use several other steps to select supervisors in addition to psychometric testing and psychological interviews. You may wish to have peer reviews completed on the individual. This is simply the process of learning what an applicant's co-workers think about the candidate and his or her ability to succeed in the position. Also, you may wish to have current supervisors interview the applicant and get their feedback. Some of the steps are summarized in Table 11-4.

The tragic fact is that American organizations—public and private—are loaded with supervisors who are abusive and authoritarian. The U.S. Postal Service, the scene of 34 murdered employees between 1986 and 1993, is a case in point. The Postal Service's own employee satisfaction surveys show a high level of dissatisfaction by craft or line employees toward supervisors—and the Postal Service has 90,000 supervisors and managers out of an employee population of more than 700,000. The Postal Service aside, there have been numerous instances where abusive supervisors have baited angry and frustrated employees, pushing these individuals to unacceptable levels of violence and aggression.

Table 11-4
Tools That Can Be Used to Screen and Select Supervisors

- Psychometric tests.
- Interviews by psychologists.
- Peer reviews.
- Interviews by current supervisors.
- Skill tests, if appropriate.

Source: National Safe Workplace Institute

In a legal context, abusive supervisors can damage an organization by establishing what lawyers call hostile environments where aggression can be anticipated. The hostile environment doctrine is based on substantial psychological research indicating that some workers in stressed situations (e.g. abusive supervisory practices) will react with frustration and aggression.

Table 11-4 illustrates sound supervisor/front-line manager selection practices. Using them will enable you to employ quality supervisors and managers that have the best chance of avoiding the types of practices that will backfire on the organization.

AN OUNCE OF PREVENTION IS WORTH A POUND OF CURE

The hiring process is very difficult, encumbered by numerous laws, regulations, and concerns. Hiring officers are often under enormous pressure from production managers who want to have all employee slots filled and fully operational. Production managers like to talk about "warm bodies" as if human beings are fully interchangeable. There are still other problems. Hiring can be polluted by nepotism and favoritism. The hiring officer is frequently urged to employ someone who knows somebody rather than to carefully and systematically consider a person's qualifications.

Large employers should carefully consider the idea of centralizing the final employment decision. There is little question that the regional or home office, often somewhat insulated from the trials of operational pressures, can take the time to systematically examine an applicant's background to ensure that potentially costly and careless mistakes are avoided.

For the next several decades it is likely that there is going to be much more research and debate about the hiring process and the qualities that hiring officers should consider. For the time being, there is a clear risk in hiring somebody with a violent past. In such situations, the hiring officer must make an effort to learn how the applicant has addressed those problems. Caution is in order if a person has committed violent acts in the past few years and has done very little to address his or her problems. Remember, there are no laws that require you to employ a specific person. So move ahead with the hiring decision carefully and cautiously, employing only the right person to meet your requirements.

12

LOOKING FOR ANSWERS

Guidelines for Investigating Acts of Violence

The purpose of this chapter is to provide guidelines for investigating acts of violence in the workplace. We have seen that harassing behaviors and threats amount to serious acts of violence and should be the subject for comprehensive investigations as well as actual assaults.

Timely investigations of serious incidents of workplace violence should begin as quickly as possible. Ideally, an investigation should be underway within a few hours of such an incident. Witnesses and participants could have difficulty recalling details if there are significant delays in conducting interviews. Failure to gain a thorough and accurate review of the facts could be a costly mistake for management.

Competent investigations often reveal factors and issues that would not be clear from a superficial review. This is only natural. As any seasoned investigator knows from his or her experience that what seems to be is not always what actually is. This is because people have selective memories or because they have a vested interest in a particular outcome. In this chapter, we will examine the framework for a competent and comprehensive investigation including inquiries that are designed to reveal the truth, no matter how painful it may be for an individual or even for an organization. The truth is always in the best interest of the organization because corrective steps can be taken to ensure that mistakes once made will not be repeated. Managers should know the truth, no matter how difficult, so that they are in a position to make an appropriate decision for the organization. If the truth is revealed in a different forum (e.g. in a court of law), the results can be both painful and expensive for all those involved.

INCIDENTS INVOLVING EXISTING OR FORMER EMPLOYEES

Any investigation should include basic "who," "what," "when," "where," "why," and "how" questions. Although seemingly mundane and often overlooked, they are crucial to establish basic facts that may be critical in a review by a regulator such as the Equal Employment Opportunity Commission (EEOC) or in litigation. Once the basic facts are established, then the investigator can focus on more detailed issues and concerns.

A very important set of questions involves employment status. Is the perpetrator a current employee? A former employee? If so, the investigator must determine the nature of the perpetrator's relationship with the organization and its relevant managers and supervisors.

For a current employee, there are a number of questions such as:

- What behaviors led to the incident?
- Did the violence or aggressiveness represent a pattern of behavior in the perpetrator or an aberration?
- Did anyone in the organization have reason to believe that violence was possible or even likely? In other words, was the event foreseeable?
- Has the perpetrator been threatened with termination or diminished employment status?
- Has there been a change in workload? Compensation levels?
- Are there any problems between home and work life?
- What is the quality of the management and supervision that the employee receives?
- Are the relevant supervisors and managers generally effective and positive in their relationships with employees?

For a *former employee,* several key questions should be raised:

- Under what conditions was the employee separated?

- How much time had passed between separation from employment to the time of the incident?
- What led to the termination of employment?
- What kind of relationship did the perpetrator have with his peers? supervisors?
- How long was the perpetrator employed by the organization?

It is crucial for the investigator to seek all sides of the story, including the side that the perpetrators have to tell. It is only human nature that people are self-serving, trying to put themselves in the best light. This can be just as true for victims as for those who perpetrate violence. Some perpetrators engaging in abuse or violent behaviors are in some other ways victims as well. For example, there are many examples of shunned workers becoming violent after they were teased and baited for long periods of time by co-workers and colleagues.

Violence has often been perpetrated by individuals with less secure positions in the organization such as part-time, season, contract, student-worker/intern. They often are frustrated by their failure, for whatever reason (including reasons beyond their control), to obtain more secure and rewarding employment.

As U.S. corporations (and now government agencies) try to right-size by cutting the organizational payroll (often for a third or fourth time), it is likely that more jobs will be shifted to people with non-permanent employment status. Individuals who lack security may consider violence as a response to a stunted career. For example, the son of a senior employee in a blue collar position became frustrated by his failure to gain a well-paid union job similar to the one held by his father. After several unrewarding months the senior employee's son, who worked as a contract employee with minimum wage pay, tried to blow up the organization's St. Louis headquarters by starting a fire in a basement room used for storing propane tanks. Fortunately, the fire was discovered and promptly extinguished by an alert security officer. The incident could have flattened the building, costing 600 lives.

EXTERNAL THREATS FROM NON-EMPLOYEES
Stalkers

Most workplace homicides are perpetrated by individuals from outside the place of employment. Stalkers or romantically disaffected parties represent a unique category of non-employee violence. As we have discussed elsewhere in this book, there are several steps that a company can take in such a case to protect an employee—assuming that this information is known to proper personnel.

Some key questions for investigating these issues:

- Were the proper authorities alerted to the stalking or threats against the employee?

- What precautionary steps were taken to protect the victim?

- Were restraining orders or orders of protection in place against the stalker?

- What can be learned from the experience that will benefit the organization in the future?

- Did the victim comply with the restraining order? (Note: Victims sometimes have a change of heart and will restore a relationship with the stalker, possibly in violation of the restraining order.)

NON-EMPLOYEES
Others

Often clients, customers, suppliers, or others will strike against an organization and its employees. In 1993, a fired California engineer became violent and killed individuals at two different state unemployment offices. Joseph Ferri went on a rampage in 1993 against the San Francisco law firm Petit & Martin (and others) which had previously deposed him in litigation. Indeed, even patients and their families in hospitals have become violent.

For these individuals, we should consider several questions:

- What relationship did the perpetrator have with the organization?

- What was the duration of that relationship?

- Was there a single event that caused the relationship to sour?

- Was the perpetrator related to an organization employee?

- Was the perpetrator a customer? If so, why was the customer angry?

- What can be learned about the motivation of the perpetrator?

WHY SHOULD *YOU* INVESTIGATE?

Of course, cases of workplace violence—whether from within or without—will be investigated by the legal authorities. But an employer should not rely on law enforcement to obtain all the facts. After all, the purpose of law enforcement is to determine if laws were broken and, to the extent possible, support prosecution of the perpetrator. An employer, on the other hand, has a different agenda:

- First, an employer should want to learn what went wrong that can be corrected in the future.

- Second, you will want to know issues that may emerge in litigation involving the firm.

These are just two of the many reasons why it is wise to conduct an aggressive investigation yourself.

Naturally, an employer should supply information about possible criminal acts to legal authorities. However, it is unwise to assume that the police will reciprocate by providing you with access to their investigative reports and other internal documents, even if that information is crucial to civil legal proceedings against your firm.

WORKPLACE STRESSORS

A quality investigation should include consideration of stressors in the work environment. Stressors are conditions or factors that place a significant amount of pressure on an individual. Occupational stress can result in a physiological reaction that may contribute to abusive or aggressive behaviors.

Examples of potential stressors that may be considered:

- Work load—How many hours did the perpetrator work per week?

- Shift changes—Had there been any shift changes? Data shows that workers who have shift changes often become stressed and aggressive from sleep loss.

- Role or job description changes—Did the perpetrator experience any job changes? Could these changes have generated more stress and pressure on the perpetrator?

- Grievance procedures—Did the perpetrator have a history of filing complaints or grievances?
- Peer relationships and pressures—Was the person shunned by his or her peers?
- Attendance record—Did the perpetrator have a good job attendance record? Were there unexplained absences?

CO-WORKER RELATIONSHIPS

It is important to establish the general nature of the relationships that the individual had with his or her co-workers, supervisors and managers, etc., as well as with other third parties (e.g. customers) in the work environment.

- Supervisors—Did the perpetrator accept supervision? Were they cooperative and productive?
- Co-workers or peers—What kind of relationship did the perpetrator have with his or her co-workers? Was he or she a loner? Why?
- Diversity—Did the perpetrator have difficulties with people of the opposite sex or of a different age or ethnic group?
- Other pertinent individuals in the work environment—Did the person get along with suppliers? vendors? customers?
- Had the general nature of these relationships shown any recent change?
- How well did the individual interact with others individually or collectively?

LIFE STRESSORS

Domestic or non-work problems can spill over into the workplace, leading to high levels of stress for some people. Consideration should be given to what types of information can be obtained without violating a person's privacy. The only objective should be to obtain information that will help establish the context for the incident.

The situations or circumstances that should be considered are called life stressors. Examples of such stressors:

- Family difficulties—Studies show that domestic or family problems spill over into the work environment. Changes in those relationships can put enormous pressure on an individual. Issues that should be examined—

1. Marital status? Have there been any problems with the person's relationships?
2. Recent trauma or death of family members?
3. Other family problems?

- Financial pressures—Has the perpetrator experienced any financial problems or difficulties that could have been brought on by external problems? (e.g. drug use, gambling)
- Legal—Is the perpetrator facing any legal difficulties such as foreclosure, custody challenge, or lawsuit?
- Physical health (information on health problems)—Is the person experiencing any physical illness? cancer? terminal diseases?
- Personal relationships with others—How well does the perpetrator get along with other individuals?

OTHER FACTORS TO BE INCLUDED

Examples of additional factors that should be included to complete a comprehensive investigation are:

- What information, if any, was available that violence was a possibility or probability?
- If the perpetrator is an employee or former employee, did he or she utilize the health services of the organization?
- If such services were provided, did the mental health professional know about the possibility of violence? Were proper warnings given?
- What role, if any, did drugs, alcohol or other substances play in the incident?

There is no "magic bullet" to conducting a proper and thorough investigation. Many investigations prove to be painful because they reveal information that management will find unpleasant, possibly including significant management lapses that could expose the organization to potential legal liabilities. However, it is almost always better to know as much as possible rather than to be blind-sided in the future. In following the counsel provided in this chapter, most organizations will discover the truth and be able to take corrective measures that will be in the best long-term interest of the organization.

13

HELP IS AVAILABLE

Getting the Most from Outside Resources

Many businesses and government agencies lack the internal resources to prevent, detect, or manage workplace violence. For example, many small companies may not have Employee Assistance Programs (EAPs), sophisticated proprietary security personnel, or trainers to train supervisors. This lack of resources doesn't mean that these organizations should surrender and do nothing to prevent violence. In fact, there are many sources of help available to the creative and thoughtful manager: from charitable agencies operating in your state; from government agencies; and, in some cases, from professional organizations and trade associations. In this chapter, we will look at some of those outside resources and how to get the most out of them.

CONDUCTING NEEDS ASSESSMENTS

Just because an organization is small doesn't mean it cannot conduct a needs assessment. Even organizations with fewer than 100 employees can obtain a needs assessment for little or no cost by contacting local universities or community colleges who are eager to provide their faculty and students with experiences that will help enrich their education and development.

As we discussed earlier, needs assessment involves learning the experiences that employees have had with violence and threats (either inside or outside the organization) and what they feel the employer should do about this problem. There is no perfect list of questions or fail-safe ways of conducting such an assessment. We simply must keep in mind the fact that management should know what concerns employees have so that it can provide an appropriate defense as part of a violence prevention program.

Even community colleges and small academic institutions have faculty in business, sociology, psychology, health and other departments who are capable of guiding an appropriate needs assessment. Typically the dean of faculty can make a referral.

In taking such an approach, the employer is making the workplace a laboratory of sorts. In return for a service, the employer is making its employees available to complete questionnaires and to participate in focus groups. The results may be worth this small price.

MENTAL HEALTH RESOURCES

Our society has numerous community mental health resources, either free or available at a very low cost to both employers and employees who want to diffuse violence and conflict in their workplaces. They can be identified by looking through your local phone directory, phoning United Way, or by contacting a member of the clergy. Some are identified in Table 13-1.

Some studies suggest that employees are reluctant to turn to their employers for such services even if they are available for free or at a very low cost. Many people would rather contact a local psychologist, family counselor or mental health agency. Vets Centers, managed by the U.S. Department of Veterans Affairs (formerly the Veterans Administration), are accepted by many Vietnam Era veterans. In general, there is a Vets Center in most large cities.

Companies may wish to consider putting together their own list of resources. If they are located in a small town, they may also wish to include resources that are in nearby communities and towns that are likely to serve their workforce.

TABLE 13-1
POSSIBLE HIDDEN RESOURCES IN PREVENTING WORKPLACE VIOLENCE

RESOURCE	ROLE
Colleges and universities	Employee surveys, focus groups Policy & procedure development
Community mental health centers	Employee counseling Abuse treatment Support groups
Vets Centers	Post-trauma disorders Support groups
Clergy	Anger diffusion Counseling services

Other resources include family counseling centers, alcohol and drug abuse treatment programs.

Also, Chambers of Commerce and trade associations often may have information on violence prevention.

SOURCE: National Safe Workplace Institute

ROLE OF CLERGY IN DIFFUSING ANGER

Most small towns and communities across the United States have places of worship staffed by members of clergy. These people often have training in psychology, counseling, and other skills that are useful in diffusing anger or hostility in individuals who have made threats.

As first reported in 1995 in the *Workplace Violence & Behavior Letter,* which is published by the National Safe Workplace Institute, many companies are now employing chaplains to help address employee problems. There is good reason to request members of the clergy from the religious community surrounding your business facilities to assist you in addressing many of your employees' emotional and psychological needs.

Chaplains representing all major denominations have traditionally served in the military, in police and fire departments, and in hospitals. Corporations are now finding that they can be a valuable resource on the factory floor and in corporate offices as well.

Rev. Rodney Brown, who works with employees at the R.J. Reynolds Tobacco Company in Winston-Salem, North Carolina, is perhaps the dean of industrial chaplains. He frequently guides employees in getting the help they need, either directly from him or from other resources, inside or outside the company. Rev. Brown has assisted many R.J. Reynolds employees in addressing their anger, avoiding potentially life-threatening episodes at the plant and ensuring that highly skilled workers remain productive.

Rev. Brown, a United Methodist minister, has been an industrial chaplain for 28 years at the nation's oldest full-time workplace ministry established in 1949. In recent years, R. J. Reynolds has been joined by General Motors, Carolina Telephone and Telegraph, Allied Systems and some fifty other major corporations which are turning to chaplains to provide a unique kind of counseling in the workplace and to diffuse and prevent violent workplace incidents.

While there are some 15,000 to 20,000 chaplains in a variety of settings nationwide, ranging from lay volunteers to ministers working full time in the field, the number of industrial chaplains working in companies grows steadily. Many Employee Assistance Program (EAP) counselors also have been trained as pastors or priests, and have proven themselves highly competent as counselors. There is now also a small professional association in the field, the American Association of Ministry in the Workplace, based in the Shreveport, La. office of its president, George Schurman, an oil executive and Methodist layman.

According to Rev. Brown, the greatest stressor in the workplace is marriage and family conflict. This is followed by alcohol or drug abuse, either by the worker or a family member; and finally by a relatively new phenomenon, the increase in job-related stress, including layoffs and fear of layoffs.

Rev. Brown, who earned a Master's degree in Public Administration (MPA) in the military before attending seminary and doing graduate work in counseling, did his residency at the famed Meninger Clinic in Topeka, Kansas. He heads a department that includes another chaplain and an alcohol and drug counselor. Since joining R. J. Reynolds, Rev. Brown has documented more than 1,000 crises, in some 300 of which individuals contemplated or planned to take violent action in the workplace.

His department consults with managers, co-workers and family members to develop an intervention strategy. For example, if a worker is having a problem with co-workers, the co-workers may help plan an effective intervention strategy. Often intervention means referral to resources in the community. Rev. Brown's department does not get involved in any long-term therapy, but when this is necessary he makes arrangements with appropriate community resources.

Corporate management has not been alone in seeing the value of chaplains in the workplace. The United Automobile Workers (UAW) union has been involved with chaplaincy programs since 1985 and now more than 200 locals have expressed some interest in such programs. They have either volunteers or a standing committee on chaplaincy, or, in the case of eight locals in General Motors plants, full-time chaplains. A major accomplishment for the UAW in the 1993 Chrysler contract was inclusion of the word chaplaincy, which referred to an area of employee assistance that should be explored.

The grass roots movement to install chaplains on factory floors began within the UAW locals in Flint, Michigan in 1985. One of the employees at the Buick Motor Division requested the services of a full-time chaplain to see if that would help diffuse some of the problems workers at the plant were having. The Rev. Lowell Lawson, a Southern Baptist minister who was Detroit city police chaplain, was transferred there by his denomination for a six-month trial period. The Home Missions Board of the Southern Baptist Convention underwrote the pilot effort. Rev. Lawson worked with an informal volunteer committee at first, and then helped establish the International UAW Chaplaincy Conference, which works with locals around the world. He stayed on as a consultant to the Conference until the end of 1993, when he was appointed Director of Chaplaincy Development and Director of Law Enforcement Chaplaincy for the Southern Baptist Convention. However, he continues to keep in touch with the program on an almost daily basis.

"A chaplain can be in the workplace situation what a pop-off valve is to a steam boiler," Rev. Lawson says. "People need that release point. A violent act is something that generally has been pent up over a period of time. After a while, the individual is going to express it. If they do not have someone to express it to, they will express it some other way . . . I'd like to see the Postal Service put chaplains in their facilities."

Neil Huiskens, Secretary-Treasurer of the International UAW Chaplaincy Conference notes that "Violence in the workplace isn't planned. If you can get to the person in advance, you may be able to prevent it." He said that in the last three years, his Buick plant experienced four incidents of violence including one suicide and three violent acts against a spouse or girl friend. "Having a chaplain on site could have helped prevent these incidents," he maintains.

Industrial chaplaincy is still a grass roots movement. But as Rev. Lawson notes, in 1985 many people didn't even know what a chaplain was. Now there is some recognition and awareness of what chaplains can do, although it is difficult to measure because true accomplishment means actions don't happen.

BUSINESS ORGANIZATIONS

There are numerous trade associations and Chambers of Commerce that have worked on the issue of workplace violence and have sponsored conferences and workshops.

Most trade organizations publish magazines that will provide members and those who will pay a small fee with articles that they have previously published. These often contain excellent and timely information and identify other resources that are available. Since most trade associations are focused on a single industry, it is likely that they will have examples of companies similar to yours that have developed effective programs.

Finally, many associations are now also managing resource centers. These centers can help you identify specialists in your industry who will appreciate your special business needs and can help you mold the program that you require.

OTHER RESOURCES TO DIFFUSE ANGER

Other resources can help diffuse anger and hostility in the workplace such as public and charitable agencies that have mental health resource capabilities and missions to help people in their communities with human needs. Often these agencies, funded by taxes or by charitable contributions by your employees, are truly hidden resources to which your employees can turn in times of need.

Recently, officials at the Norfolk Naval Air Station in Virginia informally surveyed employees about where they would turn if they had mental health, stress, domestic, or psychological problems. In only one out of four cases would they depend on programs or resources supplied by the Navy. Through this exercise, the Navy identified more than two dozen community agencies that were capable of providing such resources to employees. The vast majority were supported by employee contributions (United Way), through tax dollars, and other sources of charity and philanthropy.

Once managers have compiled a list of community resources, they should write a letter asking what each agency can do to help the organization prevent violence in the workplace. The Navy learned that there was a range of agencies with a variety of capabilities for contributing to the base's violence prevention initiatives. In general, these hidden resources could help employees with a variety of emotional needs. the survey revealed a few surprises as well: a few agencies had the capability of training managers and supervisors about how to recognize individuals with excessive anger or stress and how to deal with their needs.

The point of this brief chapter is clear: there are outside resources, even resources we don't tend to think of, that are available in the effort to prevent violence in our organizations. Many agencies have highly trained and experienced people who would be pleased to help individual employees in your company or contribute to your company as a whole. This is especially true now that mental health professionals are appreciating the severe impact that violence and aggression can have on organizations.

14

JOB INSECURITY

Avoiding a Downsizing Crisis

Companies are justifiably concerned that restructuring or downsizing will catalyze aggressive and even violent behaviors by employees. For the past several years and for a variety of reasons, both business and government have begun to anticipate ways that changing conditions—and resulting job loss—affect workers. Although generally considered ineffective, laws have been enacted that mandate companies to warn employees of pending layoffs. To soften the obvious hardship, unemployment benefits have also been extended in many situations. These humane efforts are vital to those whose dreams have been shattered by job loss.

Lurking behind the scenes in human resource and security offices is the anxiety and fear that job loss will anger and antagonize fragile individuals. While this is a salient variable in many lethal incidents, very few of those involve widespread change such as a downsizing or restructuring of the organization. Nonetheless, layoffs do trigger increased workers' compensation claims, greater sick leave utilization, and diminished productivity.

There is little question that many employees feel anger, bitterness, and even betrayal. In these situations, employers routinely increase their use of fraud and security specialists to ensure that people and physical assets are protected and that claims of abuse are minimized.

Corporations, when downsizing and cutting the labor force for any reason, often use proactive alternatives to outright layoffs to prevent extreme stress to employees. We will examine leaders in both industry and government to identify ways to ease the pain of job loss: Ameritech, the "Baby Bell" that is headquartered in Chicago, and the quasi-governmental Tennessee Valley Authority (TVA), the Depression-Era creation of the Federal Government, provide concrete examples of how downsizing has been successfully managed.

Companies are usually reluctant to directly lay off employees. They fear both aggressive reactions by some employees and stigmatization by the media. Instead of issuing mass pink slips, employers often begin by providing incentives to those who are willing to retire early or to simply leave the company. Typically, an incentive may feature adding years of service to an employee's record to trigger pension benefits or the payment of a lump sum. For example, a person 62 years-old may be able to retire with the benefits of an employee aged 65.

In conjunction with early retirement programs, corporations curtail hiring, not replacing those who leave due to retirement, death, or resignation. The combined processes of attrition and incentives for employees who leave voluntarily can help to curb the need for outright layoffs and the residual resentment and frustration. Unfortunately, numerous factors make it very difficult to predict how successful such programs will be. In fact, companies often lose employees they wish to retain while seeing undesirable employees remain behind. Employees are often influenced by family requirements (e.g. how close spouse is to retirement age), finances, and other factors.

Often downsizing or restructuring leaves employees, including those who remain behind, feeling anxious and uncomfortable. Survivors of the cuts may feel that their jobs are in danger because they understand correctly that attrition and other incentives won't necessarily reduce a work force as much as required. They fear that their employer will have to resort to more severe measures, actions that will threaten a much larger group of employees. They may be next to suffer from job loss and often these employees will become less productive for a period of time. Industrial psychologists have coined the term survivor guilt to describe the anxiety that many individuals feel.

THE ROLE OF OUTPLACEMENT AS PART OF DOWNSIZING

Outplacement programs are the most common tool in downsizing. The concept is approached in two ways. Sometimes the services are provided directly by the employer. More often than not, however, consulting or outplacement specialists are called in from outside. Details of how outplacement is handled vary but all address the issue of helping the newly unemployed find new economic life after job termination. Outplacement specialists generally conduct an inventory of the person's skills and interests in trying to chart alternatives. Sometimes the person may be encouraged to obtain a franchise or to operate an independent business. In many cases, the outplacement specialist encourages the person to become a consultant. Depending on the person's interests and the job market, seeking an existing job may be the way to go.

For the newly unemployed, severing corporate ties is a painful and emotional experience. The search for meaningful economic alternatives is just one piece of comprehensive outplacement strategies. Displaced employees need substantial emotional support. This is especially true under two circumstances. The first involves people who have been laid off more than once. Such individuals are naturally anxious and distrustful. A second situation involves families where multiple breadwinners have lost their jobs. This circumstance is reasonably common at military installations that are closing as a result of defense spending cutbacks. Without question, these circumstances create a severe burden on families and with that, an increased risk of aggression and violence.

Corporations and government agencies need to identify high-risk individuals, those employees who are likely to have great difficulty adjusting to job loss. At-risk individuals would include (1) people who have had difficulty adjusting to change; (2) individuals who have been laid off previously; (3) individuals in families who have other breadwinners who are losing jobs; and (4) persons who are considered by their supervisors or managers as individuals who are emotionally fragile. Some enlightened employers are now identifying those individuals as early in the downsizing process as possible and are taking steps to ensure that psychological and other services are readily available during a period of crisis. In fact, some employers are having Employee Assistance Program (EAP) personnel participate in one-on-one job-loss issue meetings with employees about to be terminated.

A CORPORATE EXAMPLE-AMERITECH

Ameritech, whose first layoff included over 3,000 managers leaving both voluntarily and involuntarily, provides outplacement only to managers. Union contracts control how other employees can be severed. With extensive holdings primarily in the Midwest, it is just one of the "Baby Bells" that has been cast into the post-regulation world. In just a short period of time, Ameritech employees went from secure, lifetime employment with the highly regulated and monopolistic Bell Telephone Company to an uncertain economic future in a company with diverse communications interests and holdings.

Ameritech saw an acute need to trim management ranks of many employees whose jobs were tied to regulatory functions. It chose to divide its employees into two groups. Middle-managers were provided $2,000 to enroll in group programs to help adjust to the future. These programs deal with issues such as how to conduct a job search, interviewing techniques, and employment options. More senior managers are referred to an outplacement service where they receive similar but more personalized attention and where they also have access to a temporary office and secretarial services to help in conducting their job search. The primary characteristics of Ameritech's program are highlighted in Table 14-1.

Like Ameritech, the Tennessee Valley Authority (TVA) was staffed by employees who just a few years ago could reasonably anticipate lifetime employment. TVA, which cut its work force to 19,000 from 34,000, established an Employee Transition Program (ETP) which begins when an employee is notified that his or her position is considered "surplus." At that point, the employee, regardless of status within the TVA, is told that his or her job is now one of finding new employment. The TVA's mission is especially sensitive because it is a dominant employer where it operates and because many families have multiple breadwinners working for this quasi-governmental agency.

When a person is surplused, he or she is given six months of full compensation and benefits as a financial cushion during the job search. Services provided within this period include monthly counseling on job skills and job search techniques, including how to interview, prepare a resume, etc. Employees also have access to reference libraries, extensive government job listings, data bases, computers, and fax machines to facilitate their quest for new employment. The steps taken by TVA clearly should be studied by other Federal agencies, especially those in the Department of Defense that

TABLE 14-1

FEATURES OF AMERITECH'S DOWNSIZING TRANSITION PROGRAM

- Outplacement
  - ✓ Available to management only.
  - ✓ Middle management- group workshops.
  - ✓ Upper management- full personal service through outside placement service.
- Benefits
  - ✓ Severance payment (2 percent of final salary multiplied by the number of years worked at Ameritech).
  - ✓ 6 months of company health benefits.
- Job Training Programs
  - ✓ Employees may voluntarily seek outside training and are reimbursed up to $5,000.
- Mental Health Services
  - ✓ 24 hour telephone hotline.
  - ✓ Employee Assistance Program, open to anyone, providing variety of counseling services.

SOURCE: Compiled by the Author based on information provided in interviews with Ameritech managers.

are now facing severe cutbacks. Essential features of TVA's program are illustrated in Table 14-2.

RETRAINING FOR THE NEWLY UNEMPLOYED

A second category of programs which eases the impact of layoffs and downsizing is retraining for jobs that may be different from those lost. In examining job training, employers must know the skills that their employees have as well as the demands that exist in the labor markets. In many cases, existing skill levels do not match up with current employer demands. This reality makes the process for employees far more difficult because they have to adjust to both job loss and the demands of transitioning to a new set of skills.

Ameritech offers up to $5,000 in tuition grants to those who engage in outside training. This allows employees to receive the type of training that they want provided they take the initiative to find it. This program recog-

Table 14-2

Highlights of the Tennessee Valley Authority's Employment Transition Program

- Outplacement
  - ✓ open to all employees
  - ✓ six months extensive and personal services within the T.V.A.
- Benefits
  - ✓ six months full compensation and health benefits
- Job Training Programs
  - ✓ In-house training for other TVA positions if available, or for different jobs outside the authority
- Mental Health Services
  - ✓ 24-hour telephone hotline
  - ✓ Employee Assistance Program providing variety of counseling services

SOURCE: Compiled by the Author based on information provided by the TVA.

nizes that the transition for many employees is likely to be difficult and that new skills will have to be found for available jobs.

The TVA, as a part of its ETP, first tries to retrain workers itself to fill needed positions within the authority. If this is not possible, employees learn skills different from those of their former job in order to take a position outside the TVA. This training ranges from advanced computer training to help in learning how to run a small business.

Even though many employees do find new positions after layoffs (two-thirds of those displaced, according to the Bureau of Labor Statistics), it often takes weeks, if not months, to do so. Even then, an employee may have to relocate several hundred miles to take the new job. Thus, in addition to having to look for a job, many are subjected to the added worry of having to live on little more than unemployment payments in the interim.

However, at Ameritech and TVA, employees receive substantial assistance after they leave. This assistance is in the form of severance and benefits packages. Ameritech offers employees a lump sum of two percent of their current salary per year of service, with a minimum of eight weeks payment compensation. In addition, they receive their normal health benefits for six months after leaving the company. All employees, as a result of Federal law, are eligible to receive health insurance—though without employer subsidy— for 12 months. If an employee is laid off or leaves before the end of the year, that person receives pension compensation up until the time when he or she is dismissed, rather than lose the portion of that year's benefits. Stock options are handled in either the same pro-rated manner or are accelerated so that the employee receives a whole year's options even if he or she leaves before year's end.

The TVA, as illustrated in Table 14-2, provides full benefits and compensation for six months or until a job is found, whichever comes first. At the end of this period, if the employee has not been placed, he or she is considered unemployed and eligible for Federal unemployment compensation.

MENTAL HEALTH INTERVENTIONS

Another program offered by employers—perhaps most directly related to curbing employee aggression—involves mental health services. Both Ameritech and the TVA understand that job loss imposes a severe emotional and psychological strain on most people. As a result, both organizations designed elevated mental health services into their downsizing programs.

Both Ameritech and TVA provide Employee Assistance Programs (EAP's) which provide a variety of counseling services including individual counseling and 24-hour hotlines staffed by psychologists for emergencies. Ideally, EAP's will be involved in the downsizing from the earliest stage on. With some employees, the shock of job loss is acute from the very beginning. In numerous instances employees failed to inform their spouses about losing their job until several months after the fact. For them, the embarrassment was too severe. In far too many situations, employees committed suicide rather than confront changing circumstances.

Both businesses and government agencies are slowly realizing that there are multiple mental health resources in most communities that can help employees adjust to the shock and pain of job loss. These community resources are probably in a better position to aid an employee during this transitional period than any that are business-related. For example, local clergy or United Way mental health agencies often have an understanding of how to build family and other support systems to help with this transition. The Norfolk Naval Air Station, which will close its depot in 1995 or 1996, has put together an extensive guidebook to community mental health resources which is made available to employees upon request.

Ideally, a program for employees that are casualties of layoffs, downsizings, reduced demand, or the like, would provide 100 percent success in new job placement with full compensation and benefits until the new job is found. Obviously this worthy objective cannot be achieved practically. What both Ameritech and the TVA represent are realistic attempts to ease the transition from one job to the next and prevent unhealthy buildup of stress and frustration during this process. Both programs represent concerted efforts to help displaced employees. They claim high success and are being used as models by businesses such as Martin Marietta and government agencies as well.

AVOIDING A CRISIS WHEN DOWNSIZING

Unfortunately, not all organizations can construct the types of programs set up by Ameritech and the TVA. Many executives simply do not properly interpret changing circumstances until it is too late. By that time, there simply are not the resources available to assist in such a transition.

At a minimum, employers should take great pains to ensure that lay-offs are handled as objectively and as fairly as possible. Employees understand when a lay-off is really a disguised way of shedding unpopular employees. Moreover, employees need to be told the truth. If management has misguided the marketplace, then employees should be told what has happened. Managers need to perceive employees as partners and stake-holders in the enterprise who need to share in both the gain and the pain. Studies show that managers who include employees in key decisions are taking important steps in reducing stress and tension. We cannot avoid change, but we can take steps to ensure that the process of change causes as little disruption as possible. Some of the key steps of how to avoid a downsizing crisis are illustrated in Table 14.3. We live in a difficult period that challenges the abilities and resources of both private and public sector organizations. The 21st century will likely require even greater flexibility in the ways corporations and even government agencies operate. The current speed of change suggests that our world demands creative leadership that is adaptive and forward-looking. These often harsh effects of change are going to test the wisdom, patience, and understanding of us all.

Many people are losing their jobs. Indeed, once secure employees are now learning that there is really no such thing as job security. People are finding it increasingly difficult to replace their existing jobs because of a combination of cyclical and structural factors. Not only are jobs lost but skills are quickly becoming obsolete. Many people are being forced to work in conditions of greater uncertainty, working in temporary jobs or in environments of little job security. The trend does not appear to be slowing down, as corporations continue to face tougher competition and even more brutal pace of change. In this environment, it is entirely reasonable to expect rising frustration in the workplace which may increasingly lead to aggressive outbreaks in employee behavior. It is crucial that both business and government work to prevent excessive stress, a potential factor behind workplace violence caused by the trends described in this chapter.

Table 14-3
Avoiding a Downsizing Crisis—What Employers Should Do

- Provide early warning when possible so that employees can plan.
- Offer universal severance packages.
- Avoid inconsistency in lay-off policies.
- Provide compensation and benefits for as long as possible.
- Identify at-risk employees and provide mental health services.
- Establish effective outplacement.

SOURCE: National Safe Workplace Institute

15

RISING WAVES

New Sources of Violence

Middle-aged, white males have until recently perpetrated the lion's share of lethal, non-robbery incidents at work. By comparison, women and minority group members, with a few exceptions, have yet to use violence as an instrument of aggression as much as males. There are reasons to believe that the future may be different. In all likelihood, there will be new sources of violence at work. By examining some possibilities, we can appreciate the depth and complexity of this problem and what it may mean in the future.

Violence at work is likely to attract far more attention in the future than it has until now because there is every indication that problems are increasing. White males are going to continue to be aggressive and kill in the workplace. In time, we can anticipate that women will perpetrate lethal incidents in increasing numbers as they become emotionally involved in work while crucial support systems decline in importance. Women now commit one out of three acquaintance murders (incidents where the perpetrator was married or had a romantic involvement with the victim), a statistic that surprises most people who believe women to be far less lethal than they actually are.

As with men, there may be a psychological barrier that, once crossed in significant numbers, creates a solution for women to resolve conflict or to express their anger. On the other hand, women may not yet feel as entitled to a job as a property right as men,which may retard their use of lethal force as a behavior pattern.

Perhaps more significant in the short run, young people are going to be far more violent and lethal than they have been in the past. We now have a group of young people aged 12 to 25 years-old who can be called the "zero to nuclear war in five seconds generation." Sometimes called the X Generation, they are now coming into the adult workplace. Already they have shown clear signs of willingness to use violence to resolve disputes. A decade ago, lethal violence by young people was rare; today, regardless of social class or race, they are much more violent and explosive in temperament. Older generations have been hoping that this generation will mature and become more emotionally stable. This hope appears to be more wishful thinking than reality.

As violence has been seen as a tool or instrumental act in the minds of white males, it surely will be seen in a similar fashion by other groups in the coming years. Each act of violence has a way of legitimizing similar acts of violence by emotionally fragile people. This is especially true for young people who do not have alternative models or concepts. We live in a copy cat world in both a good and bad sense. Tragically, young people are especially violent; they are impressed by what they see (and learn) from the entertainment media. They lack the emotional maturity and educational perspective with which to appreciate violence from the entertainment world for what it is.

Also, certain violence-prone industries will attract more attention for a number of reasons. Two that are especially vulnerable are the retail convenience trade and health-care industries. These are settings that not only expose employees but large numbers of customers and the public to acts of violence. People are demanding to be protected in these settings and want more protection and security, not less, from businesses. The multi-million-dollar jury verdicts in cases of violence involving these industries suggest that the public is fed up with business establishments that have done so little to prevent and control aggression. In case after case, juries have been persuaded that businesses have failed to provide adequate security for the public and for employees. Government is slowly but surely entering the equation, threatening regulatory sanctions for neglectful decisions and behavior by employers (see Chapter 20).

THE "ZERO TO NUCLEAR WAR IN FIVE SECONDS GENERATION"

Almost all of us have experienced the rebellious anger of young people. While adolescents have always had tempers, the anger that we now see and read about is often explosive beyond that which we experienced from previous generations. The difference today is that adolescents, irrespective of race or social class, appear willing to resolve problems through the use of force. In just a few short years, murders perpetrated by teenagers have more than doubled to over 1,300 per year. An increasing number of teenagers are implicated in crimes of violence, including armed assault, rape, arson, robbery, etc., in the workplace.

One can only speculate as to why this generation is so violent. Some thoughts can be found in Table 15-1. There is no question that this genera-

TABLE 15-1

CHALLENGES ON THE HORIZON—MANAGING THE NEXT GENERATION OF WORKERS

1. YOUNGER WORKERS HAVE A *SOCIAL SKILLS DEFICIT.*

   - Fewer conflict resolution and mediation skills.

   - Reduced trust in older generations.

   - Attention span deficits.

2. NEXT GENERATION (NOW 12-25 YEARS OF AGE) IS *VIOLENT.*

   - Teen murders have more than doubled to over 1,300 in 5 years.

   - Young people are seeing more glamorized violence on TV and in the movies. Teenagers watch 18 hours of TV each week.

   - Indicators of discipline reveal substantial difficulty to come.

3. INTRODUCTION TO WORK IS POOR.

   - Most teenagers are introduced to work in low-skill jobs with minimal mentoring, which may increase frustration.

   - High turnover encouraged by poor management gives poor impression of work and denigrates authority.

SOURCE: National Safe Workplace Institute

tion of adolescents has been heavily influenced by TV and the entertainment media. That they are watching has been well established. According to a 1992 Department of Education study, the average teenager watches nearly 18 hours of television each week. Not only are young people watching more TV, but the TV they are watching contains violence that is far different from that which we have seen in the past. The previous generation was reared watching John Wayne and the Marines at Iwo Jima. This type of violence presented a far different thought process involving violence and justice and purpose in life. Today, adolescents watch the "Terminator," "Lethal Weapon II" and other programs that involve heavy doses of graphic and truly mindless violence.

Every supervisor has stories about the way that many teenagers view work. Far too many young people see work as a mindless inconvenience that is necessary to make financial ends meet. Kids just don't want to exercise initiative or leadership at work. They want to be politely told what to do and when to do it. They want to make sure that the tasks they are assigned are well defined and easy to do. They don't want anyone hassling them or getting in their way. They don't want to be pressured and they certainly don't want to be coerced. They don't trust older generations, in general, and they have transferred that distrust to managers and supervisors in particular.

Today's young people have suffered from what can best be described as a *parenting deficit*. The parenting deficit even exists in children from traditional nuclear families. Instead of educating children about life and its challenges as well as the consequences of certain decisions and behavior, the kids are parked in front of the TV where they learn about life in 30-minute segments. In these TV lessons adolescents learn that conflicts must be resolved firmly and quickly (preferably before the commercial break). Often, the way that disputes are resolved on TV is through violence and aggression, with the most vicious and ruthless person winning. The use of forceful means becomes an instrument to achieving the outcome that young people think they want. Any TV program that dealt with complexity and thoughtful approaches to life would not be broadcast for very long.

Already we are seeing scores of youthful perpetrators conducting lethal acts of violence. In Miami, a 17-year old courier for a construction supply firm murdered a 31-year old receptionist and mother of four. The adolescent was angry that the receptionist had declined his romantic advances so he stalked and killed her. In Clarksville, Tennessee, a young U.S. Army enlisted man obtained part-time employment at a fast food restaurant. Within a week, he decided to rob the restaurant late one Saturday evening. He gunned down four co-workers and walked away with less than $2,000. He was captured a short time later when he bragged about his acts with friends at his Army base. In a Boston suburb, a young person stormed into two abortion clinics killing two and wounding five. The perpetrator was captured a couple of days later shooting up an abortion clinic in Norfolk, Virginia. A neighbor defended this young man as someone who is "normal" and insisted that the media was wrong to see his behavior in any other light. As an employee at a hair dressing salon, the young person's behavior appeared to be troubled. His supervisor recalls that he did just the opposite of what his customers wanted" and that he came to work "looking like a janitor. He walked away from his job more than a week before killing two anonymous receptionists who happened to be in the wrong place at the wrong time.

These are examples of the increased aggression we are witnessing from younger people. The reasons for this explosive anger and willingness to use lethal force no doubt vary from case-to-case and from individual-to-individual. What is clear is that the aggression used by younger people is a growing phenomenon that will be a serious problem for decades to come. One example of where this aggression is especially salient is the fast food industry which is heavily dependent on young people as employees. While industry-specific statistics are difficult to come by, there is strong evidence suggesting that robbery and violence conducted by employees and former employees is skyrocketing. There are scores of robbery/murders in this industry each year. As the industry grows, so does the problem. By examining violence in this industry, we can more fully appreciate rapidly emerging problems associated with violence at work by this new generation of employees.

VIOLENCE IN RETAIL CONVENIENCE INDUSTRY

The retail convenience industry—fast food outlets, convenience stores and gasoline stations—is the largest employer of adolescents in the U.S. today. It faces a host of robbers and violence perpetrators that suggest how easy it is to conduct acts of violent crime. This hard-hit industry must solve its problems or it will surely be the target of more violence that will not only affect employees but customers and the public as well. Failure to address the problem will surely result in more lawsuits and, potentially, government regulation. Often employees who commit these crimes are frustrated by their failure to go to college or to attract higher-paying jobs that awaited previous generations. They see the fast-food industry as a source of low-paying, low-skilled and dead-end jobs. Because their work is highly routinized in order to ensure uniform products, any hopes for learning and the development of discretionary judgment are dampened.

The director of security for a national fast food chain told the *Wall Street Journal* that more than three-quarters of the robberies in his chain were perpetrated by employees or former employees. Other industry experts believe that at least one-half of the robberies in the industry are inside jobs undertaken by employees. In many of these cases, the perpetrators are as young as 16 years old. Indeed, a good many perpetrators are part of the Zero to Nuclear War in Five Seconds Generation. In Sacramento, California, a robber reportedly brutally murdered a manager as he fled out the front door of a fast food place. The robbery was coordinated by an employee, the robber's girlfriend. For some time, detectives investigating the case did not believe that it was an inside job. A tip turned the case around. Resolution came only after police followed the employee in a cross-country airline flight which she took to see her fleeing boyfriend.

Young people are hardly alone in committing these crimes in the fast food industry. There are many different types of robberies, although any type can involve a young person. It pays to understand,however, the types of robbers that the industry faces in order to appreciate the magnitude of the problem at hand. It also helps us to understand that interventions are crucial in order to arrest problems before they become severe. If we fail to intervene as employers, parents, educators, or community leaders, our society will continue to pay a huge price in increased crime and violence.

TABLE 15-2

INCENTIVES ENCOURAGING ROBBERY OF A RETAIL CONVENIENCE ESTABLISHMENT

- Ease of entry and exit.
- Impeded visibility and poor lighting.
- Vulnerable (young, senior, minority) workers.
- Probability of obtaining $100 or more.
- Reasonable certainty of few or no witnesses.
- Easy to obtain "inside" information on security procedures.
- Turnover of employees discourages employee loyalty.

SOURCE: National Safe Workplace Institute

PROFESSIONALS

These individuals are likely to rob establishments that present little or no threat of arrest. Since it is not unusual for a professional to have specialized in robbing a certain type of establishment, it follows that in some cases these perpetrators got to know the industry they rob by first being employees. They know the conditions that are most conducive to a successful robbery, conditions that usually mean getting a few hundred dollars or more and escaping with little notice or chance of arrest.

In one way, professionals represent less threat of violence than many other categories of perpetrators. Because they often possess above-average intelligence, they will look for situations where there is very little chance that force will be used. In one city, a fast food robber wrapped himself in elastic bandages and would hide near restaurants on heavily congested roadways until he felt that the best opportunity was at-hand. He would wrap his face in the bandages and rob the target. He would disappear almost as quickly as he appeared. This individual, a young person, stymied police for more than a year.

ADDICTS

Addicts are very frightening perpetrators of crime because they are frequently irrational and unpredictable. They are individuals who are looking for money to sustain a drug habit and often have a desperate and frightening quality. They have often killed employees who represented little or no threat when they became nervous or alarmed. Because these individuals are highly erratic, it is very difficult to defend against them.

Industry security experts insist that employees go along with the demands of the robber. They urge employees to remain calm and comply with the robber's requests as quickly as they can. It is important that the employee try to communicate with the robber. If an addict believes that the employee or employees represent little threat, there is a greater chance that the robbery will be completed without the use of violence. However, an impaired addict is exceedingly dangerous and likely to become agitated with little provocation.

Video footage of robberies in progress exists that suggest that there is much we can learn from how robberies are conducted. This footage demonstrates that a robber is more likely to shoot if an employee is standing than if the employee has been able to get on the ground. The reason for this can be found from the science of proximics, the study of spatial relationships between people. Theory from this field suggests that people in the prone position are far less threatening than people who stand. If an employee can communicate his or her intention of getting on the floor after the robber has obtained the cash, then that employee may have a better chance of survival. Very few employees, however, are given much instruction on how to survive such a traumatic event. While some chains are making employee training tapes, it is not clear what steps are taken to ensure that they are seen. One major chain requires employees of its corporate outlets to see the videos on a regular basis, a task confirmed by E-mail. The same chain, however, asserts that it has very little control over franchisees.

GANG MEMBERS

Many U.S. cities are haunted by gangs which are increasingly greedy and correspondingly violent. Big city newspapers are filled with headlines and stories about gangs and gang violence. Las Vegas casinos were plagued in 1994 by Los Angeles gangs; gangs from Chicago, Philadelphia, and other cities have been implicated in armed robberies and assaults across the U.S. In some cases, gang members have been able to gain inside information by working for a short period at fast-food outlets. In other instances, friends provide crucial information that these gang members use to undertake violent and criminal acts.

Adolescents are driven by peer pressure from gang members to (1) prove their worth and/or (2) rob funds for gang activities. Robberies are often part of a gang's initiation ritual. If an aspiring member cannot obtain sufficient funds through a robbery, then he or she cannot join the gang. The pressure is clearly peer-driven more than an individual's desire to commit a crime.

The idea of violence as part of the initiation process is new, according to most experts. Gang members have often become incredibly violent as part of the process of conducting robberies. In some instances, aspiring members are told that they must fire their guns at innocent people (as well as rival gang members) as part of the hazing or initiation process. If a gang member kills a person, his or her stock in the organization rises. Such a member is a hero, an individual who is willing to pay the price to be a full-fledged member of the gang.

Gang robberies and violence are often marked by erratic and uncertain behavior. The unpredictable quality of many gang robberies makes such incidents terrifying for employees and customers, as we have seen too often in TV news video footage. The random and undisciplined use of force leaves little doubt that many gang members are impaired by drugs and alcohol during such incidents.

EMPLOYEES & FORMER EMPLOYEES

As discussed earlier, employees and former employees are often facilitators of such crime. These incidents often involve individuals who are looking for a quick haul and who know crime control and security procedures at the location they are going to rob. They take advantage of information to make a quick hit.

If industry estimates of the large share of convenience industry robberies are true, then we must anticipate that employees and former employees represent a very serious threat that must be addressed in a much more effective fashion. Also, because these events often involve complicity from co-workers, one must be concerned about these patterns of behavior and choices as these workers mature and enter the adult workforce. The volatile job market that awaits unskilled and uneducated younger workers can only serve to reduce loyalty and increase a person's sense of frustration. Our failure to arrest violence among adolescent populations could extract a high price for many years to come.

Fortunately, there are answers to these problems. What remains to be seen is the industry's will to take advantage of new information and tech-

TABLE 15-3
CHALLENGES AND OPPORTUNITIES TO THE RETAIL CONVENIENCE INDUSTRY

- Develop a consensus around standards for reasonable and prudent safety and security measures.
- Select and train adolescent workers more carefully. Possibilities:
  1. attitude testing
  2. thorough background checks
  3. training on security and safety procedures
- Better "survival" training against gang members and addicts.
- Effectively use interactive video and other video technology.
- Sponsor empirical studies (e.g. tradeoffs between guards and various applications of technology).

SOURCE: *National Safe Workplace Institute*

nology. We must develop creative mechanisms for this very serious yet unappreciated problem. The industry is going to have to do a better job in training more carefully chosen workers. It will also have to examine the explosion of technology (e.g. videos, silent alarms) that is coming as the defense industry converts its capabilities to civilian applications. Unfortunately, the industry seems plagued by lack of agreement on what needs to be done. As a result, few chains are willing to make the financial commitment that is crucial to preventing violence. This is understandable because firms see substantial expenditures—$5,000 per store or more—creating a competitive disadvantage in a very competitive marketplace. In the short-run, solutions are likely to come incrementally, perhaps beginning with how employees are selected.

PRE-EMPLOYMENT SCREENING

The retail convenience industry faces a terrible dilemma. It experiences very high rates of turnover and, as a result, is understandably reluctant to spend on training. Perhaps one way to reduce turnover is to hire the appropriate people in the first instance. Indeed, more and more employers are emphasizing the hiring of the right hourly workers as a major key to safety, quality and productivity goals.

Several companies are now employing job candidate profiles or prescreening examinations as a way to identify applicants with desirable traits. Pre-employment screening inventories can be completed in 20 minutes and cost about $5.00 per test, depending on volume ordered. Testing companies are now beginning to include measures that may provide employers with some indications about an applicant's likelihood of using violence and aggression.

Examination of instruments that have been validated shows that low scorers on the people-relations scales have as many as five times more arguments with customers, arguments with coworkers, and customer complaints. High scorers on the people-relations scale were significantly more dependable and better at following company policies and work schedules.

Other measurements scored by such tests include safety and dependability. Low scorers on workplace safety scales averaged five times as many on-the-job injuries while high scorers were rated significantly safer by their supervisors. Low-scorers on the dependability scale are significantly more likely to use alcohol or drugs and have missed ten times as much work.

Many chains are now exploring such instruments as a means to identify better job candidates. Use of such instruments, at least on an experimental basis, is important in order to determine if test usage will affect safety and security. Unfortunately, the reluctance to use such tests will remain high. Many retail convenience industry employers insist that they cannot employ desirable candidates in many job markets and therefore must accept whoever applies. While there is some doubt about whether or not such preemployment instruments will find wide acceptance, it is to be hoped that some employers will experiment with these instruments and make them an important part of the application process.

HORROR OF THE CLOSING ROBBERY

Closing robberies take place when an establishment (e.g. convenience store) closes. Because there are no customers to deter robbers, these incidents are some of the most horrifying incidents conceivable. For example, a closing robbery in Austin, Texas, at a yogurt shop left four young girls, aged 12-17, dead. While statistics are not kept, industry experts say that the use of violence increases at closing robberies because the perpetrators are known to the victims and they need to avoid detection and apprehension.

The industry is trying to improve security through sound procedures and by increasing the use of technology. For example, one company now manufactures a silent alarm that can be placed in a tie-clasp. Still other companies are using video equipment which is operated during the highly vulnerable closing period. Unfortunately, only a small percentage of fast food outlets use these technologies, which are reasonably expensive (but available at a small fraction of what is spent on advertising). The available technology will probably not be used effectively until there is industry agreement on acceptable security measures or such practices are mandated by state or local laws.

HEALTH-CARE SETTING

A fact that has drawn the attention of policymakers (see Chapter 20) is that hospitals, medical centers and clinics are increasingly targets for violence in our society. At the very least, people should be able to demand safety and security at a medical facility as a last bastion in an increasingly violent world. For a variety of reasons, it is very likely that the health-care community will be mandated to enforce increasing security and safety regulations while it is facing demands from employers and government to reduce or at least control the cost of health care.

It is easy to understand the enormous emotional and psychological pressures in the health-care setting that result in significant stress for staff, patients, and family members alike. Even minor injuries are very traumatic for individuals and families who have high expectations that they will be swiftly and efficiently cured. Americans have never been very good at coping with trauma and death, and now our frustration and anger have become much more intense if we do not receive the response we desire. This is especially true in large urban areas of the U.S.:there are large patient loads in trauma and psychiatry; the patient population is impoverished; staff shortages are substantial. Many of the risk factors that exist in the health-care industry are identified in Table 15-4.

TABLE 15-4
RISK FACTORS IN THE HEALTH CARE SETTING

Environment—

- Gangs

- Drug Addicts

- Acutely disturbed patients and visitors

- Availability of weapons

Work practices—

- Shortage of staff

- Work in high crime areas

- Night employment

- Crowded emergency rooms

Perpetrator profile—

- Mentally ill patients, especially during first 24 hours of hospitalization

- Associates of gang members who had experienced fatal trauma

- Distraught relatives and friends

- Social deviants or threatened individuals

SOURCE: National Safe Workplace Institute

POLICIES DESIGNED TO CURB VIOLENCE

California has now enacted a new law that requires hospitals and other health-care facilities to have proactive approaches to violence prevention (see Chapter 20 for more information). As a result of increased awareness, hospitals around the nation are beginning to focus on the problem of violence prevention. The approach that hospitals are taking seems to involve one or more of the following activities:

- Establishment of violence task forces

- Criminalizing violent acts in emergency rooms

- Injury prevention plans and procedures

- Identification of security hazards (e.g. lighting, alarms)

- Training to deal with high-risk patients and visitors

There now are numerous manuals and training videos designed especially to prevent and control violence in the health-care setting. There is every likelihood that interest in such approaches will grow in the future, especially if there is continued pressure from regulators and state policy-makers.

VIOLENCE IN PSYCHIATRIC UNITS
Dimensions of the Problem

Psychiatric units represent especially complex problems for hospitals and staffs. Part of the problem has to do with old-fashioned thinking that assaults are part of the job for nurses, attendants, and other technicians.

Surveys of psychiatric unit employees show a high level of injury and assaults. Many employees talk of the weapons, typically hand-crafted knives, that are brought by patients to the hospital. As a result, it has become commonplace for patients to be searched for weapons prior to admission to psychiatric wards. In some cases, hospitals are adding metal detectors to screen visitors.

Charter Barclay Hospital in Chicago was issued one of the first Federal job safety citations following an investigation of circumstances and conditions that contributed to the death of one the hospital's employees working in the psychiatric unit.

BUILDING A HOSPITAL
SECURITY PLAN

Hospitals are now fully realizing the importance of security. Most are having comprehensive security audits conducted on a periodic basis. They also are improving the quality of the personnel that they hire and enhancing training programs. Many hospital administrators believe that it is merely a question of time before the health-care community is subjected to substantial regulatory control. More important, hospitals and clinics worry about their reputations: they cannot afford to be seen by the public as unsafe.

The health-care community is unique in U.S. industry because of the large amount of training that goes on. As a result, hospitals appear to be much more accommodating to the need to enhance security. Table 15-6 illustrates some of the measures that the health-care industry is now exploring.

Some of the many considerations for enhancing security in hospitals. are physical layout, staffing and security personnel availability. There is also a clear need for and training related to appropriate responses to violent acts.

TABLE 15-5

SECURITY EDUCATION AND TRAINING FOR EMPLOYEES IN EMERGENCY DEPARTMENTS

1. General safety measures.

2. Personal safety measures.

3. The assault cycle.

4. Aggression and violence predicting factors.

5. Obtaining patient history from a patient with violent behavior.

6. Characteristics of aggressive and violent patients and victims.

7. Verbal and physical maneuvers to diffuse and avoid violent behaviors.

8. Strategies to avoid physical harm.

9. Restraining techniques.

10. Appropriate use of medications as chemical restraints.

11. Any resources available to employees for coping with incidents of violence.

SOURCE: National Safe Workplace Institute

TABLE 15-6

APPROPRIATE EXPERTISE FOR HOSPITAL SECURITY PLANS

1. The role of security in hospital operations.

2. Hospital organization.

3. Protective measures, including alarms and access control.

4. The handling of disturbed patients, visitors, and employees.

5. Identification of aggressive and violent predicting factors.

6. Hospital safety and emergency preparedness.

7. The rudiments of documenting and reporting crimes.

SOURCE: National Safe Workplace Institute

There are violent acts that occur in America every day in the workplace. In this chapter, we have attempted to identify emerging problems that may become more acute and apparent in the years ahead. In writing this chapter, we could have easily explored other potentially volatile industries (e.g. aerospace, energy) or issues such as the high-performance, high-stress work environments that are a source of concern. There is no doubt that other industries and problems will gain increased attention in the years ahead.

Perhaps we have been selective in focusing on adolescents and their explosive anger, the myriad of problems faced by the retail convenience industry, and violence in the health-care community. Scrutiny of these issues helps us appreciate the enormity of the challenge that we face in preventing violence in the workplace. Young people are going to be a source of aggression for many years to come. Also, the retail convenience trade and health-care industry must do more to reduce and prevent violence at work in their industries. By understanding these issues, we will have a deeper understanding of the problem of violence at work.

16

SIDESTEPPING PITFALLS

Employer Vulnerabilities in Combating Workplace Violence

Businesses are especially vulnerable to certain mistakes in preventing violence at work. These mistakes are expected. After all, violence is a new challenge for many managers. The nature of violent episodes that exists in our minds—often involving the nightmarish spectacle of gun-riddled bodies, is terrifying for many managers when they cope with workers or customers with explosive anger or erratic behavior. During periods of stress, our imaginations often take over. We fear for the worst. Thinking clearly during such periods is easier said than done. It is not surprising that managers overreact, making decisions that make little or no sense

The challenge is to arrive at a reasonable and prudent approach to violence prevention. No one can expect us to live in a perfect world: not injured victims, our superiors, or even the judicial system. But we can expect trouble if we do not have a reasonable approach to violence prevention and management. There is simply too much information that suggests that violence is a serious problem with equally serious consequences and implications for both individuals and organizations. If we overlook or reject vital information and clues that point to the prospect of violence, our failure will surely anger victims and their families. Our superiors will hold us responsible for our failure. If we are prudent in our conduct and make informed choices, we will preserve the safety and security of our work environments. Even if disaster does strike, our prudent actions will exonerate us in the minds of those who stand to lose by our failure: our co-workers, family members, and organizational stakeholders.

In this chapter, we will examine some of the vulnerabilities typical of employers. By discussing these vulnerabilities, you will be able to measure your responses and have a good sense as to what can be expected of you. No one likes getting blind-sided or surprised. Managers cherish certainty and predictability—qualities and characteristics demanded by organizations. Indeed some companies, like Motorola, are measuring and evaluating their managers for their ability to anticipate the unpredictable and to manage accordingly. It is no surprise that Motorola, a company that features a high-performance, high-work environment, is both a leader in violence prevention and in profitability.

There is no need to be surprised when it comes to violence prevention. We can seize the opportunity and examine the wise and unwise decisions of individuals and organizations to learn the vulnerabilities or blind spots that so many organizations have experienced. This chapter should help you prepare and think through the consequences of decisions and misjudgments. It identifies the ambushes that lie in wait. Don't be fooled. Be prepared by having a reasonable and prudent stance in the effort to combat violence. Vulnerabilities that exist:

1. "Violence Can't Happen Here!" or Other Management Denials

Often managers claim that their organization is immune to violence. They believe that they have the human resource and security management systems in place to ensure that they will have a safe and secure work environment. They think they know their employees and the problems that they face, that violence will remain foreign to *their* work environment.

The reality is that violence often comes from outside our organizations. Many lethal and other serious events are perpetrated by stalkers or other romantically disaffected parties. Employees are often reluctant to tell us about their fears or even the beatings that they are receiving or may have received. Employees don't tell us because they will be embarrassed, even if they work in a large organization.

The reality is far different. The reality is that stalkers and other romantically disaffected parties increasingly bring violence to work because of access and predictability. They know when and where they can attack their victims and behave accordingly. This very fact has led the California Assembly to pass legislation allowing corporations to request restraining orders blocking such parties from having access to company property.

A decade ago, many organizations thought that they were immune to charges of sexual harassment or other behaviors. In 1993, the Equal Employment Opportunity Commission (EEOC) resolved more than 10,000 claims—a fraction of the legitimate cases that exist and that are being pursued through other legal avenues (e.g. civil litigation, state regulatory agencies). Today, very few managers doubt the serious problem of sexual harassment and most companies have strong prohibitions against such behavior and abuses. Indeed, more than 30 states have mandatory training requirements for supervisors and managers.

If managers think that their organizations are immune from violence, then they may be surprised. Violence is too pervasive and the consequences can be too severe. Managers must think of violence like any other safety and health hazard, and prepare accordingly.

2. Improper management of Relationships with Psychologists and Psychiatrists

It is logical and reasonable to expect mental health providers to properly diagnose and treat mental disorders associated with violent behaviors.

The reality is that mental health providers, including well-trained psychiatrists, often cannot diagnose those behaviors or characteristics that may result in violence. To complicate the issue further, they sometimes present useless or ineffective information that may lead us to overreact against certain threats. In fact, there are cases where businesses have spent $1 million addressing threats where the perpetrator had little or no capacity to act violently.

One such case was publicized on the front page of *The Wall Street Journal*. It involved a fired Kidder Peabody bond trader who began to threaten the company shortly after he was dismissed. During the next 10 months, Kidder Peabody managers spent $1 million, according to the Journal, investigating and following their former employee. In all likelihood, the former employee did not represent a physical threat. Rather, he was threatening his former employer as a way to vent his anger and frustration.

Obviously, it is much easier to gain psychological data on employees than on individuals outside our work environment. If we believe that an employee is dangerous, we may be able to subject that individual to a dangerousness assessment or fitness-for-duty examination by a licensed psychiatrist or psychologist. Unfortunately, a referral may not lead to a diagnosis. Many mental health providers are reluctant to provide employers with information that may lead to the loss of a job, so the report is often inconclusive and the employer has to start back at square one.

There are a number of steps that you can take to prevent these and related problems. Steps include:

1. Choose the right mental health provider. Send an employee only to a psychologist or psychiatrist who is experienced in assessing dangerous personalities.

This may seem obvious but many mistakes have been made because employers don't check into the backgrounds and credentials of their mental health providers. Don't make the same mistakes. Be critical about those whom you hire for such assignments and make certain that they can do the job.

2. Once you have decided that you want to salvage an employee, make your instructions clear to the psychologist or psychiatrist. You don't want to know any more than the minimum, absolutely essential information that you need to manage your business. Specifically, you want to know:

- if a problem or condition can be diagnosed;

- what the course of treatment will be; and

- when you might expect that the employee will be returned to work.

There are two other issues that employers should insist upon when working with psychologists, psychiatrists, and other mental health providers. First, they must be available to promptly offer emergency services to employees. Ideally, an employee ought to be able to see a provider within four hours of such a request. This contrasts with the wait of one week or two that is often the case. Second, employers should insist that mental health professionals relay any warnings of violence that may be communicated to him or her by an employee. Even though court cases have indicated that a provider has a duty to warn of any specific threats, there have been instances when the provider has failed to inform a target of potential danger. Employers, for reasons that are obvious, need to know if their employees have been threatened so that they can take appropriate steps.

3. Proper and Effective Use of Legal Counsel

Like mental health providers, lawyers have to be managed as partners and members of your team, not barriers to progress. Almost every senior manager in American business (and government) has had difficult, often trying experiences with either in-house attorneys or with outside counsel. For better or worse, lawyers need to be involved in mapping out your violence prevention plan so that you are certain that your actions are consistent with the law.

Some attorneys are very proactive in encouraging employers to embrace violence prevention programs; others are not. Some worry about increasing the employer's exposure to liability. Actually, this is a legitimate concern. Lawyers sometimes embrace the notion that an employer doesn't have to address a problem that it doesn't know it has. Unfortunately, this is not true. The problem of violence is widespread and has been addressed by many businesses, trade associations, professional groups, and, now, government. The ostrich approach won't work. Businesses really can't hide.

The point is to get lawyers involved early and make them partners in the process of preventing violence in your work environment. They can become assets when it comes to issues such as mandatory counseling referrals, employee privacy, termination of employment, negligent security, and related issues. Use attorneys, but use them wisely.

4. Over-Reliance on Physical Security Measures (e.g. Cameras, Buzzers)

Far too many organizations have decided that physical security measures, such as cameras or alarms, will address their needs in preventing violence. Security magazines are loaded with advertisements lauding the effectiveness of such devices in curbing numerous abuses and ills, including employee violence.

There can be no question that physical security devices can play a constructive role in preventing violence at work. For example, cameras can often be effectively deployed to identify theft and sabotage by angry employees working in remote warehouses and other facilities. Interactive video systems likewise have proven their worth in deterring robberies and theft in convenience establishments. Such systems effectively extend the resources and capacity of security personnel.

But there is ample evidence to suggest that such systems are only as good as the people that run them. Unfortunately, employers who have placed emphasis on physical security will often rely on poorly paid contract security officers to operate such systems. There is also much evidence to suggest that these systems have limited effectiveness against determined perpetrators. Many individuals have thwarted such systems in carrying out lethal acts of violence. During a short period in 1994, for example, perpetrators skirted sophisticated key card-access systems in California and North Carolina to carry out violent homicides.

Management consulting firms are now insisting that employers replace staff security officers with contract services, but the quality of such services has proven to be very uneven. Only one state, New York, has even minimum requirements that specify standards and qualifications for service as a security officer. As a result, very marginal individuals are attracted to these jobs, often lured by the prospect of carrying a gun and wearing a badge. You should be certain that your organization has stringent qualifications regarding the people who are employed to protect you. In the final analysis, you should be as willing to rely on them to protect you against the prospect of violence as you would a well-trained public law enforcement agency.

5. Failure to Articulate a Strong Policy Against Violence

Organizations too often want to get by with policies that are known only to a few individuals. One might call this a "need-to-know" approach to violence prevention.

Policies need to be clearly and effectively articulated by senior management. That message needs to be reinforced, the more often the better, in company newsletters, internal communications, and through other mechanisms. Employees and other stakeholders must understand that a violence-free environment is a corporate value understood and accepted by all.

One advantage or reason to reinforce the message is that most workplaces are now work environments for contract employees, temporaries, or other third parties who do not normally function within the confines of what we traditionally know as employer-employee relationships. These individuals must also understand and embrace the values of the organization, even if their stay will be brief.

Senior managers need not see the expression of a clear violence prevention policy statement as an admission that violence is a problem for them. Quite the contrary. The astute manager should be able to comprehend that violence often comes from outside the work environment and that violent episodes can occur even in the best managed organizations.

6. Inconsistent Application of Rules and Policies

Managers are often reluctant to apply rules consistently. For example, employers who will dismiss line-level workers for fighting often will overlook violence by vice presidents or other senior managers. Management needs to embrace the notion that what is good for the goose is good for the gander. Anything less is inappropriate and will lead to a breakdown of social order in the organization.

Consistency is an elusive virtue. We all favor certain characteristics in our peers and subordinates which often have little to do with job performance. Managers must overcome their personal biases and prejudices and manage by performance and objective measures. An organization that fires one employee for fighting and overlooks similar acts by another employee can end up in court if a lawsuit is filed in the future.

7. Unwillingness to Use Discipline Against Abusive Employees

Managers are often reluctant to use discipline. This is especially true with younger managers who supervise older employees, a common pattern in many businesses. Other employers have hesitated to take punitive actions against employees who are known to be abusive, the bullies of the organization.

Employees who get away with rules violations often will push their luck in the future. Sooner or later, the testing of boundaries between a supervisor and employee will become more severe. The interactions may become violent, especially if conditions or problems are introduced into the equation (e.g. divorce) that upset the already fragile emotional stability of an abusive employee.

An often-chosen form of discipline is suspension without pay for a few days. Ideally, the use of discipline will occur early in an employee's career and will become more severe if abuses or patterns of behavior persist. It is far more difficult to apply discipline later in an employee's career when habits and problems have become established and tolerated by poor managers.

Emerging organizational structures for the 21st century will change the nature of work groups and the relationships between supervisors and the supervised. Milliken Industries, a textile conglomerate based in South Carolina, is now abolishing the position of supervisors in some of its plants. In their place, Milliken is turning to work groups or teams that organize themselves in the best way possible to accomplish their goals and objectives. Other companies are embracing peer review panels to address issues of punishment and sanction within the organization. While these concepts are exciting and offer promise, many organizations remain rooted in traditional structures. For these organizations, which are clearly the majority, the issue of disciplining abusive employees remains a potential problem.

8. INADEQUATE INCIDENT DOCUMENTATION

There is no excuse for failing to document incidents in an adequate manner, which means obtaining information about the "what," "when," "where," and "how" elements of an incident. Those responsible for investigating an incident should attempt as well to obtain independent corroboration of the information that has been presented. Each bit of information should be collected confidentially to encourage witnesses and participants to be honest, complete, and objective.

Employers will often fail to gain information from perpetrators. To the extent possible, you should hear both sides. While the investigator should be skeptical, there is the possibility that an employee was working in what lawyers call a "hostile" environment that would tend, in the eyes of a jury, to make that employee less responsible for his or her actions. Numerous conditions could exist to create a hostile environment, including abusive supervisors, disrespectful peers, unfair work practices, among many other possibilities.

Even if you determine that a "hostile" environment exists, you may still want to discipline an employee. Organizations must have personnel systems that result in employees being responsible for their behavior and decisions, even under difficult circumstances. But an employer may also wish to take advantage of such information to pursue punitive or corrective action for those who contributed to the problem.

Inadequate incident documentation often comes back to haunt employers. It can raise doubts about an employer's motives or facts in the eyes of a regulator or court. It is critical to obtain the facts and obtain them as quickly and as efficiently as possible.

Generally, it is a wise practice to have one or more individuals review such documentation as quickly as possible. In large organizations, this is best done by security personnel working in tandem with attorneys specializing in labor and employment issues. If an incident has been poorly or inadequately documented, reviewing officers should ask for clarification or elaborating information immediately. There is no excuse for letting a week pass between the commission of an incident and the completion of a documenting report.

Life is full of ambushes. The challenge is to avoid them and the other hidden problems that can diminish our effectiveness. Employers have certain vulnerabilities, some of which have been examined and discussed in this chapter. The list discussed here is by no means complete. Good managers can avoid such pitfalls through good management systems, policies, and procedures, coupled with sound judgment.

Let there be no false hopes. There is no guarantee that following the advice in this chapter (or even in this book) will ensure you a violence-free workplace. However, you can be reasonably assured that following this advice will increase the chance that your organization will meet most serious challenges in an effective fashion with minimal consequences. That is all that can be expected of you. The prudent manager prepares. Good managers, the leaders of tomorrow, are seldom surprised.

17

WHEN TRAGEDY STRIKES

Debriefing Following an Incident

Businesses each day experience severe incidents of workplace violence. In 1993, there were 1,063 homicides in workplaces of small, one-person, family-owned businesses right up to those of Fortune 500 companies.

The process of recovery from a traumatic incident involves skills and processes offered by a growing number of mental health providers. Nevertheless, most organizations do not systematically approach recovery from violence as a process crucial to restoring the organization to its pre-crisis performance levels. There is a choice that organizations can make. One choice is to leave recovery to chance, a risky proposition that threatens the stature of management and the confidence of your employee population. The better choice is to embrace critical incident stress debriefing (CISD), a post-trauma process typically involving psychologists and other mental health specialists.

In an increasing number of organizations, senior managers are bringing in clinical psychologists, counselors, and other specialists for CISDs to ensure that the organization is restored to its full productivity as quickly as possible. Debriefings were first conducted on behalf of law enforcement and fire protection agencies, organizations where stress and crisis go hand-in-glove. Researchers demonstrated that those who serve and protect were often traumatized by serious incidents or by an accumulation of small incidents. Indeed, many large police and fire departments across the United States have psychologists and psychiatrists either on staff or available in the event that such tragedies strike.

Dr. James Cavanaugh, M.D., of the Isaac Ray Center at Rush-Presbyterian-St. Luke's Hospital in Chicago, calls such interventions "absolutely critical for stabilizing severely traumatized individuals" including "men and women who are in positions that expose them to violence and crisis on a frequent basis." Dr. Cavanaugh, who pioneered such methods over two decades ago, fully understands the need for these services. The Isaac Ray Center is headquartered on Chicago's near West side in the heart of one of the city's most violent neighborhoods. Cavanaugh and his colleagues at Isaac Ray have treated thousands of public and private sector employees in a practice that serves a broad array of businesses and public agencies.

It is wrong to think that time heals the wounds and scars left by acutely traumatizing events. Cavanaugh's research shows that employees generally fall into three groups following a trauma. First, a few individuals will recover quickly, seemingly without the assistance of mental health interventions. Sometimes, these seemingly stoic souls are internalizing their pain and grief, only to unleash their feelings and emotions in a destructive way at a later date. A second group will require modest counseling, usually on an outpatient basis, in order to remain at their previous level of confidence, security, and safety. Finally, some people will develop serious psychological afflictions that may require more extensive therapy or clinical services. CISD practitioners are vital because they can help management identify those individuals who are likely to perform at less than optimum levels. This process will help management plan its human resource requirements in an effort to restore productivity.

Workers are often just one group that may require such interventions. Cavanaugh and other experts, including Dr. Ron Schouten of Massachusetts General Hospital and Dr. Bobbi Lambert, a San Francisco clinical psychologist, suggest that organizational stakeholders and others affected by the critical event may benefit from psychological services. Dr. Schouten explains that stakeholders include such individuals as worker family members, customers, suppliers, and others who are connected directly or even indirectly to the trauma. (See Table 17-1.)

The Pentagon is one of the nation's leaders in responding to trauma. The military now turns to post-trauma interventions following accidents or military exercises that are costly in terms of life and limb. Events that traumatize an organization can be destabilizing for individuals for months or

Table 17-1

Individuals Affected by Traumatic Events

- Injured employees
- Employees (including some remote from the scene)
- Witnesses
- First responders (e.g. paramedics)
- Family members
- Stakeholders (e.g. suppliers) that knew victims
- Others connected to the trauma

SOURCE: National Safe Workplace Institute

even years. Similar smells, sounds, and sights can bring the trauma back into the victim's mind, bringing about what experts call a post-trauma episode. The choice, as described by David Yarborough, a Lancaster, South Carolina neuropsychologist and an Army reserve officer, is to stumble into recovery or to plan your way to restoring individual and organizational health. Yarborough is just one of many experts called upon by the Pentagon to work with servicemen and women following traumas.

Compelling evidence demonstrates that adequate post-trauma care can be very effective in helping an organization regain its footing following a crisis. Indeed, many post-trauma experts work on a host of crisis situations such as natural disasters, airline crashes or motor vehicle accidents (involving employees), on-site employee fatalities, heart attacks or strokes, and numerous other tragedies. Some well-managed businesses also involve CISD specialists following non-fatal incidents including cases where employees have been abused or raped (one in ten rapes occurs at work). The damage caused to an organization from non-fatal incidents can be severe and must be addressed.

Generally, post-trauma specialists should be on the scene as quickly as possible, certainly within 24 hours of the event. These specialists will begin by engaging in triage, a process that identifies for intensive treatment and monitoring those individuals who are most acutely affected by the event. The period of time for recovery depends, in part, on the exposure that an individual had to the event. For example, a person who actually held a dying person in his or her arms is more likely to experience post-traumatic aftermath than a person several rooms or work stations away. The intensity of the experience is likely to be influenced as well by feelings toward the victims, proximity to the crisis, past experiences of a similar nature, etc.

Those who experience and survive a traumatic event can typically be triaged into different categories that will require a corresponding level of care. The three most typical categories can be labeled good, fair, or poor. The status of most, but not all, survivors can be determined within two-to-three days following the event. In some cases, survivors can reach a pre-crisis level of job performance in a very short period of time. For others, the process may take weeks, months or even years. The goal of the immediate diagnostic and treatment process is to identify what stage the survivor is in and what the followup care should be. It may even be that an individual who seems to have been only remotely connected to the trauma may require substantial, in-patient clinical care.

IDENTIFYING EXPERTS

The time to identify CISD experts is long before you have a crisis. If you know who you are going to work with long before a crisis occurs, your ability to operate in an effective and efficient fashion with that CISD professional will be greatly enhanced. Indeed, most organizations with crisis management plans are constantly reviewing potential problems and ways that they would react to a crisis. These organizational plans involve scenarios that contemplate a host of possibilities. By identifying your CISD provider on the front end, you are planning for the crisis you hope never comes.

Planning does not mean that you must have a long and complex drill with your provider. It simply means that the post-trauma specialist becomes familiar with your organization so that he or she knows how to organize critical information in the time of a crisis. During this same period, which may simply be a series of meetings, you should be building confidence in the provider's ability to work with you during periods of crisis and recovery. Again, this involves good business planning.

There are three basic ways through which businesses find post-trauma experts. In some cases, your Employee Assistance Program (EAP) professional, irrespective of whether that person is directly employed by your organization or provided as part of a contract, can make a referral to such a specialist. In fact, some larger EAP contract service providers are now offering post-trauma services to their clients.

A second way is by contacting local or Federal law enforcement agencies, especially the Federal Bureau of Investigation (FBI). Large FBI field offices have staff post-trauma specialists or local specialists on contract with their office. Also, psychologists employed by large metropolitan police departments can provide similar assistance in locating a CISD professional.

A third way to find such professionals is through occupational health centers that are a part of large teaching and research hospitals in major cities. Increasingly, these agencies are providing post-trauma services as part of their client program offerings where they operate. If they do not have this service, they often know who can provide CISD and post-trauma care.

Post-trauma mental health services are a growing field for mental health providers. You should be certain that your provider has both excellent academic and experiential credentials. You want to be as sure as possible that those who will provide you with this type of service know what they are going to do before they have to swing into action. You will want to check references to be certain that your service provider has conducted post-trauma services for companies or organizations similar to yours. If they cannot demonstrate substantial experience in successfully dealing with post-trauma events, then you should be reluctant about hiring them. You do not want your organization to be a laboratory for inexperienced individuals, regardless of how impressive their credentials. If your organization experiences a trauma, you have the responsibility to deploy seasoned professionals who have confidence in their ability to address serious and often difficult situations.

PHASES EXPERIENCED BY VICTIMS

Post-trauma experts think that victims go through three stages during the recovery process. The first stage, according to Dr. Michael Mantell, a San Diego-based psychologist, is one of shock and disbelief. A reaction of horror is only natural and to be expected given what employees have lived through. By watching television footage, we all have seen the shock and horror on the faces of co-workers who have seen a fellow employee gunned down in the workplace. Such events become etched into our minds, becoming imagery that we cannot easily forget.

In general terms, one can reasonably expect that the level of post-trauma emotions will be in proportion to the intensity and scope of the event itself. In other words, a relatively isolated event is likely to impose less serious and lasting conditions on the organization, although there can be exceptions. For example, even the loss of a single, well-liked employee to a cause such as a heart attack or stroke can traumatize substantial numbers of employees. Such a reaction is to be expected. Traumatic events, particularly those that result in death, put us in touch with our own mortality, a painful ordeal even for the most stoic among us. This first phase—shock and disbelief—can last several minutes or many months.

Employees will have different reactions to an unsettling, traumatizing event. Post-trauma specialists have stories about how employees who are only marginally in contact with a traumatic event are adversely affected for long periods of time, while others much closer to the trauma recover quickly. How victims recover during the post-trauma period is affected by numerous factors, including their life's experiences and their natural (e.g. family) support system.

This support system has been shown to have significant impact. One of the most important supports a person can have is a spouse, parent, or sibling who can work with the post-trauma victim during this period of crisis. If these individuals are caring and nurturing, they can have a positive effect on the outcome. There are others who help make up our support systems, like friends, clergy, neighbors, peers, and others.

The second phase involves the victim experiencing a range of emotions. These can include intense anger, fear, terror, frustration, survivor guilt, grief, and even confusion. During the second phase, victims are trying to accommodate their experience. They are struggling to adjust to and accept what has happened. Rage is often directed toward perpetrators as victims try to place blame. Frequently victims will begin to blame themselves. They are confused. They often feel inadequate in the face of adversity.

Some survivors will be unable to function in the work environment in any meaningful manner during this phase. They often will not be able to talk without tears or remorse or other deep emotions that may render them essentially ineffective. If the trauma involved a death it will have put the victims in touch with their own mortality, giving them a deep feeling of vulnerability. As time passes, individuals may experience one or more of these emotions with varying degrees of intensity. It is not unusual for employees to remain anxious for months.

The third stage involves restoration of equilibrium. During this period, victims are likely to have good and bad days as they struggle to stabilize their emotional footing. The amount of time that it will take them to regain equilibrium is likely, but not necessarily, based on the intensity and severity of the event. Not every person is the same.

Post-trauma providers are well schooled in these stages. They will begin to chart the recovery course as quickly as possible after the event. Following group debriefings, they will assess each individual and begin a treatment monitoring program for the more acutely affected. After a brief period, they will turn over the clinical phases to psychologists, psychiatrists, and other mental health providers. In some cases, the post-trauma expert will consult with those who provide continuing care.

POST-TRAUMA CRISIS MANAGEMENT

There are a number of steps that you should take following a crisis. You must begin the painful process of accounting for personnel while you await the arrival of a post-trauma service provider. You need to communicate the message that all personnel and family members will be provided for with utmost care and concern. You must recognize that many of your employees are unstable and that they are looking to you to restore their sense of confidence. If you cannot demonstrate leadership following a crisis, the damage can endure for months or even years to come.

The following steps are designed to help you express concern and to restore order in the organization. This may sound insensitive, but the opposite is actually true. Many employees go to work, in part, because jobs help shape their lives by providing them with a sense of predictability and stability. During this period, your employees will cherish those qualities and characteristics in your organization. In general, there are four specific steps that you may wish to consider in establishing your post-trauma program. These steps are described below. While these steps provide general guidance in different ways, you must tailor your approach based upon your organization, its mission and purpose, and, most important, your work force.

Step One. Demonstrate concern and caring for those who have been harmed by the trauma.

Show compassion for those who have been hurt and who have lost their lives. This is of paramount importance both in the short- and long-run. This is particularly true if your employees believe that management's performance may have caused or contributed to the problem. For example, it is not unusual for employees to feel that an employer had poor security or that a manager or supervisor harassed or baited an employee into homicidal anger. Irrespective of whether management is to blame, employees will expect you to show respect for those who have been hurt or lost their lives.

Your employees may wish to hold a brief service to memorialize those who have died. They may also want to collect funds to aid the families that have been affected. Some may even want to establish a scholarship fund for children who have lost a parent. You don't need to wait for your employees to show leadership. You can announce that you intend to do all of these things. Your employees will value your leadership and their faith will be renewed.

Employees go to work to earn a living to support their families. When asked, nearly all of us say that we want to die peacefully in our sleep in the privacy and security of our homes. When people die at work, there is shock and anger. We are uncomfortable because we have seen proof that things are sometimes not the way that they are supposed to be. Don't buy into the nonsense that accidents do happen or something similar. Our lives aren't a lottery. Recognize that feeling and cherish those who have paid the ultimate price.

In Japan, it is the responsibility of senior managers to attend to workers who have been injured or to the family members of those who have been killed. They will visit on a frequent basis injured workers in the hospital or the family members of those killed. It is not surprising for Japanese managers to resign if it is demonstrated that poor decisions or designs led to a worker's death. We can learn something from the way the Japanese do business. Perhaps it is no surprise that worker fatality rates are much lower in Japan than in the U.S.

There is a clear message that you want the organization to receive during this period. Employees and other organization stakeholders should know with certainty that management is going to care for those directly affected by a trauma in every reasonable way possible. This may be out of character for your organization, but nonetheless it is crucial that caring qualities be demonstrated if you expect your work force to recover to pre-trauma performance levels any time in the near future. You have to view these acts and expenditures as an investment in rebuilding a fragile organization or work unit.

There are other important steps for his period. You should report on the condition of the injured through announcements on the public address system, in company newsletters, etc. You will want to make this a priority, not a secondary responsibility, if you are sincere about acting in a responsible fashion. Also, if a small group has been intensely affected, you may want to meet with its members on a regular basis to debrief them on issues related to the event. In time, the need to communicate and debrief will decrease. You are contributing to your business, making the comeback that is vital to the enterprise and its members.

NOTIFYING FAMILY MEMBERS

Three different groups have responsibility to contact family members. If a felony has been committed, law enforcement will contact parties at the last known address of the decedent. Second, hospital chaplains or counselors often will try to contact family members. In many instances, family members have already come to the emergency room for information on their loved one. Third, you have a moral responsibility to communicate with families. You will want to contact the spouse, if any, and try to obtain additional information on other family members. What you want to avoid is for a parent or sibling to be driving down the road and to hear about the death of the family member on the radio. If necessary, you should encourage both law enforcement and the hospital to hold off on any press or official statements until all appropriate parties have been notified.

Step Two. **Open up communications channels and control rumors.**

Organizations in crisis are often paralyzed by rumors which can cause severe damage. By opening communications and controlling rumors, you are taking important steps in damage control.

Many organizations set up a crisis hotline as part of their crisis management strategy. You should encourage employees and others to contact you with questions and concerns, as frequently as necessary. In extreme cases, you will have to staff your hotline 24 hours a day until the crisis subsides. You should be certain that those individuals staffing your hotline can answer questions clearly and effectively. They must have access to senior managers who, in turn, have access to critical information. They should try to answer questions that involve clear facts. You don't want your hotline to "fix the blame" or speculate.

Organizations with excellent crisis plans will debrief employees on a periodic basis and will actively communicate with employees and families during post-crisis periods. What these organizations have discovered is that there is an information vacuum, and that filling the vacuum with accurate information in a timely fashion is in their best interest. Make communication planning a top priority.

> *Step Three.* **Assess your personnel and business requirements in order to restore business performance. Acknowledge to employees what it will take to get back to normal.**

Your employees will want you to restore order in the organization as quickly as possible. You may want to close the business or shut down production in an affected area for a brief period while you assess what you have to do to regain pre-trauma performance and production levels.

If you have to bring in temporary personnel to meet organizational requirements, so be it. Some employees may express anger and resentment toward those who have been called in to replace those injured or killed. Most employees will understand that you are trying to restore the organization to where it was before the crisis and they will support your efforts.

We must expect that some employees will want to grieve and will be unable to work. This is natural. There can be no guidelines for how much time a person should be given off from work to grieve; this is a matter that you may wish to discuss with the personnel who is handling the post-trauma counseling.

> *Step Four.* **Arrange for your post-trauma team to return to your workplace on a periodic basis to counsel and debrief employees.**

You should build time into your processes so that your post-trauma team can meet with employees, their families, and other affected parties. Some employees who seemed to do well initially may have had difficulty with the passage of time. If so, you will want to have these individuals assessed and treated. By having post-trauma counselors back at scheduled intervals, you are enhancing your organization's opportunity to recover from the traumatizing event.

Having these CISD professionals back to the worksite sends a message to your employees that you care and that you will not leave recovery to chance. In general, you may want to think about scheduling such meetings once a month for the first six months following a particularly severe crisis. This is a procedure that you will want to discuss with your provider during the planning process.

The goal for debriefing is to restore the organization and its members to health as quickly as possible. You need to develop a crisis plan that includes post-trauma care services. Ideally, you will want to identify your provider prior to a crisis and begin to think through how this professional should be used. You should think of post-trauma planning as good human resource management planning, nothing more or less.

Serious incidents of trauma inflict damage far beyond the physical injury and death that is so apparent in the event itself. In effect, sound post-trauma management is really good people management. A good post-trauma program is a sound approach to restoring pre-crisis organizational health. By following the steps outlined in this chapter, you will be providing an insurance policy that will help you contain the damage that serious incidents often inflict.

CHAPTER

18

TRAVERSING A MINEFIELD

Legal Issues
in Workplace Violence

Workplace violence has significant legal consequences and ramifications for employees and employers who ignore warning signs. Employers may wish to hide from the problem but courts are more frequently applying new and familiar doctrines to this problem. An employer law firm, Littler, Mendelson, Fastiff, Tichy & Mathiason, has 30 attorneys advising and representing clients on workplace violence issues alone. Garry Mathiason, who manages this growing practice for the firm, claims "Companies have no real choice but to be proactive and strive to prevent violence." Mathiason, whose firm has written a lengthy treatise on this subject, concludes: "Companies must have sound procedures that identify what will be done in specific circumstances. Those that fail to take even simple steps are exposing their companies to regulatory compliance problems and the possibility of litigation."

This new awareness flies in the face of the what-you-don't-know-can't-hurt-you philosophy. In reality, if employers fail to act in a responsible fashion to curb or prevent violence, the result may be not only deaths and injuries but legal consequences that can be felt for years to come. There are numerous doctrines that can be applied to the problem of workplace violence, doctrines that often spell out expensive consequences for the ill-prepared. In this chapter, we examine some of these and how they are likely to be applied to this area. The legal issues relating to workplace violence have increased in number and complexity as courts have mandated the employer's duty to provide a safe workplace for their employees. Employers simply cannot fail to recognize these concerns and adjust accordingly.

NEGLIGENT HIRING
Pre-Employment Concerns

At the hiring stage, an employer has a fundamental duty to investigate the background of applicants. This duty may be satisfied by a basic check of employment references if the position is not safety-sensitive or if it does not involve frequent contact with members of the public. At minimum, employers should confirm dates and locations of previous employment and education. References should be called and carefully checked.

The possible consequences of failing to conduct this basic reference check were demonstrated in Minnesota when Stephanie Ponticas was raped by a building superintendent hired by a company that neglected to check his references. If the company had conducted a basic background check, they would have discovered that the rapist's references were his mother and sister, and the five-year gap in his employment history was due to the fact that he was incarcerated for armed robbery.

While the courts are establishing that the employer has a duty to conduct a reasonable investigation of its applicants, what constitutes such a reasonable investigation is a more problematic question. The scope of the employer's duty to inquire into an applicant's background depends upon the position. Courts adjudicating the issue of negligent hiring generally have imposed a heightened duty of inquiry upon employers in cases where jobs involve control of weapons (law enforcement or security officers), substantial public contact, and supervision of children, e.g. school teachers. Other examples of safety-sensitive positions are a truck driver or a nuclear plant employee. In Colorado, a trucking company was held not liable for the sexual assault committed by one of its drivers because the company had promulgated rules restricting drivers' contact with the public.

Government's duty may be greater than that of a private employer. A public sector employer may be required to conduct an independent investigation instead of merely relying upon an applicant's statements.

In conducting an investigation, a potential employer will encounter several obstacles in ascertaining whether the applicant is a safe and suitable candidate for the position. For example, he or she may not be able to find out from a prior employer about workplace confrontations the employee was involved in or the reason the employment relationship ended. Previous employers may be reluctant to discuss these issues because they fear a defamation suit by the employee. When contacting prior employers, the person conducting the inquiry should be as specific as possible and avoid general questions. Confirming previous employment, dates and job titles is usually not difficult.

Some employers are now centralizing the control of hiring decisions in order to avoid the warm-body syndrome in which managers will lower their standards to fill a vacancy. There are clear advantages to centralizing employment decisions although there is little question that leaving managers short-handed has its costs.

NEGLIGENT HIRING
AND RETENTION

While employers still have a duty under the doctrine of negligent hiring to conduct a reasonable inquiry into a person's background, their discretion in choosing safe employees is markedly restricted by various anti-discrimination statutes and common law actions.

The courts have been cognizant of the limitations and economic burdens on employers in adjudicating negligent hiring cases. But they are less likely to be sympathetic to the employer when the employer ignores and fails to respond to established threat patterns or incidents of harassment occurring within the workplace. In reaching a decision in a Minnesota case, the court emphasized the public policy of providing ex-felons with an opportunity to rehabilitate themselves. The court further stated that a contrary determination would deter companies from hiring ex-criminals because of the fear of liability. However, the court found the employer, Honeywell, potentially liable for negligent retention, which it left for a jury to decide. In this case, Honeywell knew of the applicant's prior background and attempted to place him in a position with little contact with co-employees or the public.

The doctrines of negligent hiring and retention similarly have been applied to sexual harassment in the workplace. An Illinois decision, *Geise v. Phoenix Company of Chicago,* determined that a company had a duty to select and retain managers who would not commit acts of sexual harassment. The decision may be interpreted to imply that companies have a duty to investigate the background of their supervisory employees for instances of sexual harassment. While knowledge of these past acts may not warrant exclusion or termination, it does require the company to explain to the manager its policies forbidding sexual harassment and to monitor the situation closely. Courts have increasingly demonstrated a willingness to hold employers vicariously liable for sexual harassment acts committed by their employees.

INVESTIGATION OF CRIMINAL RECORDS

Criminal background checks pose a complex issue in the area of pre-employment investigation. Although a criminal record may contain past incidents of violent conduct, it may or may not accurately predict the future violent propensities of an applicant. In theory, our society remains dedicated to the ideal of criminal rehabilitation and therefore wants to provide individuals with troubled pasts a second chance. Because of this commitment, courts have been reluctant to impose a duty upon employers to conduct an investigation of criminal records.

Those employers that choose to conduct such checks should be wary as to how they use them. These records may be difficult to analyze accurately because of factors such as arrests without convictions, plea bargains, no-contest pleas, or expunged records. Furthermore, the use of arrest records by an employer has been found to be a violation of Title VII of the Civil Rights Act of 1964. Title VII's prohibition on the use of employment criteria that have a disproportionate impact on the protected classes (race, age, sex, religion, and national origin) affects an employer's discretion in using conviction records to disqualify applicants. If an applicant belongs to one of the protected classes and demonstrates that the use of conviction records has a disparate impact upon the protected group, the employer has to demonstrate that the use of the conviction record was justified by business necessity.

In order to prevail on this defense, the employer will have to show that the records were related to the job. For example, an employer could assert that the position of bank teller or cashier requires that the employee have no convictions for property theft.

Overall, the employer faces a difficult balancing act in complying with Title VII when he or she attempts to use criminal records as a basis to exclude potentially dangerous applicants.

NEGLIGENT RECOMMENDATIONS?

There also is now a high-profile lawsuit in Tampa, Florida against a major insurance company. One of the company's managers wrote a letter of recommendation for an employee who was reportedly being discharged for bringing a gun to work. The letter presumably helped the terminated employee find a new job where familiar behavior patterns once again emerged. Only this time the employee was fired and came back to kill former co-workers. Families of the victims have filed a lawsuit which has won national media attention but remains undetermined at this point. The defendant in this suit did something that has been done many times before—ease the departure of a disgruntled employee that they no longer wanted. The families of the dead employees, and their lawyers, see the matter in a much different light.

PRE-EMPLOYMENT SCREENINGS & TESTS

Title VII has effectively constrained an employer from predicating a decision not to hire an applicant on the basis of his or her prior criminal history. In addition, a host of other regulatory burdens have motivated employers to seek alternative methods for identifying and excluding applicants with undesirable traits, from dishonesty to drug addiction to a propensity to violence.

One of the most relevant statutes in the area of pre-employment screening is the Employee Polygraph Protection Act of 1988, which prohibits the use of lie detection devices. Largely as a function of this ban, many employers have since turned to various pencil-and -paper tests as a component of pre-employment screening and selection systems. A test is legally defensible if it has been properly developed and validated as job-related. To be legally defensible, a selection system (or instrument) should satisfy the following standards:

1. The procedures related to the test are based upon the Uniform Guidelines on Employee Selection (Equal Employment Opportunity Commission), case law, the Civil Rights Act of 1991, and Americans with Disabilities Act of 1990.

2. The testing service has conducted an in-depth analysis which clearly delineates the knowledge, skills, abilities, and other factors (KSAOs)

relevant to the position and essential job functions, in the context of predictive validity methodology.

Tests which fail to meet these criteria may not be legally defensible. Nevertheless, the author has personally seen examples of tests used by employers that do not meet these standards. In many cases, these tests have been developed by individuals who do not understand legal requirements or who choose not to comply with the law. Often the claims made for such tests are compelling and employers who feel that they would benefit from such instruments often become unwitting consumers.

Insofar as recent case law may be considered instructional, the weakest link in the chain for pre-employment testing would appear to be questions which applicants or employees construe as unconstitutional invasions of their privacy. Two relevant cases illustrate this concern from different perspectives.

In the most widely cited decision on this issue, Mc Kenna v. Fargo, 451 F. Supp. 1355 (D. NJ 1978) *aff'd without op.*, 601 F. 2d 575 (6th Cir. 1979), the court held that a battery of psychological tests administered to firefighter candidates, which included questions dealing with an array of private matters including but not limited to sexual preferences and religious beliefs was allowable because it met the job-relatedness standard.

The court concluded that the state's interest was sufficiently compelling to warrant an intrusion on privacy because, due to "unique psychological factors which are crucial to the life-endangering occupation, a psychological and emotional assessment of applicants has an importance that would be found in very few other occupations."

More recently, Soroka, et al v. Dayton Hudson Corp., (Alameda Superior Court CA, No. H-143579-3), illustrated the importance of job-relatedness in converse fashion. In Soroka, four plaintiffs who had been applicants for jobs as security officers claimed that a test comprised of 704 true-false questions drawn from the Minnesota Multiphasic Personality Inventory (MMPI) abridged the right to privacy guaranteed them by the Constitution of the State of California. The test items at issue concerned such matters as sexual preference and religious beliefs. The standard to which the defendant ultimately was held was the weight of the employer's compelling interest. Unlike the court in McKenna v. Fargo, however, the court in this case did not find such interest sufficiently present, and the plaintiffs prevailed.

While neither of these cases stemmed from an incident of workplace violence, they both illustrate the criticality of adherence to high standards in testing, and especially that testing which addresses psychological and/or personality issues. Equally crucial is ensuring legal defensibility, ideally by engaging the active participation of legal counsel throughout the process of developing such tests.

With regard to workplace violence specifically, psychological screening instruments may not be able to consistently predict which individuals are likely to become perpetrators of violent acts. However, it has been established that a properly developed, properly administered test or battery of tests is highly effective in assessing and identifying personality variables, including those that may suggest a propensity toward aggressive behavior.

For example, the MMPI-2 (an updated version of the MMPI which was published in 1989) is nearly universally utilized in selecting candidates for high-stress positions (e.g. law enforcement). It addresses an array of behaviors well-documented as directly associated with stress, including but not limited to drug and alcohol abuse, hypertensive symptomology and implications of depression.

Psychometric instruments like the MMPI-2 must be administered and processed meticulously, according to professionally recognized procedures which fully protect the rights of the individual. Both prior assent and written authorization of the applicant (or employee) are required. Test results must not be used to make personnel decisions to exclude individuals from a job. For example, in the nuclear power industry, where use of the MMPI is required by federal statute, an elevated score results not in the rejection of the applicant, but in his or her referral to a licensed psychologist for a clinical interview. In the majority of cases, the issues raised by the initial test results are resolved in such an interview.

Similarly, the MMPI and MMPI-2 have been of considerable assistance in cases where the potential for workplace violence was believed to exist. In these situations, test results are combined with one or more other methods of evaluation to enable an assessment of dangerousness. These other methods may include consultations with representatives of such departments as security and human resources, legal counsel and medical officers and in-person interviews with family members, as well as with the individual considered to be at risk. Again, the procedures utilized must emphasize the rights of the individual without compromising security issues, and must be implemented in a legal and proper manner. There is disagreement among assessment professionals on the value of various psychometric instruments and diagnostic procedures. Research is being done to evaluate various options and to identify what instruments are the most effective.

Like any other managerial aid, psychological testing may be misused or even abused by those who do not understand either the responsibilities its use imposes, or the legal implications, particularly under the current, evolving law. When considering the use of psychological testing and screening, the most prudent course of action is also the best: to employ the services of qualified legal and psychological professionals with experience in this highly sensitive area.

WORKPLACE HARASSMENT
Sexual Harassment

As noted in a previous chapter, sexual harassment is itself unacceptable behavior, and it also may lead to more deadly violence. Title VII of the Civil Rights Act of 1964, as amended by the Equal Employment Opportunity Act of 1972, prohibits sex discrimination in employment. Although the language of Title VII does not specifically address the issue of whether sexual harassment constitutes discrimination on the basis of sex, it is now well settled that Title VII proscribes such conduct.

Federal law, 29 Code of Federal Regulation @ 1604.11(a) provides: "Harassment on the basis of sex is a violation of Section 703 of Title VII. Unwelcome sexual advances, request for sexual favors, and other verbal or physical conduct of a sexual nature constitute sexual harassment when (1) submission to such conduct is made either explicitly or implicitly a term or condition of an individual's employment, (2) submission to or rejection of such conduct by an individual is used as the basis for employment decisions affecting such individual, or (3) such conduct has the purpose or effect of unreasonably interfering with an individual's work performance or creating an intimidating, hostile, or offensive working environment."

All employees and employers are required by federal law to enforce Title VII and to provide a working environment free from sexual harassment. As this problem has become more visible and recognized, the appropriate law has expanded. Because compliance with the prohibition on sexual harassment has not matched the growth of the law, enforcement procedures by employers must be fully implemented. Currently, numerous employees—females and males alike—suffer its consequences, and this harassment is detrimental to victims, their productivity in the workplace and the profitability of their employers. Therefore, not only is sexual harassment disgraceful to victims and American society, it is in the best interest of companies to effectively enforce its prohibition in the work-place.

CIVIL HARASSMENT

As was reported in chapter 2, employers lose $6.5 billion dollars annually as a result of aggressive and violent work environments. Substantial loss is due to diminished productivity as a result of intimidating and menacing behaviors. If the harassment occurring at work escalates into violence, workers are likely to be substantially less productive in the aftermath of trauma. They may be preoccupied by the threat of recurring violence or be afraid to return to work. It is in the best interest of the employer to respond effectively to any type of harassment, whether the subject of the harassment is male or female.

The law with respect to the liability of employers for workplace violence is still evolving; even though the employer is obligated to provide a safe workplace, laws dealing with workplace threats are obscure or nonexistent. In contrast, there is a developed body of law dealing with sexual harassment. On the one hand, in order to combat the problem of harassment, the law that is on the books must be taken seriously by employers. On the other hand, in order to combat the harassment of male and female employees which does not constitute sexual harassment, statutes and case law must be developed.

The purpose and effect of employee threats and harassment are the same—to menace the worker and violate his or her dignity. Even though sexual harassment and stalking laws have only recently been promulgated by legislatures, the right to bring a civil action based on the "apprehension of an offensive bodily contact" has been traced in the common law to 1348. Carpenter, *Intentional Invasion of Interest of Personality*, 13 Or. L. Rev. 227, 237 n. 57 (1934). Since the impact of sexual harassment and workplace threats are equally destructive, the U.S. Congress may wish to promulgate legislation similar to 29 CFR @ 1604.11, which governs sexual harassment law, to combat harassment of male and female workers which is not sexually related.

It is possible, even probable, that Congress may decide that harassment need not be *sexually* based. Harassment involves offensive behaviors and communications that can be originated by women as well as by men, although that experience has proved to be clearly less likely. Nevertheless, it is possible that our society may eventually wish to make harassment truly based on behavior or communications rather than on gender.

HOSTILE WORK ENVIRONMENT

Even if Congress does not enact workplace violence legislation, under contract law an employer who has a broad harassment policy could also be alleged to breach an employee's rights if the harassment engaged in by employees results in a hostile work environment. The Supreme Court has recognized such a hostile work environment theory in sexual harassment situations. Hostile environment sexual harassment exists where an employee is subjected to sexual harassment that is sufficiently severe or pervasive to alter the conditions of the victim's employment and create an abusive working environment [see *Barbetta v. Chemlawn Services Corp.,* 669 F Supp 569 (1987)]. By analogy, one could argue that where harassment that is not sexual in nature is pervasive enough to constitute a hostile working environment, the employer could be found liable for the contractually implied duty to provide a safe and healthy workplace. Regardless of the sex of the recipient, employers should take action to provide a harassment-free work environment.

PREVENTIVE MEASURES

The focus of this chapter now shifts to the question of what employers can do to comply with their duty to provide a safe workplace and avoid or at least minimize the risk of workplace violence. In order to reduce the risk, employers should devise a plan which will address the problem at its early stage. For example, employers can establish a threat assessment protocol that may include hotlines so employees can report threats before they evolve into harassment or escalate into physical violence. To make such a policy effective, the employer should have a threat management team (please see chapter 6) in place so that an investigation can be conducted to control the employer's response to the threat. In establishing these teams, the employer ideally should request input from the employees. With unionized companies, the company should ensure that the teams involve the participation of labor. In the case of labor unions, the union should choose, according to determinations by the National Labor Relations Board, the representative to participate on such teams.

GRIEVANCE PROCEDURES

Management and labor should establish procedures that try to protect the interests of all parties. For example, management should attempt to learn as much as it can from individuals who have perpetrated violent or aggressive acts or made threats, even though this should probably be after the employee has been safely removed from the workplace. Management must know if abusive supervisors or peer group behavior contributed to the act.

The threat management team will also have to balance the rights of perpetrators with the need for a safe work environment. The team can achieve this objective by limiting its disclosure of the threat and identity of perpetrators to involved supervisory personnel and the parties to whom the threats were specifically directed. However, the goal of protecting the reputation and confidentiality rights of a perpetrator becomes difficult when a threat is generalized or directed at the entire workplace. Depending upon the magnitude of the threat and probability of violence, the management team may be forced to sacrifice the interests of the accused and reveal both the nature of the threat and the identity of the accused to a large employee population. In some situations the company may be forced to offer the accused either a suspension with or without pay, a transfer, or even an opportunity to resign with a severance package in order to preserve the morale and productivity of the workplace. While the short-term costs of this option may appear to be a burden, the long-term benefits of a safe and secure workplace are significant.

RIGHTS OF THE ACCUSED

In protecting the rights of the accused, a threat management team also has to weigh the rights of the complaining party, which will inherently conflict with those of the accused. A victim or threatened party may feel reluctant to initiate a complaint unless the team can guarantee confidentiality. The victim may be understandably concerned that the situation with the alleged perpetrator will escalate by reporting the incident without such a guarantee. On the other hand, the employer may wish in certain instances to provide a forum to a person to know about the nature of the complaint and confront his or her accuser, particularly when there are no witnesses to verify the allegations of the complaining party. Overall, the corporate or union counsel may find itself in a position where it is privy to the privileged information of two opposing parties.

THREAT ASSESSMENT

If the initial investigation of the complaint reveals that the perpetrator does represent a threat to other employees, the employer must determine how it can monitor and control the employee (see chapter 8 for more information). An employer may choose to subject the accused to psychological evaluation to assess dangerousness. The employer should provide guidelines concerning the procedures in its employment manual or in a memorandum to all employees outlining circumstances when such procedures will be used. If it is determined that an employee has violent propensities but the behavior has not escalated to the point warranting discharge, the company could mandate that the employee enter a non-punitive counseling program.

These programs, in conjunction with Employee Assistance Programs (EAPs) could help employees deal with problems producing stress such as financial pressures, alcohol or drug abuse, domestic disputes or work-related stress. Participation in these programs could defuse the potentially violent situation and improve the morale of employees within the workplace.

Finally, mental health counseling may be required under the Americans with Disabilities Act of 1990 (ADA) for those employees with violent propensities related to a mental impairment. ADA may prohibit a company from discharging or suspending an employee who it suspects poses a danger, because ADA requires the company to make a reasonable accommodation for those employees suffering from a physical or mental impairment if they can perform their assigned duties at work. Because the ADA has only recently been implemented, these issues have not yet been contested and no legal precedent exists to guide companies.

DUTY TO WARN

A trend to hold psychologists and psychiatrists liable for the acts committed by their patients is now emerging in law. Generally, there is no duty to control the conduct of another in order to protect a third person from harm. However, an important exception to this general rule arises where there is a special relationship between two persons, which gives a third person the right to protection. In *Tarasoff v Regents of University of Cal.* (1976) 551 P2d 334, a patient threatened to kill a woman he previously dated. Because of the doctor-patient privilege, the therapist did not warn the woman or her family of the threats. The patient then stabbed the woman to death in the exact fashion he had described to his therapist. The court found that the therapist was liable to the woman's parents for the failure to warn, because the therapist failed to exercise reasonable care to protect the victim from danger. The court held that, whether or not there is actual control over an outpatient in a mental health clinic setting like that exercised over institutionalized patients, the relationship between a clinical therapist and his or her patients is sufficient to create a duty to exercise reasonable care to protect a potential victim of another's conduct.

In recent years, this duty to warn has extended to counseling services such as Employee Assistance Programs (EAP) as well as mental health clinics. Counselors, along with psychiatrists and psychologists, have a legal duty to warn a potential victim of violence. The discharge of the duty to warn varies with the facts of each case. In each instance the adequacy of the therapist's conduct must be measured against the traditional negligence standard of the rendition of reasonable care under the circumstances.

Courts have found that the burden of giving unnecessary warnings is a reasonable price to pay for the lives of possible victims that may be saved. In the court's view, the public interest outweighs the breach of trust in the revelation of confidential communications involving threats of violence. There are numerous decisions that support this view. In February of 1993, a Minnesota Court of Appeals held that an EAP counselor was immune from liability for erroneously warning a third party of a violent threat made by a patient, (Minnesota Statute 148.97 states a practitioner is immune from liability for erroneously or negligently warning a third party of a violent threat made by a patient if the disclosure is made in a good faith effort to warn a third party against the patient's behavior). Other courts and legislative bodies have confirmed that the duty to report threats against third parties of potential bodily harm or serious property damage outweighs the doctor-patient privilege.

DISCHARGE/POST-DISCHARGE

In certain situations, the magnitude of an employee's behavior will warrant discharge. However, the employer's duty to protect the threatened employee and provide a safe workplace does not end at the point of termination of the perpetrator. The discharge of the perpetrator often triggers physical violence in the workplace, although violence often is latent, remaining dormant for several months or even years. Employers must take adequate security measures to insure the safety of their workers. They should confiscate, if possible, any keys or pass cards that the discharged employee could use to access the workplace. If the employee refuses to return these items, the company should change its locks or security codes. The employer should also contact local law enforcement officials to coordinate a prevention strategy or, if necessary, to seek a restraining order.

In locations that are accessible to the general public, the company may want to consider transferring the threatened employee to another location or increasing security around the work site. If the company does transfer the threatened employee, it should take steps to insure that the new location is not disclosed to the perpetrator. These steps can divert management resources and be expensive and time consuming, but are nevertheless necessary to protect people potentially in harm's way.

Finally, employers can be creative in seeking an effective resolution to an otherwise difficult situation. Firing an employee may not be the only answer. Managers may want to consider relocating employees or suspending those who have violated rules but don't warrant discharge. Some of the options that are available are included in Table 18-1.

DEALING WITH LEGAL ISSUES

This chapter has provided a brief overview of some of the legal issues of concern to an employer struggling to confront the problem of workplace violence. There are two considerations that you should keep in mind:

1. This chapter is not a substitute for legal analysis or interpretation. While it may provide you with a general understanding of the concepts that are important with respect to workplace violence, you should always rely on a competent local attorney to help you understand the laws and regulations that apply to you.

2. Laws change. This chapter may lose some of its meaning as soon as it is written. Judges make new determinations and legislatures enact new statutes. Again, you should depend on local counsel for an understanding of the laws that apply to you.

TABLE 18-1
EMPLOYEE DISCIPLINE OPTIONS

- Grievance Procedures
- Job transfer/ relocation
- Job restructuring
- Suspension with pay
- Suspension without pay
- Discharge for cause

SOURCE: National Safe Workplace Institute

A number of the issues discussed in this chapter do not lend themselves to a clear-cut conclusion. However, there are steps that employers can take that should help them prevent violence (and avoid legal ramifications of violent acts). Certainly, employers should have preventive policies and procedures in place. By providing employees with access to good mental-health counseling programs, employers can take another important step. Likewise, through the creation of threat assessment committees, and implementation of security measures that do not unreasonably invade any employee's privacy rights, a company can take affirmative steps to comply with its duty to provide a safe workplace and address the nuances of workplace violence.

19

PARTNER OR REGULATOR?

The Role of Government in Curbing Workplace Violence

Violence at work raises vital policy questions for government. The public wants safety and security; the issue is what role government should play in accomplishing that objective. Should issues of violence at work be the domain of law enforcement? Should new labor codes and employment laws be enacted? Should government be a partner with business? Or should it promulgate standards and then enforce them? These are important questions that are bound to gain more attention in the coming months and years. There is little doubt that the public wants action and that the public will support an enhanced role for government in order to achieve a greater measure of security.

There is no question that law enforcement has an obligation to enforce laws. It is also clear that many incidents of violence at work involve unlawful acts. Beyond the role of law enforcement, government's role will evolve over time. Businesses are apprehensive that public concern about violence will result in new and expensive labor codes and regulations imposed on the private sector. Already, the U.S. Occupational Safety and Health Administration (OSHA), relying on what is known as the General Duty Clause of the Occupational Safety and Health Act of 1970 (OSH Act), has issued citations to employers who have failed to respond to recognized threats of violence at work. OSHA is now contemplating a number of strategies that would result in a more aggressive stance by government toward employers on issues related to violence at work.

The toll of death and injury from violence at work alone suggests that government will expand its role. Workplace homicide is the number two killer of workers, second only to motor vehicle accidents. How can government expend substantial resources in protecting workers from less significant sources of death and injury? Does the problem of violence deserve less attention than safety problems and risks faced by factory or construction workers? Should OSHA stay away from violence because it may be viewed as a *security* issue rather than a safety matter?

Government has the legal authority to impose sanctions on employers who have failed to provide for a safe workplace. OSHA's authority comes from the Occupational Safety and Health Act which ensures that all employees have a safe and healthy workplace. This statute includes language that requires that employers respond to recognized threats to the safety and health of employees not otherwise addressed by specific regulatory standards. This particular provision is called the General Duty Clause, which gives OSHA very broad authority to investigate and issue citations. It has been construed as giving OSHA the authority to issue a citation when an employer has failed to respond to a threat of violence.

For large businesses operating in numerous states, the problem is made more complex because there are really two OSHAs. There is the Federal OSHA which has private sector jurisdiction in 29 states. In the remaining 21 states—including California, Michigan, Minnesota and North Carolina—enforcement of the Occupational Safety and Health Act rests, by agreement, with state government. What this means is that the law is likely to be seen in a different light in different jurisdictions. Priorities for interpretation and enforcement vary from state to state. California, which has relatively meager inspection resources, has become very aggressive in trying to regulate and prevent workplace violence. North Carolina, which has more safety inspectors on a per capita basis than any state in the nation, has just now begun to consider the problem of violence at work.

Inside OSHA itself, there is a struggle to determine what government's role should be. On the one hand, there are those who insist that workplace violence is a criminal and security issue and that OSHA's role would be redundant to the role played by law enforcement and the criminal justice system. This view has been embraced mostly by organized labor, which fears that the involvement of OSHA on workplace violence problems will seriously deplete the agency's modest inspection and enforcement resources, and adversely affect safety and industrial hygiene at factories, plants and construction sites.

On the other hand, still other voices argue that workplace violence now kills more employees than any other source save motor vehicle accidents. Homicide is the second leading killer of workers, overall, and the leading killer of females. This group argues that law enforcement's approach to such issues is largely reactive and aimed at the perpetrators of crime. OSHA, meanwhile, is charged with scrutinizing the role that the employer—and the employer alone—has played in ensuring a safe workplace. It can be further argued that OSHA should determine whether or not there are factors under an employer's control that have the promise of preventing injury and death. In fact, OSHA has expertise on issues (e.g. training) that may complement law enforcement's approach to the same problem.

Also, there are those who insist that those who are murdered at work often lack an organized voice in our society. Many of the clerks and cashiers murdered at convenience stores or in fast food outlets are not represented by unions, nor are they people who have much power and influence in the halls of government. There is a sense that these employees need the protection that government may be able to provide. Government can impose checks and balances on business, as partner and regulator, that should reduce workplace deaths and injuries. There is little question that government will expand its role to include greater scrutiny of factors within an employer's control that may prevent or reduce harm done by violence.

CALIFORNIA
Leading the Way on Violence Prevention

While the jury is out on the larger question of how general OSHA's role will be, there can be little question that OSHA has already begun to act. Patterns are beginning to emerge. California's state OSHA program is the undeniable leader in workplace violence prevention, although other states and the Federal OSHA program may not be far behind. In California, policymakers have become involved on numerous fronts. The state is seeking to educate while it is beginning to enforce the law. It is seeking to be both a partner and a regulator. In many ways, California could be emerging as a model for the remainder of the nation to emulate.

Take, for example, the role of education. Cal/OSHA held two conferences in Los Angeles and San Francisco that attracted standing-room only crowds of more than 1,000 people. The purpose of these conferences was for policymakers to hear the concerns of employers and the public and to share their ideas on what might be done by government. The resounding message from these twin conferences was that employees demand protection and that employers want guidance on what they should do. The conferences may have raised more questions than they answered but these events have stimulated action by the state and have built a supportive foundation by the public for an expanded government role.

California, it should be said, has many unique qualities when it comes to job safety laws. One of the key features in California job safety law is the injury prevention planning requirement that was enacted in 1991. This statute mandates that all businesses have a plan in place. If an accident occurs or if enforcement officers conduct an inspection, they will determine, in part, if the business establishment has complied with the plan and if the plan was adequate in relationship to the risks faced by the firm's employees. Inherent in this concept is the notion that a security hazard is a safety hazard. Because of this fact, a business with a high security risk (e.g. past robberies) must address such risks in its injury prevention plan. This law, the philosophy of which is evident in the state's approach to violence, compels businesses to think in a proactive or preventive fashion. Highlights of California's approach can be found in Table 19-1.

Cal/OSHA has moved in a systematic and careful fashion to attack the problem of violence at work. Beginning on August 1, 1994, the state began investigating all workplace homicides. Four months later, in December, Cal/OSHA issued its first citations arising from workplace violence. California's opening salvo of citations demonstrated the state's resolve to shift businesses toward a proactive approach on violence prevention and control. It is likely that California will be even more aggressive in the future in cases where businesses have failed to show even minimal concern for violence prevention.

California is not only leading in the development of a general approach to workplace violence, but is focusing on specific industries. After a rash of terrifying incidents in hospitals, California's Emergency Room nurses began advocating for a special hospital program. They went to the state's General Assembly where they found a receptive audience. In 1994, the Assembly passed S. 508, legislation which requires that certain preventive measures be taken to curb violence in the health-care setting. There are several key features of this new statute, shown in Table 19-2.

Special emphasis is placed on emergency rooms and psychiatric wards, where many violent incidents have taken place and where employees apparently are most at risk. Much of the thrust of the new legislation

TABLE 19-1

WORKPLACE VIOLENCE PREVENTION IN CALIFORNIA

- In 1992, 159 workers were murdered in the workplace, about one out of four of the 644 total fatal workplace injuries that year.

- In 1991 California enacted S.B.198, legislation that requires businesses to have workplace injury prevention plans.

Required procedures:

   1. workplace security hazard assessment

   2. assault investigation

   3. hazard correction

   4. emergency action plan

- In 1994, the state held workplace violence conferences in Los Angeles and San Francisco which attracted large audiences.

- After August 1, 1994, Cal/OSHA began investigating all workplace homicides for data collection purposes.

- Employers have a responsibility to record homicides. However, such records do not imply employer was at fault.

SOURCE: National Safe Workplace Institute

TABLE 19-2

CALIFORNIA'S NEW LAW TO COMBAT WORKPLACE VIOLENCE IN HOSPITALS (EFFECTIVE JANUARY 1, 1995)

- Emergency room training—

   ✓ general safety measures

   ✓ aggression and violence predictive factors

   ✓ verbal and physical maneuvers to diffuse or avoid violent behavior

- By July 1, 1995, all general acute care, acute psychiatric, and special hospitals would be required to conduct a security assessment and to develop a security plan.

- All assaults must be reported to law enforcement within 72 hours. Any individual obstructing this process could be found guilty of a misdemeanor.

SOURCE: National Safe Workplace Institute

is for training. The statute's advocates believe that training in how to identify dangerous situations and how to diffuse anger and aggression is one
of the real keys to violence reduction in hospitals. Perhaps one of the most
controversial features of the law is the requirement that hospitals must
report assaults to law enforcement within 72 hours. This provision is in
contrast with the past practice of ignoring violent acts or rationalizing
them on the basis of stress. This provision upset many hospital administrators who fear that mandatory reporting will alienate their patients and
their family members.

The fact that California enacted its injury prevention law and took
action on the problem of workplace violence while Republicans were in
power suggests that the issue of violence at work is one that cuts across par-
tisan lines. The coming months and years will determine if California is
going to move in a more comprehensive fashion. On many matters,
California has been seen as the leader and futurists are fond of pointing at
California in order to see what the future holds. We can expect more pervasive government action on workplace violence, even if other political
trends point to less government and less regulation.

A GROWING CRISIS-ROBBERY AND VIOLENCE IN THE RETAIL TRADE

Another industry group that has been the focus of attention by state and
local government is the retail convenience industry. There are 300 employees murdered each year in robberies and many of these involve fast food
outlets, convenience stores, and gasoline stations. In Florida, local statutes
have been enacted that require stores that stay open past 11 P.M. to have at
least two employees on duty.

The retail convenience industry faces a host of complex problems that
almost defy solution. A crisis of brutal murders has drawn increasing attention to robbery and violence in the retail trade: establishments where robbers think they can make an easy hit and escape with several hundred dollars. A 1994, front-page article in the *Wall Street Journal* described how robbery and murder has grown rapidly in the fast food industry in numerous
cities nationwide. Along with convenience stores and gasoline stations, it is
wrestling with how to prepare against robbers and violence.

While the industry talks about security there are limits to what it is willing to deliver. The industry, for example, has difficulty placing security val-

ues over marketing values for fear that it will lose the customers that are its very lifeblood. Obvious physical security measures such as clear visibility from streets (so that people passing by can call the police) are typically a low priority for an industry that wants to tout fast food, convenience products, and gasoline. To make matters worse, corporate executives usually feel that they have little control over franchisees who they say are independent business operators.

Tragically, employees and customers sometimes get in the way and the robber(s) turn to violence and aggression to complete the incident. Because of the nature of the industry and its employee population, it is inevitable that government regulators and the civil litigation system will require far more from this industry than it has to date. There is little question that OSHA, Federal and the state programs, will bring its specialized resources to focus on violence in the retail trade. The fact that women, minorities, senior citizens, teenagers and other vulnerable populations are victims of crime at these establishments is especially poignant and will certainly be used as a reason why intervention and regulation are necessary.

There are no guarantees in life and there will always be robbery and violence wherever money or goods of value are exchanged. As we saw earlier, there are many problems and conditions affecting this industry that make it very difficult to prevent violence. While this is true, it is equally evident that much more needs to be done. The issue is how to best arrive at a solution which guarantees a reasonable degree of safety and security. Some of the reasons why OSHA must regulate are highlighted in Table 19-3.

TABLE 19-3
WHY OSHA MUST REGULATE SECURITY IN THE RETAIL CONVENIENCE INDUSTRY

- Violence is the second leading source of workplace death overall and the leading job-killer of women. More than three out of five people murdered at work are employed in the retail trade.

- Many homicide victims are young, seniors, or women.

- Some experts believe that many workplaces can be protected through corrective measures and training.

- California is beginning to regulate . . . pacesetter for Federal action.

- Businesses want a "cover" from the growing threat of lawsuits.

SOURCE: National Safe Workplace Institute

OPPORTUNITIES FOR PARTNERSHIP?

There are opportunities for partnership between the retail convenience industry and OSHA. By working with OSHA and other independent agencies, employers can formulate guidelines that will help establish what constitute reasonable and prudent measures to prevent violence. Simply put, once agreement can be reached on what should be done, employers who comply with the guidelines (or regulations, if necessary) would be shielded from enforcement actions or civil litigation.

The way that this could be achieved is by recommending that employers implement security and safety measures commensurate with the degree of risk they face that would be determined by location (low-, medium- or high-risk). While robbery and crime can occur at any location in the U.S., corrective actions would be taken corresponding to the statistical level of risk. In most cases, high-crime locations in urban areas would be high-risk and, as a result, we would anticipate need for a higher commitment to violence prevention. Many fast food outlets already have very aggressive measures in place in high-risk areas. For example, it is fairly common to see a uniformed security guard present at fast food outlets in high-crime neighborhoods.

There are two ways in which government could emerge as a partner with the retail convenience trade. First, government could publish guidelines that would not constitute a standard but would reflect appropriate actions by the industry. A second alternative would be to train OSHA consultation personnel to provide advice and guidance to the industry on an informal basis. The Federal Government currently funds job-safety consultation in all 50 states that could provide this service to businesses. New Jersey, for example, in what may be seen as a model pilot program, has already begun to train its consultation personnel on workplace violence issues and appropriate strategies. Washington, on the other hand, has taken a different approach. The state distributes an 18-minute video, "Is It Worth Your Life?" designed to help businesses prevent robbery and violence and to instruct employees caught in a robbery about how to survive without being harmed. Both states have shown leadership and creativity in this area.

A NEW ROLE?
Preventing Violence in the Health-Care Industry

As we saw previously, the health-care industry is experiencing too much violence for a public that feels deeply that hospitals should be safe havens in a violent world. Earlier in this chapter, we examined how California, as a result of new legislation, is now taking action toward preventing violence in the health-care setting. There are signs that indicate that Federal OSHA may be inclined to investigate violent incidents at hospitals and to issue citations under certain circumstances.

Perhaps ground was broken in 1993 when U.S. OSHA issued a citation to Charter Barclay Hospital in Chicago. The language of the citation, which relied upon the OSH Act's General Duty Clause, Section 5(a)(1), suggests that threats and the existence of violence are reasons enough to adopt preventive measures. OSHA fined Charter Barclay $5,000, which was later reduced to $2,500, but also identified 20 abatement measures that the hospital had to undertake to demonstrate compliance. As seen in Table 19-4, health-care facilities should take steps to ensure that employees who deal with potentially violent patients are trained to do their jobs with minimal risk of injury.

REDUCING THE IMPACT OF CIVIL LITIGATION

Perhaps an unappreciated role for OSHA is to reduce the need and impact of civil litigation. Currently, there are very few standards or guidelines that

TABLE 19-4
OSHA ABATEMENT MEASURES REQUIRED
OF CHICAGO'S CHARTER BARCLAY HOSPITAL

OSHA imposes a $5,000 fine (later reduced to $2,500) for conditions that led to the death of an employee.

OSHA requires that Charter Barclay undertake certain abatement measures in order to comply with the citation.

1. Plan that identifies risk factors of assaultive behavior.

2. Mandatory training on crisis prevention techniques.

3. Training on restraint/seclusion procedures for emergency staff.

4. Training on multi-cultural diversity to develop racial sensitivity.

5. Identification of patients with increased potential for violence.

6. Staffing levels increases during emergencies.

SOURCE: National Safe Workplace Institute

employers can easily embrace to demonstrate that they had adopted preventive measures considered to be prudent defenses. Without these guidelines, businesses must face the risk of having to rationalize decisions and performance to juries. In many situations, plaintiffs assert that an employer's failure to adopt certain physical security measures or training programs, for example, indicated neglect or thoughtlessness by the employer. As one might imagine, it is hard to overcome such arguments to juries who are tired of violence and believe that much more should be done.

No one can expect perfection from an employer. There will always be newer technology or superior training methods and programs. The issue is to have independent authorities issue consensus guidelines or standards that suggest that certain measures are prudent and necessary. The existence of such guidelines or standards would, in effect, transfer the judgments that are currently being made by juries to individuals who have far more expertise and knowledge. This initiative would level the playing field and establish clear ground rules for employers.

THE ROLE OF ORGANIZED LABOR IN CURBING VIOLENCE

Organized labor has not been especially visible in the workplace violence prevention dialogue. This is unfortunate because policy development, by either individual businesses or by government, would benefit from the perspective of working people—those who are most often at-risk of violence at work. After all, it is line people—customer service representatives, shift workers, support staff, etc.—who are often the likely targets of angry coworkers and demented or hostile customers.

The thinking of certain individuals within the AFL-CIO is that there is too much blame-the-worker thinking in workplace violence prevention. Many voices within the labor community also see a real conflict between policies that terminate hostile workers who have made threats and the obligation of the union to represent and grieve workers who the union thinks have been treated unfairly by management. These points of view can be appreciated but should not result in a lack of participation by the union in the policy formulation and implementation stages. By understanding the need for these initiatives, unions can understand the need to ensure safe and healthy work environments for all workers. Labor has supported many workplace anti-drug and alcohol programs as well as policies aimed at curbing sexual harassment. Perhaps the AFL-CIO can adopt similar approaches to preventing violence at work.

Labor's views are very important to the Federal Government, especially Democratic administrations. The U.S. Department of Labor, for example, has been reluctant to pursue policies on health and safety issues without the tacit support of the AFL-CIO. However, the development of policies by states such as California, and probably by other states in the future, will place considerable pressure on the Federal Government. This is especially true because large corporations prefer that Federal policy preempt the various state policies and programs on the same issue.

GOVERNMENT AS EDUCATOR

The Federal Government, should, at a minimum, assume a more assertive policy as educator of industry and workers on the important problem of violence at work. Developing a role as educator will require thoughtful planning, communication with industry, labor and academia, and, most important, a willingness to lead. With each workplace killing, the Federal Government has lost an opportunity to protect and to serve the citizens it has been obligated to represent.

The National Institute for Occupational Safety and Health (NIOSH), a research arm designed to provide OSHA and the Secretary of Labor with scientific studies to promote safe workplaces, has expended substantial resources on the problem of violence at work. To this point, most of NIOSH's studies and research have been focused toward commercially motivated violence. Even its research efforts in this area have been incomplete inasmuch as very little work has emphasized the demographics and backgrounds of people who perpetrate violence, a necessary component in order to establish sound survival training.

Also, NIOSH has expended very few resources on the problem of angry workers, disgruntled former employees, or hostile customers. Perhaps this oversight has been a function of NIOSH's National Traumatic Occupational Fatality (NTOF) program. Scientists working in this program have studied death certificates to learn about how and why workers were killed. NIOSH's NTOF program, in reality, has provided very little insight into the problem of violence. Its researchers have drastically under-estimated the amount of violence, suggesting that about 750 workers were being murdered each year at work when the actual number exceeded 1,000.

Past mistakes aside, NIOSH should revisit the issue of violence and formulate a more comprehensive and creative research program. It could begin by calling together scholars and researchers to develop a more comprehensive approach. Once the problem has been properly understood NIOSH then could target specific projects that have the best means for producing life-saving information.

GOVERNMENT-PARTNER & REGULATOR

Government must emerge as a partner and regulator on the issue of violence at work. Anything less would clearly fail the public interest and guarantee that needless death and injury will continue. It is time that Federal and state officials demonstrate the commitment that makes the OSH Act's promise of a safe workplace a reality for all employees.

The Federal Government has the legal authority to act against employers who have failed consistently to provide for safe workplaces. OSHA will continue to issue citations when egregious acts of neglect by employers demonstrate the convincing need for enforcement. However, OSHA appears reluctant, for political and budgetary reasons, to embrace a more ambitious agenda. The Secretary of Labor needs to carefully consider his priorities in order to ensure that OSHA's resources are being used in an appropriate fashion. The Secretary, perhaps with Congressional prodding, should ask why this most important agency has been so piecemeal in addressing the second leading cause of worker death. Presumably a government agency dedicated to workplace safety would want to allocate its resources in a fashion that corresponds with the magnitude of the problem it is mandated to address. This has not been the case with this agency.

Like NIOSH, OSHA can play an important educational role. In the case of OSHA, however, this agency has the resources through its consultation program to provide advice to business on how best to prevent violence at work. It needs to begin training its consultation staff in this area and determine how best to deploy its members. There is no question that employers who want to embrace good programs could benefit from OSHA's counsel in this area. If OSHA is reluctant to embrace violence prevention as a primary objective in its programs, it may wish to establish pilot programs in New Jersey and other states that embrace this approach.

Government can be both regulator and partner in preventing violence at work. To date, however, government has not been effective in assuming this long-neglected role. Past mistakes and oversights, though, should not determine current and future policy. Government must address violence prevention and provide the expertise and insights that can save lives and reduce injuries.

PLOTTING THE FUTURE . . .

For the immediate future, violence will continue to infect our lives because of societal and demographic conditions already in place. These conditions cannot be changed in the near-term. The United States, as much as we love this nation, is the most violent advanced civilization on earth. The repercussions of this violence will be felt at work, at home, and at play. The U.S. is violent because of our inefficient legal system, because of the failure of our economic system to replace good jobs, because our entertainment industry glamorizes violence, and because we are unwilling to discipline abusive employees. Just because violence exists, we don't have to tolerate it. Instead, we must strive to prevent it from entering our workplaces by utilizing the ideas and concepts outlined in this book.

The problem of violence, as we have seen, is complex. Many employers resist the need to embrace values that can make the goal of violence-free a real possibility. To be fair, some of these corporations are good companies with otherwise sound human resource procedures and policies. These employers feel that they have workplaces where the rules are fair and where the compensation and benefits are competitive. Employers do not realize that violence is often *beyond their control*. They equate violence with disgruntled employees (a small part of the problem) while they cherish customers who are abusive. The challenge for employers is to embrace values that oppose violence. They need to implement procedures and processes that are consistent with the violence-free values and objectives. This book has attempted to provide a road map for how this can be accomplished.

There is a danger that we will become complacent about violence and begin to accept it as part of life itself. With each violent incident, we become more numb to the harsh realities that are part of a violent culture. To resist the impulse to become complacent, we must realize that we have choices that can improve our prospects. This book has been about those choices. It has been about the possible options to help us build organizations embracing positive values that will make violence a less likely prospect.

That we have violence in our lives is a cruel reality. The path to removing violence is far beyond the mission of this book. Table 20-1 reveals the scope of the problem which demonstrates the work that must be done at the level of culture and nation. We can learn a lot about what needs to be done by examining our cousins in other advanced nations. To them, the violence we have is foreign, totally alien to their way of life. In building our nation, we have made choices that have had consequences. Our pursuit of justice has left our criminal justice system comparatively inefficient. Our demand to have the right to possess weapons has led to liberal gun control laws that make it easy for criminals and the mentally incompetent to obtain firearms. Our wish for free speech has produced an entertainment industry that glamorizes violence, giving our young totally inappropriate ideas about resolving conflict and disputes. We need to understand what we have bought before we can appreciate the choices that must be made.

THE REAL ISSUE
Using Health Values to Shape New Boundaries

While violence is likely to persist as a national problem, increasing numbers of employers are electing to adopt violence prevention strategies as part of their efforts to have violence-free work environments. Their motives are as much practical as anything else. Employers understand that most workers, especially women and educated employees, who often have choices, desire work environments free from intimidation and menacing behaviors.

Employers are also starting to articulate new health values in their organizations that include violence prevention as a foundation. They realize that

TABLE 20-1

COMPARISON BETWEEN THE U.S. AND OTHER ADVANCED NATIONS

	CONTROLS PRESENT IN OTHER INDUSTRIALIZED NATIONS WITH LOW HOMICIDE/CRIME RATES	*CONTROLS ABSENT IN U.S.*
LEGAL SYSTEM	Emphasizes prevention of crime, efficiently apprehends and punishes violators.	Comparatively inefficient criminal justice system and extremely liberal gun laws.
CULTURAL SYSTEM	Promotes norm of good behavior.	Glamorization of violence in popular culture, especially media.
ECONOMIC SYSTEM	Generally lower unemployment; long-term safety net for unemployed; few working poor.	Minimal safety net; large numbers of unemployed or underemployed; large numbers of working poor.

SOURCE: National Safe Workplace Institute

the best organizations in which to work will be those free from fear, intimidation, and menacing behaviors. They realize that attractive and positive workplaces offer a real alternative.

There is a health values gap in the U.S. that is easier to understand than it is to measure. Studies show that many of our brightest and most productive employees are individuals who exercise, eat right, watch their weight and pursue the foundations of a healthy lifestyle. They embrace these choices and see the results in the lives. Yet, when they go to work, they sometimes find that senior managers embrace a different set of values. The result is a gap that frustrates many creative, intelligent, and able employees.

The health values gap illustrated in Table 20-2 must be closed. The most successful organizations in the 1990's and beyond will be those that intuitively appreciate this need. They understand and know that the fabric of a healthy lifestyle at work can be woven into the fabric of a healthy lifestyle away from work. When this is accomplished, management and the employee both are winners. In the future, this weave will no longer be a luxury, but a requirement. The organizations that fail to understand and act upon these distinctions will decline more quickly than ever before. The cor-

TABLE 20-2

UNDERSTANDING THE HEALTH VALUES GAP

- At home, health values are important. Survey data show that health issues are of increasing importance.

- At work, our employers may not believe that health is so important.

  This gap will be increasingly important to employers trying to find and retain productive employees. Employees want their employers to embrace health values more consistent with the values they hold away from the work environment.

  This is especially true with educated workers and women.

SOURCE: National Safe Workplace Institute

porate landscape is littered with organizations that failed to adapt to contemporary conditions and challenges.

We live in a world of dramatic change which is often very stressful. As the speed of change is accelerated, the pressures are increased. There now are numerous high-performance, high-stress workplaces that are testing the limits of our most effective human resource managers. Individuals are constantly on the edge of breakdown. Some, as we have said, react by trying to eat right, exercise, and rest when they can; others try to cope without changing their lifestyles. They are on a collision course with disaster. Since stress introduces physical changes in the way our bodies work, these individuals are at risk of emotional breakdowns, strokes, heart attacks, and other physical ailments.

Not only are organizations changing, but employees' attitudes are changing as well. In the 1950's, 1960's, and 1970's, individuals were blindly loyal to their company. They felt employed for life. The Chief Executive Officer of General Motors was moved to tell the country that "what was good for GM was good for the country." The decade of the 1980's was a transitional period when U.S. companies could no longer assure ever-growing profits. These companies dumped thousands of employees, bringing about greatly diminished organizational loyalty.

We live in a far different world in the 1990's. We have whole new classes of employees—contract and temporary workers who do not really know from day to day what their jobs will be. Many employees are demoralized and untrusting. They are at work solely to make a living. The notion of a secure retirement is increasingly abstract. The willingness of many employees to jump ship to a new job around the corner or across town grows on a daily basis. Some employees are much more clear about what they want than about what they are willing to give. It could be decades before we evolve into a set of circumstances where people are settled and willing to trust.

Then there are younger employees who apparently lack the social skills and graces of their parents. Many are quick to blame and to question any voice of authority, either at home or at work. In many ways, managers are now presiding over a tinder box that could explode at any moment. We are just beginning to realize that this generation of young people is unlike any other preceding it.

The burdens of good management are growing. Many corporations have abolished management layers which has increased the ratio of workers to managers. While improved access solves problems, it creates others. A manager cannot spend as much time in person supervising 50 employees as he or she can supervising eight or nine. Critical elements of communication get lost when communication burdens increase. When times are good, the problem may not be as noticeable as it will surely be when times are bad.

Some organizations will have more problems with change than others. Those that know their employees as well as they know their customers are likely to achieve better results than those who ignore their employees or whose priorities are imbalanced. It is no surprise that demand for industrial psychologists is on the rise. It is no surprise that we have instruments called "employee opinion surveys" or "climate assessments" that act as barometers for employee thoughts and feelings. The future will demand that

TABLE 20-3

A WINDOW ON OUR THINKING—THE WAY PEOPLE SEE WORK & HOW THAT WILL INFLUENCE BUSINESS

1. Quality of work and conditions of work will become a competitive factor for business in obtaining and retaining qualified workers.

2. Employees will be less loyal and more mobile.

3. Younger workers will be difficult to manage.

4. Temporary and contract employees will feel little or no loyalty to temporary employers.

5. The demands on front-line managers will increase, making good communication more difficult.

SOURCE: National Safe Workplace Institute

we learn more, not less, about our employees and what makes them function.

As we move into the next century, high-performance, high-stress organizations are going to be the norm, not the exception. There will be more Motorolas and fewer General Motors. A number of management strategies and paradigms are being introduced to help us adjust to this new world. Some of these concepts and techniques could introduce a new set of unintended problems. Let's look at some of the new management approaches and how they will affect the way our organizations work and deal with violence. By looking at these issues, we will be in a better position to understand the concepts and strategies that will best work to prevent violence.

REBUILDING ORGANIZATIONS AND DECISION-MAKING PROCESSES

There are few large organizations in the United States today that are not in a period of rapid change. In fact, those that are not changing are organizations either in decline or in mature industries. Terms such as re-engineering, TQM (Total Quality Management), Work Teams—among others—are entering the lexicon of American business. These processes are attractive to corporate boards and senior managers because they promise larger profits from more productive and efficient organizations and decision-making structures. Indeed, in many corporations, the number of outside consultants and contract employees at work is often larger than the number of permanent employees.

More and more organizations are following the lead of such innovative firms as Milliken, the textile giant, in moving to team-decision making. Milliken has eliminated hundreds of supervisor positions, moving the authority for numerous decisions to work teams. There are admittedly risks that teams will engage in behaviors that will shun or ostracize team or group members. But there are also risks that exist from abusive supervisors. Management can take two steps to insure against these abusive practices by work teams. First, managers should insist that teams be sensitive to practices that isolate certain members (especially by sex, race, or creed). They should encourage team members to be honest with each other, and there should be procedures where concerns about inner-team practices can be raised and effectively addressed. If abuses occur, escape valves must be created so that word reaches senior management which can then impose remedial training or discipline to correct the situation.

The crush of global competition has led to the embrace of Total Quality Management (TQM) and still other advanced management techniques. TQM will indirectly support violence prevention by increasing management's awareness of costs, including many of the hidden costs (e.g. lost productivity) of aggressive behaviors. Therefore, management styles involving TQM would logically include a focus on the behaviors and processes counter to maximizing productivity such as any dysfunctional behavior like anger, aggression, and violence.

ADDRESSING THE DIVERSITY CHALLENGE

Racism and the failure to appreciate cultural and other differences between people can contribute to tension in many workplaces. Corporations are now addressing diversity problems through training, reassignment, and other strategies that will help employees appreciate differences. Diversity training has been criticized by some individuals who do not understand the nature of the problem and what has to be done. The reality is that corporate America is increasingly made up of females and minority group members who are assuming prominent positions. We simply must appreciate our diversity as a strength and not a weakness.

Many lethal incidents have occurred because some white males have felt that "inferior" minority group members and females had been promoted at their expense. The perception that such individuals are being unfairly promoted feeds on itself and intensifies their frustration and anger. We need tolerance and understanding by all parties, not hatred and tension; sound diversity training is the only real solution to meet this challenge.

Promotions are only one aspect of the diversity challenge. A growing minority population (African Americans, Hispanics, Asians, and others) will mean a much different work force on the shop floor for the remainder of this century. What does this mean? Possibilities include:

- Training (e.g. hazard communication) burdens will increase.
- The jobs of supervisors will be much more difficult.
- Some jobs may be ghetto-ized isolating those job-holders.
- New immigrants may be increasingly frustrated with differences between rich and poor.
- Pressure for quotas and minority contracting will increase.

Many corporations are including diversity training for their workplace violence threat response teams. They should be congratulated because it reflects the importance of this issue to violence prevention. While it is impossible to quantify racism as a source, it probably looms large. Hence, any and all efforts to improve racial, ethnic and gender harmony should serve to reduce the violence threat.

THE ROLE OF SAFETY & HEALTH PROFESSIONALS

Safety and health professionals will play an increasingly important role in shaping the future of workplace violence prevention. As we move into the 1990's, we are seeing a dramatic change in how safety is viewed within the organization. Businesses are increasingly empirical or bottom-line driven when it comes to safety; re-engineering programs are shifting the focus from safety engineers to professionals such as risk managers. While safety managers and risk managers both have safe work environments as a goal, an engineer will try to eliminate or reduce a hazard through engineering strategies while a risk manager will find *the* way to best manage the problem. Risk managers, by nature of their profession, are far more interested in behavioral issues than are safety engineers.

Corporations are also placing more emphasis on professionals such as industrial hygienists, human factors specialists, trainers, and environmental health physicians. All of these professionals are intellectually suited to work along with human resource managers and security specialists on violence prevention strategies and programs. Each of these safety professions brings a unique perspective that is very important and can add richness and validity to programs and policies.

EXTERNAL PRESSURES ON MANAGEMENT

There are a number of forces external to the corporation that are likely to influence the development of workplace violence prevention policy.

Historically, unions have had considerable clout with corporations and government. There is a growing debate about whether unions have waned or whether they will return to positions of power and influence as new waves of change roll through our lives. History shows that the labor movement exerted new influence in the past even when managers and the intellectuals of the day concluded that the time for organized labor had passed.

Unions could again be a force in the last part of this century. To understand how they impact our lives, one need only consider a simple fact. By defining the terms of the social contract between managers and the managed, unions exert influence far beyond what their numbers would indicate. Many companies will base their salary structure on what companies with unions will pay despite the fact that the influence of labor on compensation is waning.

Historically, unions have pressured for government intervention in the workplace to compel employers to embrace new responsibilities. Organized labor was directly responsible for passage of the Occupational Safety and Health Act of 1970. It also contributed to the shaping of our labor laws and the social agenda of our nation. While in general decline, organized labor remains an influential part of many industries—aerospace, steel, autos, food processing, and transportation—to name a few. We can't write off unions just yet.

Despite its influence, organized labor has been slow to combat workplace violence. There are serious internal conflicts in labor's leadership on the subject. For openers, many unions feel that they must grieve (petition management to restore lost jobs) workers who are fired because of threats or violent acts. Some labor union leaders feel that it is their most important obligation to protect their membership, whatever the cost. In theory, this may pit the interests of the security of the work force against individual perceived rights and liberties.

In one important case, a national union has ignored a call from management to combat violence. The American Postal Workers Union (APWU) has resisted calls from the Postmaster General to join a common strategy with other postal unions to combat violence. The Postal Service is hardly blameless. It has made decisions that have alienated the APWU and continues to do so, isolating influential labor voices.

On the other hand, different voices in labor are beginning to push for a more proactive violence strategy. They recognize that teams offer an inclusive strategy for managing aggressive employees where the voice of labor will be heard rather than ignored. For example, the United Auto Workers union (UAW) is now cooperating with manufacturers on various anti-violence strategies. While these discussions are in the early stages, there is hope for common ground. Yet, in general, it is likely that labor leaders will remain conflicted and ambivalent when it comes to employee violence and violence prevention.

Like unions, courts are another external factor. Courts are likely to play an unwitting role in how anti-violence programs are shaped and implemented. By interpreting the law, courts transform statutes into social structures that have far-reaching impact. Furthermore, courts are used to define the boundaries and responsibilities between individuals and organizations. Conservatives think that courts are likely to be more restrictive in their interpretations and application of laws in the future. There is just as much justification for thinking that they will go the other way. Courts often have the last word on the way things are done and the choices that are made. That reality alone gives them enormous power. In accepting this burden, they are likely to want to remedy wrongs and balance the score between opposing sides. Courts also are often bound by the findings of juries, which are oriented more and more toward individuals and causes and against corporations and government.

THE MEDIA AND WORKPLACE VIOLENCE

The media likewise will exercise influence in several ways on how, when, and where violence programs are embraced and adopted by private and public sector organizations. Most important, they act as a filter that sorts through the information of life and determines what is important to the public. Like it or not, and many people don't, the media shape public opinion and play an important role in our lives by deciding what is important for us to know. Shaping public perceptions by screening out information that they do not want us to receive, the media also set the political agenda for the nation through the same set of decisions.

To understand this subtle reality, consider the fact that a typical news outlet in Washington, D.C. will receive about 40 press releases for every story it will pursue. In the minds of the media, most news is not news. Major news organizations, including the television networks, *The New York Times*, *The Wall Street Journal*, etc., will have even more impact because less influential news organizations, following a herd instinct, are afraid to find different or competing news.

Most senior business executives live in fear of the media. They realize that a hostile press can be as destructive to corporate morale and profits as a hostile takeover attempt. Senior managers dread stumbling into an incident or comments that will attract intense media exposure. They know of executives who have lost their jobs, and sometimes their careers, because of press coverage. It is no wonder, then, that many surround themselves with a palace guard of media advisors and public relations gurus. As the

TABLE 20-4

A WINDOW ON OUR THINKING—THE MEDIA WILL PLAY A MAJOR ROLE IN THE WAY PEOPLE SEE HEALTH ISSUES

1. In general, the media will give more coverage to *health issues.*

2. The media have become *segmented.* There will be many media outlets (e.g. newsletters, cable TV programs) where health is the sole focus.

3. The way the media see issues *shapes the political* agenda of the nation—Federal, state and local.

4. The media will continue to hold *government and employers accountable* for problems and failures.

5. The media will continue to have a *liberal bias.*

6. The media will continue to have a bias towards *women.*

SOURCE: National Safe Workplace Institute

clout of the media grows, so does the impact of media and public relations specialists.

The power of the media is now shifting, although the impact of these changes has yet to be fully realized. The media are increasingly segmented. There are a lot more specialists covering business, including individuals who focus strictly on workplace issues. Added to the general news media are specialized publications—cable TV programs, news and trade magazines, newsletters, etc. Segmented programming is growing by leaps and bounds, challenging the influence and domination of the major media in many important ways.

The media have taken an enormous interest in workplace violence, unfortunately misinterpreting events in a way that does the subject a disservice. In reaching for conclusions, the media sometimes talk with a perpetrator's friends or co-workers who often share his or her agenda and objectives. Too often they then will conclude that a lethal perpetrator engaged in an act of justice or retribution against an unfair or even autocratic employer. While internal stressors or poor supervision may have contributed to a problem, society simply cannot tolerate abusive and criminal acts of violence.

Reporting on the status quo does not sell advertising, controversy does. This fact suggests that there will continue to be erroneous or sensationalized reporting on some cases of workplace violence. This is only logical, given the fact that human beings want safe and secure lives. We desperately want to avoid danger, especially in places like work.

All negative considerations aside, it is hoped that media scrutiny, in the final analysis, may be positive to the understanding that we have about violence and its perpetrators. Quality reporting will focus attention and, hopefully, clear heads and good thinking will prevail. Specialized reporting from the health and business press is also likely to have a positive impact. This type of reporting will often go into detail, trying to provide an in-depth understanding of what has transpired.

TABLE 20-5

WHAT ROLE WILL SOCIAL INVESTORS AND PENSION FUNDS PLAY IN THE CONDITIONS OF WORK?

The Department of Labor is now trying to persuade the investment community that the conditions of work are related, long-term, to organizational profits and effectiveness.

Many "social investment" firms are pursuing similar strategies. These changes could have enormous impact in the way organizations work.

Observations—

- For the past decade, socially responsible investors have pushed businesses to provide information on environmental and social issues.

- In June, 1994, Calpers (the huge California state pension fund) announced that it was developing workplace issues criteria for its investments.

- A number of socially responsible investors appeared poised to move in this direction, including Calvert, Dreyfus Third Century, etc.

Possibilities include scrutiny of—

- Internal stressors (e.g. EEOC complaints, labor-management disputes).

- Workplace safety and health data-injury rates, fatalities, etc.—and workers' compensation data experience modification ratings.

- Performance in hiring of women and minorities.

- Contracting with women and minorities.

SOURCE: National Safe Workplace Institute

THE IMPACT OF WALL STREET
AND SOCIAL INVESTORS

The financial community, if it so desires, can have substantial impact on the way people are managed in the United States. Because a share of the funds available for investment comes from employees and their investment funds, there is reason to think that social investors could play a major role in shaping organization human resource strategies. This is most likely to occur first with corporations that have labor unions but could occur in virtually any business that is publicly traded. Closely held, private firms are most likely to avoid scrutiny, simply because of their independence from traditional capital markets.

The logic behind social investing is that corporations exist for reasons that extend beyond profitmaking and, as a result, are obligated to a variety of stakeholders. When the Secretary of Labor claims that effective human resource strategies are likely to yield greater profits, then people—senior executives as well as investors—are likely to listen. A senior manager who does not believe that a program or policy will achieve its desired effect is still reluctant to ignore approaches that appear to have the promise of positive results. In this world, the risk and cost of acting is often less than failing to act.

The prospect of a mega-incident such as an explosion that kills hundreds of people could easily stimulate a movement by investors toward violence prevention. As discussed earlier, in 1994, a frustrated temporary employee tried to start a fire in a room where propane tanks were stored. The employee nearly blew up the *St. Louis Post-Dispatch*, an incident that would have cost hundreds of lives.

In the short-run, it is unlikely that specific violence-prevention measures will escape the focus of social investors. The approach that this community is likely to take in the short-run will be limited by information that everyone can agree is important. For example, minority hiring practices, because the truth is easy to determine, are likely to attract more attention than the quality of a threat assessment protocol. But this will change, either over time or because of a major incident that captures everyone's attention. As investors become comfortable with general questions, they will begin to ask more detailed questions about specific policies and procedures. When workplace violence increases as an important issue, it will surely attract more attention.

VIOLENCE PREVENTION
The Time Has Come

Several good reasons have been enumerated throughout this book why managers should want violence prevention as an organizational objective. There is virtually no legitimate reason for management—or anyone else—to oppose implementing sound programs and procedures. In the old days, organizations would defer simply because they resisted *all* change. The fact that we now live in a world marked by rapid change makes the embracing of new organizational values even more likely.

Corporations that are people-driven will have little difficulty embracing violence prevention as an important organizational objective. This simply has to be done. When a 1994 Gallup poll reported that two-thirds of the American people did not feel safe at work, alarms went off in many organizations. For moral, legal, and competitive reasons they will have to strive to implement procedures and policies ensuring that they are free of violence. The risks for failing to act are just far too great.

People are any organization's most important asset. Companies cannot enhance the value of that asset if people feel threatened, abused, or frightened. Violence prevention ultimately can be thought of as an insurance policy that most organizations cannot afford to be without, one designed to protect this most important resource. If current trends hold, this will be even more true in the future.

Violence prevention likewise is a way to redefine the boundaries between people at work while re-writing the rules for how business is conducted. These are unpleasant tasks required by new circumstances that are beyond the control of otherwise enlightened and forward-looking management. The winds of change are blowing. The prudent and wise will respond to the challenge at hand. In doing so, our organizations will be better places to work and our human resources will be more productive.

ENDNOTES

INTRODUCTION

1. Testimony by Professor Ed Donnerstein, Ph.D., Chairman, Department of Communications, University of California at Santa Barbara, before the California General Assembly Women's Caucus, May 9, 1993.

2. National Institute for Occupational Safety and Health, Centers for Disease Control, October, 1992.

3. Legislation has been introduced by Senator Tom Campbell and Assemblywomen Barbara Friedman and Dede Alpert.

CHAPTER 1

1. Data provided by Dr. Robert Harrison, M.D., California Department of Health Services, who conducted the research under contract with the National Institute for Occupational Safety and Health.

2. Statement by Ken Hunter, Chief Postal Inspector, U.S. Postal Service, in testimony on August 5, 1993, before the Subcommittees on Census, Statistics, and Postal Personnel; and Postal Operations and Services, U.S. House of Representatives.

3. "Fear and Violence in the Workplace," October, 1993, Northwestern National Life Insurance Survey (Employee Benefits Division), Minneapolis, Minnesota. Available upon request.

4. Census of Occupational Fatalities, Bureau of Labor Statistics, U.S. Department of Labor, May, 1994.

CHAPTER 2

1. Scott, John Paul (1992). Aggression: Functions and Control in Social Systems. Aggressive Behavior, Vol. 18, 1-20.

CHAPTER 3

1. Gardner, Jennifer M. "Recession swells count of displaced workers." *Monthly Labor Review*. U.S. Department of Labor Statistics. June, 1993. p. 14.

2. Ibid.

3. See Department of Labor Press release, USDL 92-530, Wednesday, August 19, 1992. "Worker displacement increased sharply in recent recession."

4. Gardner, pp. 14-15.

5. Richman, Louis S. "CEOs To Workers: Help Not Wanted." *Fortune*. July 12, 1993. pp. 42-43.

6. Uchitelle, Louis. "Strong Companies are Joining Trend to Eliminate Jobs." *The New York Times*. July 26, 1993.

7. Press Release, USDL 92-530

8. Belous, Richard S. *The Contingent Economy: The Growth of the Temporary, Part-Time and Subcontracted Workforce*. The National Planning Association. 1989. pp. 16-17. Estimates based on statistics from the Bureau of Labor Statistics.

9. Henkoff, Ronald. "Winning the New Career Game." *Fortune,* July 12, 1993, pp. 46-47.

A

ANNOTATED WORKPLACE VIOLENCE PREVENTION POLICY

NOTE: The information in brackets has been prepared to explain the policy.

LAW

Federal, state, and local laws require that employers provide their employees safe and healthy workplaces. Many require that employers respond to recognized hazards that are not specifically addressed by standard,and have been interpreted as applicable in circumstances relating to violent acts in the workplace.

[Note: The Occupational Safety and Health Act of 1970 (Act) provides the Secretary of Labor (Secretary) with broad police powers to investigate conditions in businesses that may contribute to injury of employees. In 21 states, the Secretary has conditionally delegated enforcement of the Act to the State. As a result, there are different interpretations, from state to state, of the types of safety concerns that should be a focus for OSHA enforcement. Until recently OSHA officials generally regarded homicide as a criminal and security issue rather than a safety matter subject to OSHA's jurisdiction. This de facto interpretation, however, is in a state of change. There are numerous citations that now show that it is within OSHA's clear authority, at either the Federal or State level, to investigate and issue citations following homicides. In 1993, Federal OSHA cited a Chicago hospital that failed to train its psychiatric staff in how to deal with dangerous patients and in crisis management (Secretary v. Charter Barclay Hospital, 4700 North Clarendon, Chicago, OSHA No. 102992021). In addition, Federal OSHA has cited other employers for violence-related matters. In 1992 State OSHA cited a retail establishment in Indiana (Indiana Department of Labor vs. Stationers, Inc., 36 N. Pennsylvania, Indianapolis, Inspection No. 108597691) for exposing employees to the "recognized hazard of robbery and/or death . . . while working in a retail establishment." Perhaps more importantly, the citation went on to say that Stationers, Inc., had failed to develop a deterrent program that included employee training in robbery deterrence. The use of the general duty clause does carry a different set of sanctions than if a promulgated standard is not followed by an employer. For example, OSHA cannot use the general duty clause as authority to issue a willful citation (which carries a fine of up to $70,000) nor can the government impose criminal penalties.

[There are a number of civil doctrines that apply to workplace violence in the contest of this policy. The most salient civil doctrines are negligent hiring, retention, and supervision; foreseeability; civil harassment; duty to warn, workers' compensation, and invasion of privacy. For a review of legal doctrines and case law, please consult:

- the monograph *Terror and Violence in the Workplace,* (San Francisco: Littler, Mendelson, Fastiff, Tichy & Mathiason, 1993).

- Chapter 9, "Maneuvering Through a Legal Minefield: Legal Issues in Workplace Violence," from the author's *Breaking Point—The Workplace Violence Epidemic & What to Do About It* (Chicago: National Safe Workplace Institute, 1993).

- For laws that apply to New England in general see *Workplace Violence and the Law* (Springer, F.J., Alquist, Elizabeth A.; et al, A Review of the General Legal Issues and Specific Connecticut Statutes, ©1993 by Day, Berry & Howard).

- For laws and cases that are applicable for Massachusetts, in particular, see "Violence on the Job" (*Massachusetts Employment Law Letter,* Vol. 5, No. 8, November, 1994).

Also, there are issues concerning the accommodation of mentally disabled individuals (see Hindman v. GTE Data Services, Middle District of Florida, U.S. District Court) that must be considered. In this case, which will go to trial in early 1995, Hindman filed a lawsuit alleging that GTE Data Services had an obligation to accommodate his mental disability. Hindman was reportedly terminated for having a gun on company property. During the period when the company was terminating Hindman, his attorney contacted GTE Data Services urging an accommodation and reporting that Hindman had been under psychiatric care, a fact apparently unknown to the company. This case and others will help more define more clearly what rights employers have in circumstances where weapons or aggressive behaviors are a matter of concern.]

POLICY

(Employer) complies with, and wholeheartedly supports, the language and spirit of laws as they relate to the safety and health of employees and customers. (Employer's) workplace violence policy includes the recognition that a place of employment safe from the fear of violence is fundamental to the health and well-being of both employees and customers alike. (Employer) hereby affirms its policy that its employees should work in environments that are free from physical attack, threats, and menacing and harassing behaviors.

As used in this policy, violence is defined as unwanted or hostile physical contact.

Physical attack is an unwanted or hostile physical contact such as hitting, fighting, pushing, shoving or the throwing of objects.

Threat is the expression of a present or future intent to cause physical or mental harm. An expression constitutes a threat without regard to whether the party communicating has the present ability to do harm and without regard to whether the expression is contingent, conditional or future.

Harassment is behavior or communication designed or intended to intimidate, menace, or frighten another person.

Property damage is behavior or acts that contribute to the destruction or damage of private property.

[Note: The harmful effect that violence has on employees is just now being understood. The Bureau of Labor Statistics (see Census of Occupational Fatalities, Bureau of Labor Statistics, U.S. Department of Labor, May, 1994) reported that 149 employees were murdered in non-robbery homicides in 1993. These individuals were murdered by employ-

APPENDIX A

ees, former employees, or by individuals who had a romantic involvement with the victim. The total number of homicides in 1993 was up by 23 from the previous year, the first year for which comprehensive statistics were collected and reported. Other data demonstrate the magnitude of the problem that violence has become. A Department of Justice survey (National Crime Victimization Survey, July, 1994) revealed that there are 100,000 crimes committed at work each year, including 16% of all assaults and 8% of all rapes. Finally, one additional source of data helps us appreciate the scope of non-lethal aggression. A survey by Northwestern National Life Insurance Company (*Fear and Violence in the Workplace,* NLIC Employee Benefits Division, October, 1993) revealed that one out of four employees considered himself or herself to be the recipient of harassing behaviors.]

[The cost of violence to employers is far more difficult to quantify. The author has identified cost factors from elsewhere in this book. He previously wrote in *Breaking Point— The Workplace Violence Epidemic & What To Do About It* (Chicago: National Safe Workplace Institute, 1993) that a serious incident of violence can easily cost a company $250,000. There is no doubt that much of the cost of violence is absorbed by victims as well as by employers. A number of cost factors have been identified by the Author at the conclusion of this Appendix.]

Violence, threats, and harassment are always prohibited, especially whenever:

1. The act, behavior, or communication is abusive and could cause another person physical or psychological harm.
2. The act, behavior, or communication damages company or employee property or disrupts the work tasks of an individual or group of people within the (employer's) workforce.

[Note: This statement has been so formulated to provide you with wide latitude in interpreting how individuals have been harmed, as long as it is clear that physical or psychological harm has been caused. While harm may be clearly understood if a person is physically injured and must miss time from work, psychological harm is more difficult to evaluate. Examples of psychological harm include depression, phobia and panic disorders.]

PROCEDURE

1. Any employee who experiences or witnesses such acts, conduct, behavior, or communication must immediately contact his or her supervisor, Corporate Human Resources, Corporate Security, or the (employer's) hot-line at the employee's election.

[Note: There are at least four logical options that employers may wish to provide to employees for reporting threats and other acts of violence (including property damage). These include:

Supervisors. Unfortunately, supervisors are sometimes the cause of violence. Moreover, supervisors sometimes are reluctant to take appropriate action for a variety of reasons (e.g. the supervisor may like the perpetrator or be fearful of retaliation).

Corporate Human Resources. There are many reasons why Human Resources is a reasonable choice. The most obvious is that many companies with remote locations or facilities have a person trained to perform human resource management functions. On the other hand, it is possible that a particular manager may be the source of the problem or that the employee will fear retaliation from such a manager.

Corporate Security. In most cases, security professionals have good investigative skills. However, it may be inappropriate for Corporate Security to investigate cases in locations that are geographically remote.

Hot-lines. Many employers may wish to provide a toll-free 800 phone number as a valid way for employees or others to report information on violence confidentially. There are at least two reasons why such a hot-line may be desirable: (1)

APPENDIX A

some individuals may fear contacting Corporate Security, Corporate Human Resources, or their supervisor. This is not unusual when a senior person is intimidating or menacing a subordinate. (2) The existence of such a mechanism is considered not only to be effective but is also a mitigating factor under the Federal Sentencing guidelines. There are reputable vendors who offer toll-free hot-lines. If you consider out-sourcing for such a service, make certain that the vendor's employees are well-trained and can effectively handle reports of violence. In general, those answering a hot-line should be college graduates and people who have law enforcement or employee counseling experience.

[(Employer) may wish to consider allowing the person to go to any one of the above sources. The important factor is to get information to someone who can act upon it in an effective and timely fashion.]

2. Any supervisor or manager who receives a complaint of violence, threats, or harassment, or who has reason to suspect that these acts or behaviors are occurring, must notify Corporate Human Resources or Corporate Security.

3. Upon being informed of an allegation of violence, threat, or harassment, the Corporate Human Resources, Corporate Legal, and Corporate Security will investigate the matter.

4. Upon the conclusion of this investigation, the Company will determine how to respond. In the interim, the Company will make responses as appropriate. Thereafter, Corporate Human Resources will notify the employee of the outcome of the investigation and advise the employee of any corrective or preventive action taken.

[Typically the most appropriate action involving someone who has perpetrated violent acts or made direct threats is removal until an investigation has been completed. This is especially true in situations where a manager believes that the continued presence of an employee represents a danger to employees or customers. There are rare circumstances when an employee can return after an appropriate period of time has passed. Such situations may be where: (1) an investigation has revealed that the employee had reacted to a hostile work environment; (2) the employee was determined to have been suffering from a medical affliction or remedial psychological disability; and (3) the facts do not support permanent removal from the workplace.]

5. Appropriate disciplinary action, up to an including termination, will be taken in instances of misconduct, as judged by the Company.

6. Employees who knew of information about violence, threats, or harassment, but did not act consistent with this procedure, will be subjected to appropriate discipline, up to and including termination.

   [Note: The Author believes that it is intolerable for individuals who know of violence, threats, or inappropriate aggression or conduct to withhold this information from the personnel who can take corrective action. Unfortunately, many employees do not believe that they have a responsibility to enforce discipline. As a result, it is becoming more difficult for management to achieve compliance with a truly effective violence prevention policy. The enforcement of this provision should be especially severe for personnel in positions of responsibility and trust.]

   [An alternative policy would state: "Employees who know of information about violence, threats or harassment have a moral obligation to notify an appropriate person consistent with this procedure." A third option would be to say nothing, assuming that employees will comply with the policy without being mandated or advised of their moral obligation.]

7. An employee will not be retaliated against by the Company for reporting violence, threats, or harassment.

RESPONSIBILITIES

Corporate Human Resources, together with Corporate Legal, Corporate Safety & Health and Corporate Security, hold the

APPENDIX A

responsibility for planning, designing, and implementing this policy. The Vice Presidents of Corporate Human Resources and Corporate Security will assist the senior executives of each business unit in acquainting all employees with this policy.

MANAGERIAL RESPONSIBILITIES

Specifically, managers should:

1. Support (employer's) principle of, and rationale for, encouraging work environments safe from violence, threats, and harassing/aggressive behavior.

2. Inform subordinates on a periodic basis about (employer's) policy and procedures on encouraging work environments safe from violence, threats, and harassment.

3. Be aware of potential situations where violence, threats, and harassment of employees might occur, and take preventive and/or corrective steps including, where appropriate, disciplinary action up to and including dismissal. Corporate Security and Corporate Human Resources should be notified immediately of any allegations of violence, threats, and harassment, and consulted regarding the proper investigation or response.

4. Be alert to the possibility of violence, threats, and harassment on the part of employees, former employees, customers, and other third parties (e.g. stalkers). Take preventive and/or corrective action up to and including dismissal. Corporate Security and Corporate Human Resources should be consulted regarding the proper investigation or response.

5. Be alert to conditions that may lead to violence, threats, or harassment. Corporate Security and Corporate Human Resources should be consulted regarding the proper investigation or response.

HUMAN RESOURCES RESPONSIBILITIES

Corporate Human Resources should:

1. Post in an appropriate manner (employer's) policy prohibiting workplace violence and otherwise communicate the company's policy to all employees and applicants.

2. Investigate claims of violence raised by employees or others.

3. Advise managers on how to address and resolve concerns in their areas.

4. Monitor policies and practices for compliance with (employer's) workplace violence policy.

5. Provide training on workplace violence prevention matters and otherwise ensure compliance with (employer's) policy.

6. Refer appropriate matters to Corporate Legal.

7. Assist Corporate Legal as necessary in supporting this policy and responding to concerns.

8. Establish an ongoing committee including Corporate Legal, Corporate Security and other appropriate business units and divisions to ensure effective implementation of this policy in various circumstances.

LEGAL RESPONSIBILITIES

Corporate Legal should:

1. Advise Managers, Corporate Human Resources and Corporate Security regarding workplace violence laws and regulations.

2. Respond to inquiries from governmental agencies or courts.

3. Coordinate with outside counsel as necessary.

SECURITY RESPONSIBILITIES

Corporate Security should:

1. Review security measures as appropriate to ensure that this policy is effectively implemented. Specifically, Corporate Security should review physical and human factor security

measures during the course of audits or assessments to ensure protection of the company's employees and property.

2. Advise Managers, Corporate Human Resources and Corporate Legal on security procedures necessary for preventing workplace violence and for implementation of this policy.

ADDENDUM

HOW WORKPLACE VIOLENCE AND CONDITIONS THAT LEAD TO VIOLENCE HARM WORKERS AND ORGANIZATIONAL EFFECTIVENESS

Physical harm:

- Death
- Injury

Psychological:

- Trauma
- Mental health services
- Suicide and suicide prevention
- Substance abuse
- Survivor guilt

Property damage

Property theft

Productivity impediments:

- Lower morale
- Absenteeism
- Labor-management conflict
- Increased turnover

Diversion of management resources:

- Response to crisis rather than profit-making activities
- Costly litigation

Increased security costs

Increased workers' compensation costs

Increased personnel costs (employment and training)

SOURCE: *Joseph a. Kinney, consultant*

APPENDIX A

B

EMPLOYEE ASSESSMENT PROCESS

QUESTIONS & ANSWERS:
Assessment of Potentially Dangerous Employees

If there is specific evidence that an employee has engaged in or threatened to engage in violent behavior in the workplace, a behavior assessment must be conducted. However, a report of possible violence which is not substantiated by direct evidence cannot be used to justify extraordinary measures such as those rationalized in this discussion. In evaluating the seriousness of the threat, it is important to recognize that no single indicator can be considered highly significant unless it occurs in conjunction with other indicators.

Indicators which have been found to be associated with violent behavior in the workplace are presented below as a series of questions which should be raised when there is a concern that an employee may be a danger to himself or others. The questions below appear in order of importance. Affirmative answers to the first three questions would call for answering the remaining questions.

1. Is there any official or documented record that the perpetrator or suspected party has been known to act in a violent or assaultive manner?

In answering this question, you should consider as most important any documented criminal history or conviction for violent offenses such as assault and battery, armed robbery, rape, domestic assault, etc. However, *any* criminal history involving charges that have been placed (not including convictions), even for property offenses, should be considered as an indicator of past behavior of a violent nature. A history of traffic violations may indicate a drug or alcohol problem, poor impulse control, or other behavioral issues. If a thorough pre-employment examination has been conducted and verified, then post-hiring events should be

APPENDIX B

the focus of an inquiry. If there is some question, however, about the completeness of the pre-employment scrutiny, then a more exhaustive review should be made.

Although conviction is the most definitive historical evidence of past violent behavior, any information which can be legally obtained regarding contacts with law enforcement, which did not result in conviction, but were the result of violent actions should be weighed in the assessment.

In addition to convictions, other possible official sources of information regarding past violent behavior are military records, particularly those relating to court martial and discipline. School records also will frequently highlight behavioral problems and time gaps perhaps indicative of institutionalization. Previous work history may suggest that the person was disciplined, removed or left employment due to fighting, possession of weapons or aggressive behavior.

Information directly received from family members or intimates regarding violent, aggressive or assaultive behavior directed against family or associates should be fully weighed; of special importance would be a recent divorce or separation from spouse or family, if it occurs in conjunction with other indicators. Unofficial, but reliable reports from associates and co-employees regarding past violent behavior should also be weighed particularly if the information provided is consistent with other documentation.

Impressionistic assessments of violence, even if they cannot be precisely defined by specific facts or events, are possibly important. A family history of violence may suggest a predisposition to consider violent or unacceptable or undesirable behavior, but should not be overemphasized. In view of the fact that past behavior is the single best predictor of future violence, the search for information which will provide a definitive answer to this question should be as exhaustive as necessary.

2. Has the perpetrator or suspect been diagnosed as violent or been hospitalized or treated for aggressive or antisocial behavior?

Hospitalizations or outpatient psychiatric treatment may be associated with violent behavior. Whenever possible, the cause for such treatment should be identified. In the course of determining if a person has been treated for aggressive behavior, treatment with antidepressants, mood elevators or tranquilizers should be examined for possible association with disruptive behavior.

Any descriptions in health or other personal records which include any of the following or similar terminology should be a matter of concern:

explosive,

impulsive,

hostile,

aggressive,

agitated,

angry,

belligerent,

abusive,

homicidal or

suicidal.

These characterizations should be taken as an indicator that a mental health professional has considered the person as possibly violent even if this diagnosis is not explicitly stated.

3. Does the perpetrator or suspect own, have easy access to and/or familiarity with weapons or other dangerous devices such as explosives?

Possession of a weapon does not necessarily indicate potential danger, although a fascination with weapons and possession of multiple weapons should be a matter for concern. Evidence that the employee has recently obtained a weapon, and further indication that the person has brought a weapon to the workplace should be a cause for great concern.

Where recent acquisition of a weapon has been confirmed, the nature of the weapon obtained is of prime significance. Relatively lethal weapons such as semiautomatics with a magazine capacity of 20 rounds or greater (e.g. AK-47, SKS, M-16) present greater cause for alarm. In addition, ownership of semiautomatic

APPENDIX B

pistols of 9mm or larger caliber (e.g. .357 magnum) should be considered serious.

In determining the ability of a person to use a weapon, familiarity with weapons should be presumed if the person has a military history or is known to be a hunter or marksman. Any indication of recent activity associated with weapons, such as an unusual obsession with practicing or cleaning should be taken seriously.

An indication of preoccupation with weapons must be considered in the context of a systematic assessment process. Preoccupation can include people who:

- talk at length about weapons,

- subscribe to magazines covering firearms,

- have a local reputation as someone who knows a great deal about weapons,

- wear military type clothing,

- visit shooting or target ranges,

- often practice with weapons, or

- are members of paramilitary or survivalist organizations.

Individuals who fit in one or more of the above categories and who have made threats or have behaved in an otherwise aggressive manner should be considered at risk.

4. Has the perpetrator or suspect indicated or appeared to harbor resentment or anger toward the company, its managers or co-employees?

In addition to employees who openly threaten or express anger, any employee who is terminated or separated by mutual agreement may be thought of as harboring some degree of resentment. The depth of resentment and anger should be determining factors. The longer the period of time the person has been associated with the company, the greater the likelihood that such hostility will be strong.

Moreover, employees who do not find other work or interests after separation and who continue to be preoccupied with perceived grievances or actions of the company, present a greater danger. Those whose severance from the company has been preceded by long-standing disagreements or differences with management, or who have repeatedly filed grievances and lawsuits are likely to harbor deep resentments, as are employees who believe they have been unfairly treated.

Such employees who are known to be extremely resentful and angry should be considered as possibly dangerous even if they had not made open threats. The possibility of violence increases if they have named or shown an inclination to hold a particular individual responsible for some perceived mistreatment.

5. Has the perpetrator or suspect been known to express sympathy, fascination or interest in publicized actions involving violence?

There is evidence to suggest that many actions involving extreme violence are derivative. In general, workplace violence tends to occur in clusters in that a single event can trigger similar events in other locations. This is because unstable people are often prompted to engage in violence similar to something they have read about, seen on TV or the movies or heard about from others. When this occurs, there is usually a time lapse of months or weeks between the time the person is originally exposed to the idea and the time of the violent act. In the interim, the person will be fantasizing about the action and may attempt to discuss details about the event with others.

Thus any written or verbal allusions to a serious, highly publicized violent episode, particularly one which occurred in the workplace, should be taken as an indication that the person may be fantasizing about such an action.

6. Has the employee's separation or action which has precipitated concern been preceded by increasingly deteriorating work performance and attendance problems?

An affirmative answer may suggest alcohol or drug abuse, both of which have a high correlation with violence, or some other form of personality disorder, according to a sample of incidents studied by the National Safe Workplace Institute. However, such a pattern should be considered as an indicator for violence only if it occurs in conjunction with other indicators of dangerousness.

APPENDIX B

APPENDIX B

7. Is there any indication of extremely low self-esteem, severe depression or suicidal tendencies?

In cases examined by experts, where an employee has engaged in extremely violent behavior in the workplace, many employees either committed or attempted to commit suicide. Although few people with suicidal tendencies are inclined to engage in aggressive behavior, the reverse is not true. Homicidal behavior does have a correlation with suicidal tendencies. Therefore an employee who is being evaluated because he has demonstrated aggressive behavior would be considered more dangerous if he also displayed suicidal tendencies which are often revealed in self-deprecating statements. Any statements of a fatalistic nature, or which would suggest that after a defined time period nothing will be important, would also be considered a possible indicator of such tendencies.

There are certain other actions which may be signs of potential danger: closing out bank accounts; transferring assets; writing a will; giving away or selling treasured belongings; clearing an office desk of personal possessions. Consult with the local police and request that they visit the employee's home to check for signs of finality (i.e. painting walls black). If the police observe any of these signs, they will be able to implement preventive measures immediately. This technique will complement the assessment by revealing any signs of preparing for an end and by interrupting the person's thought pattern.

The presence or suggestion of depression or suicidal tendencies should be considered an indicator of dangerousness only if it occurs in conjunction with the other indicators discussed above.

8. Is there any indication of new or increased stress which might precipitate a violent action at this time, as opposed to some other time?

Persons who are beyond or near the edge of control are sometimes propelled into action by stressful changes in their environment. Precipitating factors may be a death in the family, a divorce, the loss of a child as a result of a divorce adjudication, a financial setback, the loss of a job. Such factors would be a cause for concern when a person is already considered as a possible danger for other reasons.

9. Is there any indication of mental deterioration?

Mental deterioration is not necessarily a precursor to violent behavior; in fact, it may preclude such behavior if the person is so disorganized as to be unable to carry out an aggressive act. Nevertheless, practitioners dealing with violent behaviors have observed that violent outbursts are sometimes associated with mental deterioration. In particular, paranoid delusions in which the person appears to feel that he or she is being picked on, talked about, discriminated against, or in some way singled out by co-employees or managers, can be a sign of possible dangerousness.

10. Are there any contrary indicators to violence or an indication that the person is so seriously disorganized as to be unable to carry out a coordinated violent action?

Contrary indicators to violence would be confirmed negative responses to the above questions. For example, evidence that the person has refrained from using violence in the past, even when provoked, would be considered evidence suggesting that the person is not likely to engage in violence in the future. Along the same lines, a person who has taken a new job or found a new interest or made what appears to be a long-term commitment to something, would be unlikely to engage in serious violence.

MODEL BEHAVIORAL OBSERVATION PROGRAM

A Behavioral Observation Program (BOP) is used typically by supervisors and first-line managers to document employee behavior and productivity. A BOP involves observations of an employee over a period of time, in order to properly assess employee fitness and performance. Completed BOP forms are kept by the Human Resources Department and by an outside vendor.

XYZ CORPORATION
(fictitious name)
BEHAVIORAL OBSERVATION PROGRAM
INSTRUCTIONS AND FORM

Instructions for Responding Supervisor or Front-Line Manager*

1. If the subject employee has been under your supervision for a period of time, please review the last BOP form you have completed. This form will help you in recalling the employee's previous on-the-job behavior. While completing this form, realize that you are responding to observed changes since the last evaluation. If this is your initial evaluation of the subject employee, then you should comment on behavior you have seen since becoming his or her supervisor.

2. Carefully read and respond to each question. Complete all spaces. If you cannot comfortably make a determination or response, please mark "unknown" and provide a brief explanation as to why you cannot complete the question.

3. While completing this form, please keep in mind you are not being asked to evaluate or diagnose the individual. However, you are being requested to use your supervisory skills and record your observations for further professional review.

APPENDIX C

4. Upon completion of this form, make a copy for your file (if you wish), and promptly return the original to:

NSWI Behavior Consulting (fictitious)
1234 Avenue A
Nome, Alaska

* I have read and followed the above instructions. My responses are true and accurate to the best of my knowledge.

_____   _____   _____

Name (Print)   Signature   Date

EMPLOYEE NAME: _____

DATE OF BIRTH: _____

PRESENT POSITION: _____

LENGTH OF EMPLOYMENT: _____

Directions: Circle your observation for each behavioral category.

PART I
WORK PERFORMANCE

1. Work quality: Improved Worsened No Change Unknown

2. Work quantity: Increased Decreased No Change Unknown

3. Mistakes: Increased Decreased No Change Unknown

4. Judgment: Improved Worsened No Change Unknown

5. Effectiveness: Improved Worsened No Change Unknown

6. Concentration: Increased Decreased No Change Unknown

7. Absenteeism: Increased Decreased No Change Unknown

8. Compliance
   with rules: Increased Decreased No Change Unknown

9. Cautiousness: Increased Decreased No Change Unknown

10. Commitment: Improved Worsened No Change Unknown

11. Safety
    mindedness: Improved Worsened No Change Unknown

APPENDIX C

12. Coopera-
    tiveness: Improved Worsened No Change Unknown

13. Responsibility: Improved Worsened No Change Unknown

14. Ability to work
    independently: Improved Worsened No Change Unknown

15. Tardiness: Improved Worsened No Change Unknown

Overall Rating: Employee's overall behavioral performance during this period:

Improved   Worsened   No Change   Unknown

Please discuss any commendations received or disciplinary actions taken against the employee during the observation period:

Additional comments that you may wish to make:

PART II
PERSONAL AND SOCIAL
INTERACTIONS AT WORK

1. Level of anger: Increased Decreased No Change Unknown

2. Manipulation
   of others: Increased Decreased No Change Unknown

3. Rate of
   speech: Increased Decreased No Change Unknown

4. Complaints
   about others: Increased Decreased No Change Unknown

5. Irritability: Increased Decreased No Change Unknown

6. Activity level: Increased Decreased No Change Unknown

7. Sociability: Increased Decreased No Change Unknown

8. Maintains
   friends: Improved Worsened No Change Unknown

9. Complaints
   by others: Increased Decreased No Change Unknown

10. Socially
    Isolated: Increased Decreased No Change Unknown

11. Accepts
    criticism: Improved Worsened No Change Unknown

12. Level of
    maturity: Increased Decreased No Change Unknown

13. Honesty: Increased Decreased No Change Unknown

APPENDIX C

Overall Rating: Employee's overall ability to get along with others during this period:

Improved   Worsened   No Change   Unknown

Please note or describe any significant changes in the employee's social behavior during this period:

PART III
EMPLOYEE HEALTH

1. Complaints
   of personal
   health: Increased Decreased No Change Unknown

2. Energy level: Increased Decreased No Change Unknown

3. General
   appearance: Improved Worsened No Change Unknown

HEALTH CHECKLIST

1. Adjusted to new shifts   Yes   No   Unknown
   (if applicable):

2. Facial changes (red faced,
   paleness, dry mouth, dilated
   pupils, hearing loss, etc.):   Yes   No   Unknown

3. Weight loss: Yes   No   Unknown

4. Weight gain: Yes   No   Unknown

5. Shakiness: Yes   No   Unknown

6. Nausea/vomiting: Yes   No   Unknown

7. Increased use of antacids,
   coffee/tea, aspirin, cigarettes: Yes   No   Unknown

8. Dizziness: Yes   No   Unknown

9. Breathing problems: Yes   No   Unknown

10. Unusual behavior or thinking: Yes   No   Unknown

Please describe any significant changes in personal health at work as noted above:

PART IV
MISCELLANEOUS

1. Have there been any instances in which the employee demonstrated unwarranted anger, suspicion or hostility?

   None   One   More than one

2. Any additional comments you wish to offer:

Supervisor Name   Signature   Date
(Print or type)

ORGANIZATIONAL ASSESSMENT PROCESS

Organizations often make the mistake of deciding that they will establish a policy and program without first identifying any special problems that they may have. They believe that they can simply declare a policy in place without any special understanding of what will work with their work-force and how management can best make employees aware of policies and procedures.

Ideally organizations will follow a number of steps in determining what they need to fix to have an effective program. To the extent possible, organizations should conduct a *needs assessment* of the special or unique problems or requirements that exist. The following steps are crucial to this process:

Step 1. Conduct an *employee opinion survey* to learn what problems and concerns employees currently have about violence at work (see draft questions below).

Step 2. Undertake *focus groups* to explore in detail any issues or concerns that came up based upon the surveys.

Step 3. Conduct an evaluation of:

- existing programs, policies, and personnel.

- past incidents and threats of violence.

- role of the existing personnel in investigating and designing preventive measures involving workplace violence or threats of violence.

- security policies, procedures, and physical security systems to determine whether existing policies and systems are well-suited to controlling violence at or around plants and other facilities.

Step 4. Provide *briefings, reports, and memoranda* in order to build understanding of key executives and managers on workplace violence, management considerations, need for policy, etc.

Step 5. Summarize *what is known* about occupational stress and workplace violence within the work environment and what is being done to address those conditions.

Elaboration of some of these points may clarify the importance of any specific component.

APPENDIX D

Attitude/climate surveys. Employees are much more aware of violence than are middle- and senior level managers. This is true because line-level employees are often exposed to situations and circumstances where aggression or violence is much more likely.

To learn what employees think, a survey should be conducted asking key questions. If possible, the survey should be pre-tested with a sample of the work force to ensure its validity.

Employees often see violence not only as a problem that is increasing but as one more serious than other safety and health concerns. In fact, while acceptable national surveys have not been conducted, we believe that most employees see violence as a serious problem that is neglected by management.

Often it is appropriate and useful to follow surveys with focus groups. While surveys are useful instruments in identifying the scope of the problem, focus groups can help to identify the intensity of the feelings that exist.

Sample questions:

Employee background information . . .

- Age _____

- Years employed by company _____

- Job classification _____

- Sex (circle one)   M   F

1. Have you witnessed or experienced violence during the past two or three years?

   Yes _____   No _____

   - If the answer is yes, was the violence from . . . (check all that apply)

   a. employees _____

   b. former employees _____

   c. employee family members _____

   d. customers _____

   e. others _____

2. How would you describe the violence that you witnessed or experienced? (Please check all that apply.)

   a. Fighting _____

   b. Pushing _____

   c. Shoving _____

   d. Other physical contact _____

   e. Threats _____

   f. Harassment _____

3. Did management know about the violence that you witnessed?

   Yes _____   No _____

4. Is violence at our workplace . . . (check one that applies most)

   a. Increasing _____

   b. Staying the same _____

   c. Decreasing _____

5. Do you feel that you are working in a safe atmosphere?

   Yes _____   No _____   Uncertain _____

6. Do you believe any of your co-workers are capable of becoming violent?

   Yes _____   No _____

   If yes, why? _____

   _____

   _____

APPENDIX D

7. Would you know what to do if a co-worker became violent?

   Yes _____   No _____

8. On a scale of 1 to 10 (with 1 being the most important and 10 the least important), how would you rate violence as a safety and security problem at our company?

9. Do you feel that our company has adequate security against the possibility of violence (including violence from outside the workplace)?

   Yes _____   No _____

10. What security problems do you worry about?

    _____

    _____

    _____

    _____

11. What experiences have you had while working here that you consider to be violent?

    _____

    _____

    _____

    _____

12. What do you believe causes violence at our company? (Check all that apply.)

    a. Overly controlling management/supervision _____

    b. Fear of job loss _____

    c. Problems at home (e.g. money) _____

    d. Lack of health or counseling _____

    e. Poor management _____

f. Poor discipline _____

g. Other (please specify) _____

13. What types of violence do you believe we experience from *outside* the company?

   _____

   _____

   _____

   _____

14. What types of violence do you believe that we experience from *inside* the company?

   _____

   _____

   _____

   _____

15. What perceptions or opinions do you have, if any, on the effectiveness of *security services* in handling threatening situations?

   _____

   _____

   _____

   _____

16. What perceptions or opinions do you have, if any, on how first-line managers handle difficult employees?

   _____

   _____

   _____

   _____

APPENDIX D

SECURITY ASSESSMENTS

Employers should contract with security experts, especially those who have experience with violence and violent behaviors, for thorough evaluation of physical and human factor security concerns. It is only natural that existing personnel will have a stake in the status quo and be reluctant to deeply evaluate programs that they or colleagues have managed. On the other hand, an independent assessment, including some of the key issues discussed below, may disclose vulnerabilities previously unknown to your company.

PHYSICAL SECURITY

1) *Physical measures for people and property protection.* A realistic security assessment will carefully examine physical measures (e.g. cameras, card entry systems) that provide security to employees and customers. This list is by no means comprehensive. Your company may or may not use the systems or technology that is implied in the following questions. Moreover, new technology and personal protective systems are becoming available that may not have been known to the author when this was prepared. However, a well-trained security consultant should know of recent applicable technological developments.

- How accessible are your employees and your customers to individuals who become violent?

- What systems, if any, can you put into place if there is an emergency?

- Do you use card access systems or other entry controls?

  ✓ How secure are these systems?

- Are cameras properly located and operative?

  ✓ Are monitoring stations well equipped and properly staffed?

  ✓ Do you use interactive video for remote facilities?

- What kind of alarms or panic buttons do you provide for threatened employees? What is the response time by security?

- Are parking lots and entry and exits properly lit and patrolled?

- Are employee ID cards updated on a regular basis?

- What physical security measures are available and applicable in your workplace that you have not previously considered?

- Are systems audited on a regular basis to ensure that they are operative?

HUMAN FACTORS SECURITY

The role of people in security. There are many companies that have spent a lot of money on physical security but have not properly invested in the people that can make the systems work. Violence, to a large degree, is a people-management issue where physical security plays a very important but supportive role. If an organization experiences a serious threat or violent behavior, the role of your security professionals in controlling and stabilizing the environment will be critical. In the event of such emergencies, time is crucial. With each passing minute, employers lose control and the potential for harm and damage to people and property increases. An outstanding security staff is tantamount to having adequate insurance.

- How well-trained is your corporate security director?
  - ✓ Has he or she been trained in behavioral emergencies?
  - ✓ Does your security director know how to deal with dangerous employees?
  - ✓ Does your security director know how to manage threats?
- Are security staffing levels adequate?
- Have security officers been trained in anger diffusion and other techniques that are appropriate for angry employees? customers?
- How well-trained are contract security officers who work for your company?

APPENDIX D

- Do you have a plan for controlling the environment in the event of an emergency?

- Do you have adequate communications capability in the event of an emergency involving violence?

- What joint plans has your security director worked out with local law enforcement?

- Does your security director know about restraining or civil orders that involve company employees?

- Do front-line managers and employees have easy and ready access to crisis management plans?

- How effective was security in handling past incidents of violence?

- Do employees have confidence in your security department to handle aggressive or violent employees or members of the public?

EXECUTIVE LEVEL/ SENIOR MANAGER BRIEFINGS

Senior managers should learn as much as possible about the subject of workplace violence and how this menace can be prevented. Many consultants and organizations provide senior-level briefings to inform managers about programs and policies that can be implemented to deal with this growing problem. Below is a sample format of such a program, including learning objectives, that you may wish to consider. Each heading includes a discussion of the awareness and learning objectives for that part of the briefing. If your company or organization has unions, you may wish to invite representatives from each union to attend. This is important because union leaders and members need to have an understanding of both the problem and what your company intends to do about it.

I. INTRODUCTION—
What Is Workplace Violence?
What Is the Scope of the Problem?

Objectives: This part of the session should provide the audience of managers with an understanding of the types of violence (harassment, threats and attacks) that occur at work. Homicide, as emphasized throughout this book, is just the tip of the iceberg. It should also include a discussion of non-physical violence such as theft, property damage and sabotage.

Moreover, this part of the seminar should demonstrate how costly violence is to the organization and its employees. Most of these costs are hidden from management and, as a result, go unappreciated.

III. CONTEXT—
Causal Variables and Risk Factors Present in Incidents of Violence

Objectives: This segment will examine the psychological characteristics of individuals who have committed violence at work.

It also should discuss how (a) external variables mix with psychological factors in an individual and (b) how behavior evolves sequentially in perpetrators of violence.

III. PREVENTION—
Key Issues in Early Intervention of Violent Individuals

Objectives: This part of the program should examine methods that an organization can use to identify potential problems. Unless some consideration of early intervention methods is given, it is likely that your company will remain crisis-driven and reactive.

This session should explore the important role (and training needs) that supervisors and front-line managers have in violence detection and prevention.

Finally, some time should be set aside to review issues such as downsizing, domestic violence, and any unique problems or characteristics in your company.

IV. CRISIS MANAGEMENT—
Assessing and Dealing with Threats

Objectives: Examination of methods that an organization can use to identify potential problems and prevent violence is critical.

While experience shows that some-not all-threats are complex and warrant attention from a team approach, most employers should carefully evaluate the need to assemble and train such a team.

Finally, some attention should be given to the role of outside resources including mental health providers, lawyers, security consultants, and others who have a role in workplace violence prevention issues.

V. LEGAL BARRIERS—
Maneuvering Through the Legal Minefield

Objectives: There are numerous laws that determine how organizations should address and deal with the problem of violence and with aggressive employees. A good workshop will review legal issues such as privacy, employment and retention, inadequate security, safe terminations, etc.

Likewise, some discussion of emerging civil tort and regulatory implications should be included so that managers are aware of the legal implications of workplace violence.

VI. QUESTIONS & ANSWERS

You should insist that any presenter allow time for questions and answers. A good workshop leader will always encourage questions and try to facilitate increased awareness by appropriate managers and employees. Since you do not want key managers to leave with unanswered questions or concerns, workshop leaders should be encouraged to take questions in private during breaks and after the workshop.

APPENDIX D

INCIDENT DOCUMENTATION FORM

Serious incidents and all threats must be comprehensively documented in a timely fashion. Adequate documentation is important for legal and moral reasons; without it your characterizations of past incidents are likely to be challenged. These documentation forms should be kept in a secure manner. Only those managers with a need-to-know should have access to this very sensitive information.

Finally, it is essential that an individual from Human Resources and/or Security thoroughly review each Incident Documentation Form for accuracy and completeness. If the Form is insufficient, then it should be sent back until it is completed satisfactorily.

1. Today's Date: _____

2. Name of person completing this report: _____

3. Title: _____

4. Phone Number: _____

5. Person who reported the incident/threat: _____

6. Name of victim(s) or targets of threats:

   • _____

   • _____

   • _____

   • _____

7. Have targets or recipients of threats been notified? (Check one.)

   Yes _____   No _____

   If yes, who notified the target(s): _____

APPENDIX E

8. Name of the alleged perpetrator:

_____

9. Perpetrator's employment status:

_____

10. Names of witnesses:

    • _____

    • _____

    • _____

    • _____

11. Date of incident or threat: _____

12. Where did the incident happen? _____

13. Describe in detail what happened:

    _____

    _____

    _____

14. Are there any conflicts in the information provided by wit-
    nesses?

        Yes _____   No _____

    If yes, explain or document possible conflicts:

    _____

    _____

    _____

15. Has the alleged perpetrator been involved in previous incidents of violence?

    Yes _____   No _____

    If yes, please explain what corrective or preventive measures were taken in response to the previous incident:

    _____

    _____

    _____

16. Did the incident involve the use of physical force?

    Yes _____   No _____

    If yes, please document:

    _____

    _____

    _____

17. Did the alleged perpetrator make a threat or threats?

    Yes _____   No _____

    If yes, was the threat a *direct* threat?

    Yes _____   No _____

    A conditional threat?

    Yes _____   No _____

    A veiled threat?

    Yes _____   No _____

APPENDIX E

AN EXPERT'S VIEW ON TERMINATING DANGEROUS EMPLOYEES

A nightmare for every manager is the issue of handling terminations of dangerous employees, especially those who have made threats or been very aggressive. One of the foremost experts on managing such matters is Frederick A. Foster, a former southeastern Michigan law enforcement officer. Foster is executive vice president and chief of operations at Seventrees Corporation, a specialized protection services company based in Benton Harbor, Michigan. Seventrees provides direct intervention services to corporate and institutional clients who face difficult security challenges, and Fred and his team are often called upon to advise, assist and protect managers who must terminate potentially dangerous employees.

Rather than write about such a delicate issue, we have turned to Foster for insights into this area. What follows is an interview with Foster in 1994. He believes that it is important for human resource and other managers to understand how to deal with potentially dangerous individuals and this interview is designed to provide that critical information.

Q. Fred, as you work with your clients in removing disturbed or threatening persons from the workplace, do any common themes emerge?

A. Yes. Often these individuals have gotten their way for some time through manipulation and intimidation; others are so unstable that their behavior changes from unpredictable to bizarre. This conduct can instill a very high level of fear and concern among co-workers and managers which may cloud the decision-making process. Our first task after gathering initial information is customarily calm and assure the affected individuals that the situation can be brought to a safe and successful conclusion.

Q. Do you find that many managers question whether they are doing the right thing?

A. Separating a person from his or her employment is a tough call under the best of circumstances. When you add an element of threat that the removal may trigger violent reprisal, it's only natural for doubt and apprehension to arise.

Sometimes line managers and the human resources, security and law departments find themselves at cross-purposes. We urge each client to seek a cross-disciplinary team-based solution to these problems with guidance from a qualified mental health professional. It is important to limit the effect of personal feelings and arrive at a consensus decision on a course of action that everyone can live with. One thing is certain, though, if the decision-makers conclude that an individual represents a threat to those around him or her, the person *must* be removed from the work force.

Q. Does this always mean termination?

A. No. In some cases, the employer may wish to provide counseling or other therapy in an attempt to enable the worker to correct the cause of his or her inappropriate behavior and return to the work force. However, it must be made clear that the individual can only return when a skilled and objective mental health professional concludes that it is safe to allow it. Most of the time when we are called in to assist, the situation is so egregious that termination is the only reasonable conclusion.

Q. Are there general guidelines to follow when terminating an employee who is unstable or who has made threats?

A. As with all dismissals, it is best to be brief. We generally recommend that the entire termination interview take no longer than fifteen minutes, and to be direct, with no room for confusion. Tell the individual of the firing in the first sentence. Have at hand all the materials necessary to complete the termination process, including a written explanation of any severance benefits or any counseling or outplacement service that may be offered. Refer to general rather than specific issues. Avoid debate, negotiation, personal comments, and resist the temptation to justify the termination or lecture on behavior and attitude.

Q. What if additional threats are made during the session?

A. The manager must be prepared to respond reasonably to unreasonable conduct. It does no good to counter-threaten or to communicate concern over the potential for violence. It is much better to turn the conversation toward the future, and to express understanding that the employee is upset, while leaving room for him or her to de-escalate by remarking that he is too reasonable a person to carry out the threatened action.

Q. *Are some threats more significant than others?*

A. All threats should be taken seriously, but without knowing the specific circumstances, that's difficult to answer. In general, intimidating remarks early in the interview may be an attempt to manipulate the outcome of the proceedings, but unconditional threats coming at the end of the termination session are serious danger signs.

Q. *What security measures do you recommend?*

A. If threats of violence have preceded the termination, we recommend that a protection team of police officers or security professionals in plain clothes be available during the termination and any subsequent hearings, and remain on site for a reasonable period of time to assure that the individual does not return. Sound, common-sense perimeter security measures should be present at every workplace, and should be stringently observed. It is especially important to inform all gatekeepers, such as receptionists and security posts, not to allow readmittance to the terminated worker.

Q. *Are there special considerations for the security team?*

A. In order to avoid injury to anyone, including the person who has made the threats, it is important to have at least two protection officers present. If lethal threats have been made, the protectors should be armed, and body armor is a good idea. These personnel must be trained to manage and diffuse confrontations, and should be skilled in disarming, weapons retention, take-down, and restraining techniques. They should be equipped with radio communications, and have a portable metal detector available to search a person for weapons without touching him or her. The manager who is

doing the termination should know in advance how to signal the team that help is needed.

*Q. Don't many companies have a policy against armed secu-
rity?*

A. Yes, and in most circumstances this may be acceptable and
even desirable, but here we have a situation in which the
only effective protection against armed assault may be armed
response. The protection officers must be specifically
trained, though, in close quarters shooting techniques.
Bystanders are inevitable in these scenarios, so the responders must absolutely know when *not* to shoot.

Q. What about the site of the interview?

A. We recommend a private room as close to the entrance as
possible, with minimum glass and few furnishings. It is
preferable to choose a room with two or more doors, but if
only one door is available seat the person to be terminated
closest to it to avoid psychological cornering, and to enable
responding protection officers to encounter the assailant
first, if the situation degenerates. Avoid cubicle-style offices;
they afford no privacy and, if violence erupts, the assailant
may be loose in a maze of cubicles, which makes things difficult for everyone. A room equipped with a silent duress
alarm to enable the manager to signal for help is a plus. In
some situations, it may be wise to choose an off-site location,
but beware of third-party liability issues that might arise if
someone gets hurt.

*Q. Speaking of liability, do you have any advice for a manag-
er faced with the dilemma of either being held liable for
damages if an employee is harmed by a co-worker or being
sued by the co-worker for wrongful discharge?*

A. We always urge our clients to seek legal advice from qualified counsel, but I would suggest that the safety of people
comes first. Strong personnel policies with zero tolerance for
threats and harassment build a strong base for firing an
assaultive employee, but when a manager is faced with a

choice bearing responsibility for a foreseeable injury or death, I think that decisive action for the protection of others is the only acceptable course.

Q. Once the termination is complete, what's the best way to escort the individual off the premises?

A. First of all, whenever practical the firing should take place at the end of the shift or of the business day, so that the worker does not face embarrassment in the eyes of fellow employees. The individual must not be allowed to go unescorted to his or her workstation to retrieve personal belongings; a weapon could be hidden there. We recommend that the protection officers, who can maintain a relatively impersonal stance, be sent to remain with the terminated person until he or she has left the premises, but it may be necessary for a manager to go along to prevent the removal of company property. In these cases, the manager must refrain from confrontation and debate; the whole object here is to complete the dismissal quickly and smoothly. It must be made clear to the employee that he or she is not to return to the place of business, and that all communications with the company will be accomplished through a specified manager. Extreme care must be taken not to humiliate the person unnecessarily.

Q. Why is this important?

A. Troubled employees offer suffer from an inflated sense of their own importance and even irreplaceability. Firing may represent an almost unbearable provocation, against which their own sense of dignity and self-esteem may be the last and final inhibition to violence. It is very important that these individuals leave with their dignity intact.

Q. Do you recommend keeping the ex-employee under surveillance in serious cases?

A. Absolutely not. We have conducted this type of surveillance under unusual circumstances, but as a rule most experts agree that the risk that an angry and possibly delusional per-

APPENDIX F

son may realize that he is being followed outweighs any possible benefit. We are trying to prevent violence in the workplace, and the workplace is the appropriate venue for protective measures.

Q. Is there reason for concern at the homes of threatened individuals?

A. We are often asked this question, and it's another difficult call. Although companies frequently arrange for some level of protection for the homes and families of managers and co-workers who feel themselves at risk, the anecdotal evidence is overwhelming that lethal assaults by terminated employees occur almost exclusively at work. Sometimes, though, the need to preserve peace of mind overrides other considerations.

Q. In your experience, do the measures we have talked about here pay off?

A. Although no broad formal study has been done, I would have to say that I am not aware of a single fatal attack by a terminated employee in the face of protective preparations like the ones we've described here.

Q. How long do you recommend leaving these measures in place?

A. That is the question I dread the most, because there is no definitive answer. While we generally concentrate on the first three to seven days after what management perceives as a potential triggering event, no one can measure the internal perception of a disturbed individual except the person himself or herself. We are all aware of shootings that have occurred eight or ten years after an apparent provocation. Any decision on the duration of protective measures must be made by consensus, preferably with the informed advice of a mental health professional. In the case of significant threat, we strongly recommend an extremely discreet inquiry into the life circumstances of the threatener from time to time to determine whether additional steps are necessary.

Q. Anything else?

A. Just a reminder that, as with all terminations, it is essential to retrieve all keys, company identification and access control cards, credit cards, computer and communications equipment, company books and materials, customer lists, and any other company property assigned to the individual. These will be difficult to get back at a later date. Cancel immediately all access to computer systems, long distance telephone services, and facilities. Be careful, be humane, be consistently fair, and base all actions on common sense and sound management judgment, not fear and overreaction.

INDEX

Violence prevention, *(cont'd)*
    intervention system, early, 65-67
    managers and supervisors as defense, 63
    needs assessment, 53-54, 56-58 (*see also*
        . . . . requirements)
    options for threat reporting, analysis of,
        61
    peer review, 65-67
        grievances considered by, 67
    personnel, qualified to act, 60
    physical security, evaluation of, 58-59
    policies, typical, 54
    policy, communication of, 59-60, 64
    post-incident debriefings, 63
    proactive policies, shifting to, 55-58
    rationales for programs, 55-56
    reactive strategies not sufficient, 55
    reporting threats, encouraging, 60, 61
    requirements of organization, assessing,
        53-54, 56-58
        attitude/climate surveys, 56-57
        briefings of executives/senior
            managers, 58
        evaluation/assessments, 57-58
        focus groups, 56-57
    rights of individuals, protecting, 81-82
    senior managers' role, 60
    statement of policy, 64
    steps, 57
    trauma debriefings, 63

W

Wall Street Journal, 96, 166, 179, 220, 238
White-collar workers, lay-offs of, 36

Women in the workplace, violence against,
        109-16
    domestic violence, spillover of, 111
    as homicide victims, 109-11
    lay-offs of, 36
    rapes, 110
    reasons for, two, 112-15
        advancement of women, 113-14
        convenience stores, 113
        economic factors, 112-14
        low-wage high-risk positions, 113-14
        sexual harassment, 114-15 (*see also*
            Sexual harassment)
    security measures, 110-12
    as sources of violence, 161-62
Working poor, high numbers of, as
        contributory to workplace
        violence, 26
Workplace stressors, 139-40
Workplace Violence & Behavior Letter, 145
World Trade Center bombing, 8-9

X

"X generation," 162

Z

"Zero to nuclear war in five seconds"
        generation, 163-66
Zero-threat-tolerance policy, 85